PENGUIN BOOKS

ALL THE WRONG PLACES

James Fenton was born in Lincoln in 1949. He was educated at the Chorister's School, Durham, Repton and Magdalen College, Oxford, where he won the Newdigate Prize for Poetry. He has worked as a political and literary journalist on the *New Statesman*; was a freelance reporter in Indo-China; spent a year in Germany working for the *Guardian*; was theatre critic for the *Sunday Times* for five years and the chief book reviewer for *The Times* from 1984 until 1986. He is now the South-East Asian correspondent for the *Independent*. His first collection of poems, *Terminal Moraine*, was published in 1972. His poem 'A German Requiem' won the Southern Arts Literature Award for Poetry in 1981. His collection of poems *The Memory of War* won the 1984 Geoffrey Faber Memorial Prize and was published, together with *Children in Exile*, in one volume by Penguin. He is also co-author, with John Fuller, of *Partingtime Hall*. James Fenton was elected a Fellow of the Royal Society of Literature in 1983.

ALL THE WRONG PLACES

Adrift in the
Politics of Asia

JAMES FENTON

PENGUIN BOOKS

PENGUIN BOOKS

Published by the Penguin Group
27 Wrights Lane, London W8 5TZ, England
Viking Penguin Inc., 40 West 23rd Street, New York, New York 10010, USA
Penguin Books Australia Ltd, Ringwood, Victoria, Australia
Penguin Books Canada Ltd, 2801 John Street, Markham, Ontario, Canada L3R 1B4
Penguin Books (NZ) Ltd, 182–190 Wairau Road, Auckland 10, New Zealand

Penguin Books Ltd, Registered Offices: Harmondsworth, Middlesex, England

First published in the USA by The Atlantic Monthly Press, New York 1988
Published simultaneously in Canada
First published in Great Britain by Viking 1988
Published in Penguin Books 1990
1 3 5 7 9 10 8 6 4 2

Portions of this book originally appeared in *Granta*

Made and printed in Great Britain by
Richard Clay Ltd, Bungay, Suffolk

To Bill Buford

vii

THE PHILIPPINES

KOREA

Introduction: A Western Observer

I make no attempt, in the course of what follows, to offer anything more than a partial, personal view of some events in the Far East (as it used to be called). Astonishing changes have taken place in the last decade and a half, and many of them are quite beyond my scope, although not without their consequences for the countries I describe. For instance, had the Chinese taken a different view of their global interests, the whole story would have been radically altered. China trades heavily (albeit so far indirectly) with South Korea. It withholds support for the Philippine insurgency. Had its priorities been the other way around, all the signposts would have had to be changed.

At the time of writing, many key countries are in the process of some kind of democratization or reform: China itself, South Korea, the Philippines, Taiwan, and even Hong Kong. Optimists might wish to add North Korea and Vietnam to the list. In each case, the pressures for reform are markedly different in character, as are the chances of success. A democrat in South Korea stands, I think, a good chance of realizing his ambitions; his equivalent in Hong Kong, I'm afraid, has his work cut out.

Chance has played a large role in this story—none of it seems to me inevitable in character. It is by chance that the expiry of the Hong

Kong lease *coincides* with governments of a certain character in London and Beijing. It was by chance that a certain view of the situation in the Korean peninsula led to certain military decisions that eventually determined the political geography of the place. Chance pitched Cory Aquino against Marcos.

Just as the current movements toward democracy differ from each other, so too were the old regimes and their opposing insurgencies radically different. The military dictatorships founded the fortunes of Korea and Taiwan, but plundered the Philippines, never really achieved control in Cambodia, failed in South Vietnam. In the rhetoric of the insurgencies, like calls to like around the globe. But the Khmer Rouge were not like the Vietcong. When the Communists won in Indochina, the domino theory would have predicted that Thailand would be the next to "go." Instead, the Thai insurgency completely failed.

If I think back to what this part of the world was like in 1973, I have to say that nothing has happened as expected—except perhaps that Vietnam would try to rule Cambodia. Of course a materialist view of history can indicate the way a certain class or a certain economy might be expected to behave. But it cannot tell us the way an individual member of a certain class will behave. Cory is not the inevitable product of history: Had she lost courage or come down with measles, she might not have deposed Marcos. Had one of the two Kims been incapacitated last year, the other might have succeeded in thwarting the plans of President Chun to hand over to President Roh.

And if the present book has a haphazard, aleatoric element, some of that is intended, some not. The section on Vietnam was written in the years following the fall of the South. During that time, I had intended to include a full account of my experiences in Cambodia. But I found it too painful, during the years of the Khmer Rouge regime, to touch that subject, and by now it is too late. For the rest of the matter, I have deliberately stressed the part played by chance in the composition of the book.

The publication history of this material is as follows. In 1984, the Cambridge magazine *Granta* was compiling an issue devoted to travel writing. There was a part of my unfinished book that described a trip to the Cambodian areas of the Mekong Delta, which I was happy to see published because, anecdotal though it is, it happens to be rather unusual. I believe I was the only Westerner to visit the smuggling/gambling village of Prek Chak, and I was told that not much else had been written about the ethnic Cambodians of South Vietnam. This came out in *Granta 10*.

The next year saw the tenth anniversary of the fall of Saigon, and at the last moment (after a brief extract had been taken by *Vanity Fair*) *Granta*'s editor, Bill Buford, offered to run what amounted to an abridged version of the unfinished book. This was *Granta 15*—a generous abridgment (I have now restored most of the original cuts).

The fact that there is now an English magazine capable of taking a work of such length has been extremely beneficial—to me. And to Bill too, come to think of it. The success of the Saigon issue made both of us think, from our different perspectives: "What if *Granta* were able actually to *commission* a long, ambitious article? What about *that*, eh?"

Suddenly, and for the first time in a long time, I had become interested in foreign reporting. If I could have space to write as I pleased, I could invent my form as I went along.

In conventional journalism, form is length. Six hundred words, twelve hundred, fifteen hundred, forty-five hundred—all these figures denote familiar forms. They may be brilliantly or prosaically employed, but they are determined by extraneous considerations: what space is to be filled, who else is filing that day, how many ads there are, and so forth. One longs for an elastic magazine, in which content can determine new forms. One longs to get back to reporting.

By reporting I mean something that predates journalism—the fundamental activity. Those "narratives" of previous centuries, which found publication as pamphlets or in magazines, often had their origin in some natural, functional activity. An English merchant in Lisbon writes to his mother to tell her of his experiences in the earthquake. A member of a missionary society reports to his London office with an account of the macabre and piteous deaths of two of his fellows. A ship's captain gives an account of a remarkable, hazardous voyage.

In these examples, the mother wants news because she is a mother. The missionary society needs the details, maybe edifying, of its members' last moments. The owners of the ship need to know what happened to their investment, and why. This is reporting in its natural state.

Journalism becomes unnatural when it strays too far from such origins. It is quite astonishing to me how much interesting material is jettisoned by newspaper reporters because they know they will not be able to write it up, *because to do so would imply they had been present at the events they are describing*. And not only present—alive, conscious, and with a point of view.

On a trip through the sub-Sahara I shared a vehicle with an American reporter who wasn't enjoying himself at all. It was a rough journey and at one point, alarmingly, we broke down. I remember my companion banging his head against the seat of the car and groaning: "We're fucked, we're fucked."

Weeks later I saw what he had written about the trip, and was amused to see that his only personal appearance in his narrative was under the rubric, "a Western Observer." Under the rules of his newspaper, he was not allowed to say: I saw this, or I did that, or even—at this moment I really believed we were all finished.

But the rules under which he was working were invented, decades ago, by horrible old men obsessed with the idea of stamping out good writing. And the horrible old men passed on their skills to a series of young men who would never have become horrible without training, and these guys proceeded to attempt to make life as horrible as possible for us. Of the author of any of these American newspaper stylebooks, one could say, as Blake wrote of Reynolds: "This man was hired to depress Art."

It was after the Sahara trip that I had begun to wonder whether a daring raid might not be made on the Philippines. I discussed it with Bill and we began our preparations. *Our* preparations? Well, I soon began to see that Bill had formed an alarmingly clear notion of what I was going to do and when. In the first week I would cover the elections. In the second I would visit the guerrillas. In the third (I had only three weeks at my disposal) Bill said that, if I happened to storm any palaces, he wanted me to come back with clear documentary evidence.

Good editors are a blend of the bully and the altruist—and both types have a habit of invading your life. So, although I raised an eyebrow, I was not entirely surprised, on phoning Bill from the

Philippines, to find that he was currently staying at my house in Oxford. I thought: Oh, he's probably just going through my drawers to see if there's anything else he can publish, should this project fall through.

When I contacted him again later, to ask whether my possession of one of Imelda's monogrammed towels could count as documentary proof that I had stormed Malacañang, the response was disappointingly relaxed. "Very funny," said Bill. Then his voice went gratifyingly gelid. "You're not serious," he said. . . .

The Snap Revolution, in contrast to the Vietnam material, was written, edited, and set up in the course of six weeks, and I have left it more or less unchanged, adding "The Truce" as a pendant, to give a better perspective of the New People's Army. Parts of "The Truce" and the final "Kwangju and After" appeared first as daily journalism in *The Independent*. Parts of the Vietnam material owe their origin to the *Washington Post,* the *Guardian,* and the *New Statesman*. Other "founders and benefactors" will be thanked in private.

VIETNAM

Journey

In the summer of 1973 I had a dream in which, to my great distress, I died. I was alone in a friend's house at the time and, not knowing what to do, I hid the body in her deep freeze. When everyone returned, I explained to them what had taken place: "Something terrible happened when you were out. I . . . I died." My friends were very sympathetic. "But what did you do with the body?" they asked. I was ashamed to tell them. "I don't know where it is," I said, and we all set out to search the house for my corpse. Upstairs and downstairs we looked, until finally, unable to bear the deception any longer, I took my hostess aside and confessed. "There wasn't anything else in the compartment," I said, "and I just didn't know what to do." We went to the deep freeze and opened it. As the curled and frozen shape was revealed, I woke up.

I was glad to be going off on a journey. I had been given an award for the purpose of traveling and writing poetry; I intended to stay out of England a long time. Looking at what the world had to offer, I thought either Africa or Indochina would be the place to go. I chose the latter partly on a whim, and partly because, after the Paris Peace Agreement in February of that year, it looked as if that region was in for some very big changes. I wanted to see Vietnam for myself. I wanted to see a war, and I wanted to see a communist victory, which I presumed to be inevitable. I wanted to see the fall of a city. About Cambodia I knew next to nothing. It was very much in the news at the time: The Americans had stopped bombing it in August; afterward there had been the siege of Kompong Cham. The correspondents had been writing as if the Lon Nol regime had only a few days to go, and I remember wondering whether I would get to Phnom Penh, my first port of call, before the place collapsed.

Although I had a few journalistic commissions, I was not going primarily as a journalist. I wanted time and solitude to write, and knew that travel would tend to make me fall back on my own company. I wanted to see a communist victory because, as did many people, I believed that the Americans had not the slightest justification for their interference in Indochina. I admired the Vietcong and, by extension, the Khmer Rouge, but I subscribed to a philosophy that prided itself on taking a cool, critical look at the liberation movements of the Third World. We supported them against the ambitions of American foreign policy. We supported them as nationalist movements. We did not support their political character, which we perceived as Stalinist in the case of the Vietnamese, and in the case of the Cambodians . . . I don't know. The theory was, and is, that where a genuine movement of national liberation was fighting against imperialism, it received our unconditional support. When such a movement had won, it might then take its place among the governments we execrated—those who ruled by sophisticated tyranny in the name of socialism.

Reduced to this, our attitude may look cynical in the extreme. In fact it was the formulation of a dilemma. After all, we had not invented the Indochina War, and it was not for us to conjure out of thin air a movement that would match up to our own aspirations for Britain. To remain neutral concerning Vietnam was to support the Americans. To argue for an end to all U.S. involvement, and leave the matter at that, was to ignore the consequences of one's own argument. If there was a conflict about which one had to choose sides, then it was only right to choose sides honestly, and say: Stalinists they may be, but we support them. The slogans of the Vietnam movement were crude stuff indeed—"One side right, one side wrong, victory to Vi-et-cong!"—but the justice of the cause was deeply felt.

It was felt by many people who were not socialists or communists by any stretch of the imagination, and who did not have any other political axe to grind. Such people had merely to look at what was being done to Vietnam in the name of the Free World to know that the Free World was in the wrong. The broadest support for the antiwar movement came from disgust at what the Americans were doing. But the movement itself brought into being, all over the world, political groups that took the lessons of Indochina a stage further. In Britain, the Communist Party made precious few gains in this period. The tradition to which the students looked was broadly or narrowly Trotskyist, a fact which no doubt intrigued the Vietnamese communists, who had taken care to bump off their own Trotskyists a long time before. The Trotskyist emphasis—the general emphasis—was on opposition to American imperialism. Very few people idolized the Vietcong, or the North Vietnamese, or Uncle Ho in quite the same way that, for instance, the French Left did. Indeed, it might be fairly said that the Left in Britain was not terribly curious about or enamored of the movement it was supporting.

By the time I was about to go to Indochina in 1973, the issue had fallen from prominence. When the Indochina Solidarity Conference was held in London that year, my own group, the International Socialists, did not bother to send a delegation. There were other, more important campaigns: against the Tories, against the Industrial Relations Act, against racism. Our movement had grown up; it was to be working class in character, it had graduated from what it thought of as student issues. It had not abandoned Vietnam, but it had other fish to fry. At the conference itself, I remember two speeches of interest. One was by I. F. Stone, who was hissed by the audience (which included an unusually large number of Maoists) when he attacked Chairman Mao for shaking hands with a murderer like Nixon. The other was by Noam Chomsky, who warned against the assumption that the war was over, and that direct U.S. intervention in Vietnam would cease. Chomsky also argued that members of the Left were wrong to dismiss the domino theory out of hand. As stated by the Cold Warriors it might not measure up to the facts, but there was another formulation which did indeed make sense: that it was U.S. foreign policy, rather than Russian expansionism, that had knocked over the dominos. Countries might be forced into positions where the only alternative to acceptance of American domination was to go over to the opposite camp and they hence might be drawn into the power struggle whether they liked it or not.

There was, and is, an argument on the Left to the effect that Stalinism was not a simple equivalent of fascism, that it contained what was called a partial negation of capitalism. Further, it was argued that under certain conditions it might even lay down the foundations for a socialist organization of society. Stalinism, in the Third World, might do the job that the bourgeois revolutions had done in Europe. Even Stalinism had its progressive features.

I mention such arguments because I do not wish to give the impression that I was completely wide-eyed about the Vietnamese communists when I set out. I considered myself a revolutionary socialist, of the kind who believe in no Fatherland of the Revolution; who have no cult hero. My political beliefs were fairly broadly based and instinctively grasped, but they were not, I hope, religiously held.

Nonetheless, I wanted very much to see a communist victory. I wanted to see a war and the fall of a city because . . . because I wanted to see what such things were like. I had once seen a man dying, from natural causes, and my first reaction as I realized what was happening was to be glad that I was *there*. This is what happens, I thought, so watch it carefully, don't miss a detail. The first time I saw a surgical operation (it was in Cambodia) I experienced the same sensation, and no doubt when I see a child born it will be the more powerful. The point is simply being there and seeing it. The experience has no essential value beyond itself.

I spent a long time on my preparations for going abroad and, as my dream of dying might indicate, I had developed some fairly morbid apprehensions. The journey itself was to be utterly selfish. I was going to do exactly as I pleased. As far as political beliefs were concerned, they were going to remain "on the table." Everything was negotiable. But the fear of death, which had begun for the first time to enter my calculations, followed me on my journey. As I went through the passport check at Heathrow, I glanced at the Sunday papers and saw that the poet I most admired, W. H. Auden, had just died in Vienna. People were talking about him in the passenger lounge, or rather they weren't talking about him, they were talking about his face.

I kept seeing the face, on the plane, in the transit lounges, on the empty seat next to mine, and I kept remembering Auden. From the start he had willed himself into old age, and it was not surprising that he had not lived longer. He had courted death, cultivated first eccentricity and then what looked to the world very much like senility. It was not senility, but it was a useful cover for his despair of living, the deep unhappiness which he kept concealed. He had held the world very much at arm's length; and had paid a heavy price for doing so.

Between sleeping and reading, I found myself passing through a depression compounded of one part loneliness, one part uneager anticipation, one part fright, and two parts obscure self-pity. In Bombay the depression began to lift: I slept all morning at the Sea Palace Hotel, then, surrendering to the good offices of a driver and guide, set off to see the sights. The evening light was first a muddy yellow, next it turned green. On the Malabar Hill, I paid my respects to the spectacular view, the vultures picking the bones on the Parsee tower, the lights along the waterfront ("Queen Victoria's Necklace"), and the couples sitting on the lawns of the Hanging Gardens in attitudes reminiscent of a Mogul miniature. The most impressive sight was a vast open-air laundry, a yard full of boiling vats between which, through the dark and steam, one could scarcely make out the moving figures of the workers. There was a steamy warmth everywhere, which I immediately liked. Waking the next morning, I looked down on a wide meandering river, either the Salween or the Irrawaddy, whose muddy waters spread out for miles into the sea. As we flew over Cambodia, I waited for the signs of bombing. The landscape was dazzling, silver and blue, but eventually, as we approached Indochina, we came upon lines and lines of yellow circles, where muddy water had filled the bomb craters. We were losing altitude. The flooded fields were marked out by lines of palms. Then we began our descent.

Fear of Madness

"I know not whether others share my feelings on this point," wrote De Quincey, "but I have often thought that if I were compelled to forego England, and to live in China, and among Chinese manners and modes of life and scenery, I should go mad."

I read this sentence the other day, for the first time, and as I came to the last clause I was struck once again with the full nausea of my first trip to Saigon. "The causes of my horror lie deep," De Quincey went on. But he set them forth:

> No man can pretend that the wild, barbarous, and capricious superstitions of Africa, or of savage tribes elsewhere, affect him in the way that he is affected by the ancient, monumental, cruel, and elaborate religions of Indostan, &c. The mere antiquity of Asiatic things, of their institutions, histories, modes of faith, &c. is so impressive, that to me the vast age of the race and name overpowers the sense of youth in the individual. A young Chinese seems to me an antediluvian man renewed. . . . Man is a weed in those regions. The vast empires also, into which the enormous population of Asia has always been cast, give a further sublimity to the feelings associated with all Oriental names or images. In China, over

and above what it has in common with the rest of Southern Asia, I am terrified by the modes of life, by the manners, and the barrier of utter abhorrence, and want of sympathy, placed between us by feelings deeper than I can analyze. I could sooner live with lunatics or brute animals.

Indochina—well, Indochina no longer exists. The name was a Belgian fiction made actual by the French. All the foreigners who lived there, or visited it for any length of time, would invariably form preferences, becoming partisans of either the Indo or the China aspect of the area. Laos and Cambodia represented the former, Vietnam the latter. Laos was the third of the countries I visited, but I may as well deal with it now. I very much sympathize with the man whom Richard West knew: Having lived for years in Laos, he became determined to write a book about it, went back to France to do so and found, when he sat down at the typewriter, that he couldn't remember a blind thing about the place. It was completely relaxing; you might almost be invisible as you walked down the street, and though you might seek out sin, sin did not seek you out with the same diligence as elsewhere in the East. If you wanted to be duped, you could go to the market and buy a gem: I bought a star sapphire which, when unwrapped, turned out to be a piece of plastic. I didn't bother to take it back.

This was in December 1973, when the Pathet Lao were already garrisoned—alongside the army of their former opponents—in most of the major cities. You might see them passing through on trucks, but they did not seem to cause much stir, either in Vientiane or in Luang Prabang, the royal capital. Luang Prabang lived up to the beauty of its name, and it had, among the Méo tribesmen, the pleasantest beggars in Indochina. They would sidle up to your table and indicate your leftovers with a conspiratorial smile. They were the most mysterious thing I had yet come across in my journey, apart from a popular Chinese medicine called "Fishing Pills." The beggars were treated with a proper respect by the waiters, who would provide them with polyethylene bags for their pickings: It was like a Chinese take out. Alternatively, if you so indicated, they would sit down with you and polish off the food on the spot.

Most of the time, they paid a minimum of attention to their benefactors. But I met one French teacher who was wretchedly working out his *coopération* (the alternative to military service) in Luang Prabang, and who had formed a little court of dependents. Every evening he would provide a meal for two young boys and a madwoman. As night wore on, he would become quite enveloped in his charity. A crowd of children gathered around the table, then the madwoman would get up and stagger amorously around the café, shrieking with laughter. Finally, as the chill set in, the more desperate cases would arrive, moaning, praying, and kissing the floor. The Frenchman hated Luang Prabang, he felt that his behavior was continually scrutinized by the Lao upper crust. But, for those who had come to Laos by choice, life passed by in a pleasant drugged haze.

I found the country beautiful, interesting, and utterly unalluring. I was afraid, perhaps, that if I stayed too long I would succumb to a final lethargy. The lethargy was common. A year and a half later, when I left Saigon, I found that the lethargy had completely overcome the British Embassy in Vientiane. I had spent three months in a city where banking facilities had come to a standstill. Consequently I had no money. I thought that my case might interest the consul—after all, I had just lived through a revolution. But no, it would be impossible to lend me the air fare to Bangkok, even though I carried proof that there was money waiting for me in Thailand. What they *could* do, if I wanted, was lend me the bus fare. But it would be extremely awkward. My visa specified that I should leave by air, but the consul reckoned that he might be able to get it changed in a few days. The bus fare was about five pounds. Everyone was very sorry that they couldn't help. They gave me two gin-and-tonics and a signed copy of the ambassador's authoritative work *Fish and Fish Dishes of Laos*.

By this time, the Pathet Lao had almost completely taken over, and most of the foreign community had left. I was walking back to my hotel that evening when I heard a most terrifying noise. Standing behind a bush was a Pathet Lao soldier, and he was snarling—I mean really snarling, like a tiger—at me. There was obviously something about me that excited his deepest, instinctual disgust. I was rather chuffed. It was the first time that something had actually *happened* to me in Laos, and it was my last night in Indochina.

* * *

My first experience of Vietnam was quite different. I was impressed, overawed, by the scale and age of the subject: a war that had been going on for longer than I had been alive; a people about whose history and traditions I knew so little. I had read some books in preparation, but the effect of doing so was only to make the country recede further. So much had been written about Vietnam. I hadn't even had the application to finish *The Fire in the Lake*. The purpose of the book seemed to be to warn you off the subject.

De Quincey's "barrier of utter abhorrence, and want of sympathy" was up. I could well have believed that somebody was trying to tell me something when I came out of my room on the first morning in Saigon and stepped over the decapitated corpse of a rat. I was staying, as most British journalists did, in the Hotel Royale, but even there I felt myself to be something of an intruder. I had to find work, I had to sell some stories, but I was afraid of trespassing on somebody else's patch. There was an epidemic of infectious neurosis at the time: As soon as one journalist had shaken it off, another would succumb. It would attack without warning—in the middle of an otherwise amiable meal, in the bars, in your room. And it could be recurrent, like malaria.

The reason for this neurosis was not far to seek, indeed it sought you out, and pursued you throughout the day: Saigon was an addicted city, and we—the foreigners—were the drug. The corruption of children, the mutilation of young men, the prostitution of women, the humiliation of the old, the division of the family, the division of the country—it had all been done in our name. People looked back to the French Saigon with a sentimental warmth, as if the problem had begun with the Americans. But the French city, the "Saigon of the piastre" as Lucien Bodard called it, had represented the opium stage of the addiction. With the Americans had begun the heroin phase, and what I was seeing now were the first symptoms of withdrawal. There was a desperate edge to life. It was impossible to relax for a moment. Saigon was a vast service industry clamoring for the attention of a dwindling number of customers: "Hey you! American! Change money, buy *Time* magazine, give me back *Time* magazine I sell you yesterday, buy *Stars and Stripes*, give me back *Stars and Stripes*, you number one, you number ten, you number-ten-thousand

Yankee, you want number-one fuck, you want *Quiet American,* you want *Ugly American,* you give me money I shine shoes, number one, no sweat. . . ." On and on, the passionate pursuit of money.

The bar at the Royale was half open to the street. The coffee at breakfast tasted of diarrhea. You washed it down with Bireley's orangeade ("Refreshing . . . and no carbonation!"). Through the windows peered the shoeshine boys—"Hey! you!"—it was starting up again. One morning I was ignoring a particularly revolting specimen when he picked up a handful of sand which he pretended to eat: "You! You no give me money, you want I eat shit!" His expression, as he brought the dirt to his mouth, was most horrible. It was impossible to imagine how a boy of that age had acquired such features: He was about ten years old, but his face contained at least thirty years of degeneration and misery. A few days later I did give him my boots to clean. He sat down in the corner of the bar and set to work, first with a matchstick and a little water, meticulously removing all the mud and dust from the welt, then with the polish. The whole process took about half an hour, and the barman and I watched him throughout, in fascination. He was determined to show his superiority to all other contestants in the trade. I was amused, and gave him a large sum. He was furious, it wasn't nearly enough. We haggled for a while, but I finally gave in. I gave him about a pound. The next day, at the same time, he came into the bar; his eyes were rolling back in their sockets and he staggered helplessly around the tables and chairs; I do not know what drug he had taken, but I know how he had bought it.

Of all the ingenious and desperate forms of raising money, the practice of drugging your baby and laying the thing on the pavement in front of the visitor seemed to me the most repulsive. It did not take long to see that none of these children was ever awake during the day, or to notice from the way they slept that something was amiss. Among the foreigners, stories circulated about the same baby being seen in the arms of five different mothers in one week, but the beggar who regularly sat outside the Royale always had the same child, a girl of eighteen months or so. I never gave any money either to the girl and her "mother," or to any other such teams.

One day, however, I was returning from a good lunch when I saw that a crowd had formed around the old woman, who was wailing and gesticulating. The child was more than usually grey, and there were traces of vomit around her face. People were turning her over, slapping her, trying to force her eyes open. At one point she and the old woman were bundled into a taxi. Then they were taken out again and the slapping was repeated. I went into the hotel and told the girl at reception to call a doctor. "No," she replied. "But the child is sick." "If baby go to hospital or doctor"—and here she imitated an injection—"then baby die." No," I replied, "if baby *don't* go to hospital maybe baby die." "No."

I took the girl out into the street, where the scene had taken on the most grotesque appearance. All the beggars I had ever seen in Saigon seemed to have gathered, and from their filthy garments they were producing pins and sticking them under the child's toenails. "You see," I said to the girl, "no good, number ten. Baby need number-one hospital." "No, my grandmother had same thing. She need this—number one." And the receptionist produced a small phial of eucalyptus oil. "That's not number one," I said, "that's number ten. Number ten thousand," I added for emphasis. But it was no good insisting or appealing to other members of the crowd. Everybody was adamant that if the child was taken to the hospital, the doctor would kill it with an injection. While I correspondingly became convinced that a moment's delay would cost the child's life.

Finally, after a long eucalyptus massage and repeated pricking of the fingers and toes had produced no visible results, I seemed to win. If I would pay for taxi and hospital, the woman would come. I pushed my way through the crowd and dragged her toward the taxi—a battered old Renault tied together with string. The baby was wrapped in a tarpaulin and her face covered with a red handkerchief. Every time I tried to remove the handkerchief, from which came the most ominous dry gaspings, the woman replaced it. I directed the taxi-driver to take us to number-one hospital and we set off. But from the start everything went wrong. Within a hundred yards we had to stop for gas. Then a van stalled in front of us, trapping the taxi. Next, to my amazement, we came to what must have been, I thought, the only level crossing in Saigon, where as it happened a train was expected in the near future. And around here we were hit by the side effects of Typhoon Sarah, which at the time was causing havoc in the northern provinces. We also split a tire, though this was

13

not noticed till later. Driving on through the cloudburst, the taxi driver seemed strangely unwilling to hurry. So I sat in the back seat keeping one hand on the horn and the other attempting to alleviate the restrictions around the baby's breathing apparatus. I also recall producing a third arm with which to comfort the old woman from time to time and I remember that her shoulder, when my hand rested on it, was very small and very hard. Everything, I said, was going to be number one, okay: number-one hospital, number-one doctor, babysan okay. We were traveling through Cholon, the Chinese quarter, on an errand of Western mercy.

All things considered, it took a long time for it to dawn on me that we were not going to a hospital at all. We even passed a first-aid post without the driver giving it a glance. In my mind there was an image of the sort of thing required: a large cool building dating from French times, recently refurbished by American aid and charity, with some of the best equipment in the East. I could even imagine the sententious plaques on the walls. Perhaps there would be a ward named after the former U.S. ambassador. It would be called the Bunker Ward.

It was when the old woman began giving directions that I saw I had been duped. We were now threading our way through some modern slums, which looked like the Chinese equivalent of the Isle of Dogs. "Where is the hospital? This is no hospital," I said. Yes, yes, the taxi-driver replied, we were going to hospital, number-one doctor. We stopped by a row of shops and the driver got out. I jumped from the car and seized him by the arm, shouting: "I said number-one hospital. You lie. You cheap charlie. You number-ten-thousand Saigon." We were surrounded by children, in the pouring rain, the taxi man tugging himself free, and me gripping him by the arm. It was left to the woman, carrying the little bundle of tarpaulin, to find out exactly where the doctor lived. Finally I gave in, and followed her up some steps, then along an open corridor lined with tailors and merchants. At least, I thought, when the baby dies I can't be blamed. And once I had thought that, the thought turned into a wish: A little cough would have done it, a pathetic gurgle, then a silence, and my point about Western medicine would have been proved to my own satisfaction. I should have behaved very well; of course I should have paid for, and gone to, the funeral.

In retrospect it was easy to see how the establishment would command confidence: the dark main room with its traditional furnishings, the walls lined with photographs of ancestors in traditional Vietnamese robes, a framed jigsaw of the Italian lakes. And in the back room (it would, of course, have to be a back room) a plump, middle-aged lady was massaging the back of another plump, middle-aged lady. They paid hardly any attention when we came in. There was not the slightest element of drama. Indeed, I began to see that I was now the only person who was panicking. When she had finished the massage, the doctor turned her attention to the baby. First she took some ointment from a dirty bowl at her elbow, and rubbed it all over the little grey body. Then from another bowl she produced some pink substance resembling Euthymol toothpaste, with which she proceeded to line the mouth. In a matter of minutes, the child was slightly sick, began to cry, and recovered. I had never been more furious in my life. To complete my humiliation, the doctor refused any payment. She provided the old woman with a prescription wrapped in newspaper, and we left. We drove to the miserable shelter in which the old woman lived. "Sit down," she said, indicating the wooden bed which was the only feature of her home apart from the roof (there were no walls). In any other mood I might have been moved by the fact that the only English she knew beyond the terrible pidgin currency of the beggars was a phrase of hospitality. But I so deeply hated her at that moment that I could only give her a couple of pounds, plus some useless advice about keeping the baby warm and off the pavements, and go.

I left the taxi-driver at a garage not far from the Royale, where I also gave him some money toward repairing the split tire. "You number one, Saigon," he said, with a slight note of terror in his voice. The weather had cleared up, and I strolled along past the market stalls. You could buy U.S. Army foot-powder in bulk, K-rations, lurp rations (for Long Range Reconnaissance Patrols), souvenir Zippo lighters (engraved "Yea though I walk through the valley of the shadow of death I shall fear no evil, for I am the evilest sonofabitch in the valley"), khaki toothbrushes and flannels, and model helicopters constructed out of used hypodermics. You could also buy jackets brightly embroidered with the words "When I die I shall go to heaven, for I have spent my time in hell—Saigon," and a collection of GI cartoons and jokes called *Sorry 'bout that, Vietnam.* As I approached the hotel, people began asking how the baby was, and smiling when I replied "Okay."

And I began to think, supposing they were all in it together? Suppose the old woman, the taxi driver, the man whose van stalled, the engine driver—suppose they were all now dividing out the proceeds and having a good laugh at my expense, congratulating the child on the way it had played its role? That evening I would be telling the story to some old Saigon hand when a strange pitying smile would come over his face. "You went to Cholon, did you? Describe the doctor . . . uhuh . . . Was there a jigsaw puzzle of the Italian lakes? Well, well, well. So they even used the toothpaste trick. Funny how the oldest gags are still the best. . . ."

Indeed I did have rather that conversation a few days later, with an American girl, a weaver. It began "You realize, of course, first of all that the taxi driver was the husband of the old woman. . . . But I do not think it was a conspiracy." Worse, I should rather conclude that the principals involved were quite right not to trust the hospital doctors with a beggar's child. It was for this reason that the hotel receptionist had countermanded my orders to the taxi man, I learned afterward, and many people agreed with her.

When the old woman came back on the streets, I hardly recognized either her or the child, who for the first time looked conscious and well. "Babysan okay now, no sick," she said, gazing at me with an awful adoring expression, though the hand was not stretched out for money. And when I didn't reply she turned to the child and told it something in the same unctuous tones. This performance went on for the rest of my stay: Whenever I was around, the child would be made to look at the kind foreigner who had saved its life. I had indeed wanted to save the child's life, but not in *that* way, not on the old woman's terms.

I was disgusted, not just at what I saw around me, but at what I saw in myself. I saw how perilously thin was the line between the charitable and the murderous impulse, how strong the force of righteous indignation. I could well imagine that most of those who came to Vietnam to fight were not the evilest sons-of-bitches in the valley. It was just that, beyond the bright circle illuminated by their intelligence, in which everything was under their control and every person a compliant object, they came across a second person—a being or a nation with a will of its own, with its own medicine, whether Fishing Pills or pink toothpaste, and its own ideas for the future. And in the ensuing encounter everything had turned to justifiable ashes. It was impossible in Saigon to be the passive observer. Saigon cast you, inevitably, into the role of the American.

Elsewhere it was possible to breathe more freely, but I was conscious always of following in somebody else's steps. Coming toward Quang Tri and asking my driver how far away the town was—"This is the main street," he said, indicating the overgrown rubble. We stood on the edge of the river, looking across to the liberated zone and the still figures of the soldiers on the Other Side. I had heard endless stories of people's exploits in Quang Tri, but it meant nothing to me. There was no point in my being there. Hue, yes. Walking around the Imperial City in the rain, through the beautiful, shabby grounds which looked like nothing so much as the vegetable gardens of an English country house. But I was nothing more than a tourist there. I thought I was actually going to meet someone, when a Vietnamese took me to see his girlfriend, to whom he was hoping to get married. She worked in a chemist's shop, but when we arrived the drill was simply that I should go in, buy some aspirin or something, look at her, and tell her boyfriend what I thought. He waited outside for my opinion. I gave the girl a warm recommendation.

I went also to Dalat, and walked through the forests among the tall red poinsettias, the Vietnamese called them the Man of Genius Tree. In my hotel room, there were poems scrawled in ballpoint on the walls:

> *I am a fairy from the moon.*
> *You are my happiness.*
> *When the sun sets*
> *The river will be without water*
> *And the rocks will scrape.*
> *Our promises will be forever.*

The nearest I got to the war was in Gia Nghia, a former American base in the Quang Duc region. It had been a great feat of engineering: The wide roads of red earth cut through the jungle to make the vast clearing. There were little signs of America everywhere, the half-caste children, even the dogs of the area were mongrels from the American trackers. There was a dog's footprint on a concrete floor, with the words "Our Mascot (MACV)" scratched beside it. There were drunken Montagnards wandering around, and in the marketplace (which sported two billiard saloons) a soldier was smoking marijuana through a waterpipe made out of an antitank shell. There was music and the sound of motorbikes from the Wall of Death, but when we went in the evening and asked them to open it up we found the family asleep on the track.

The USAID compound had a commanding view of the town. A Montagnard soldier, with huge stretched earlobes, stood on guard outside. Inside, leaning over a shortwave radio, was Ed Sprague, the local USAID official; he was marking positions on a map. There was a rifle propped against the wall and a neatly polished revolver on the table. The rest of the room was magnificently equipped with photos, souvenirs, stereo tape-recorder, cocktail bar, Montagnard girl, soft furnishings. Above the bar, engraved on copper and nicely framed, were the sayings of Sprague himself: "The Special Forces have done so much for nothing for so long that now we are expected to do everything for nothing forever," and "If you kick me once in the back when I'm not looking I'll kick you twice in the face when you are looking—Sprague '71."

He was very polite, but the USAID compound had no room to put us up, so we went to the local hotel in town. The helicopter pilots were billeted there, and I spent the evening playing Co Tuong ("Kill the General"), the Chinese and Vietnamese version of chess. The round wooden pieces were engraved with Chinese characters, and the board was made of paper. A river flowed down the middle of the board, separating the two rows of GIs, who had to move forward, one square at a time, until they crossed the river, after which they might move in any direction. Just behind the GIs lay the two artillery pieces, which might fire in straight lines at any of the pieces, as long as there was some single obstruction in between. The horses made knight's moves, and could cross the river, as could the tanks, which were the equivalent of rooks. But the elephants, which always moved two squares at a time, diagonally, were unable to cross the river and were reserved for the defense. The general was protected by his officer escort. He lived in a compound of four squares along whose sides he moved, while the two officers stuck to the diagonals. The red general might never "see" the black general—that is to say there must always be something in between. The best, the classic, way to kill the general was with a horse in front and a tank behind. Next best, with two horses. "This is the black general," said my teacher. "He is Ho Chi Minh. This is the red general. He is Thieu." "But Ho Chi Minh is dead." "I know. I killed him in the last game." Black always moved first. Throughout the evening I allowed Uncle Ho to be ambushed a thousand times, and die a hundred deaths.

I also spent some time in the billiard saloons collecting Vietnamese jokes from the pilots. The jokes were different in character from Cambodian jokes, which were all about sex. Vietnamese jokes were all about tactics. Here is a typical Cambodian joke: A mosquito is caught in a storm and takes shelter in an elephant's cunt. (Roars of laughter.) After the storm, the mosquito meets a friend. "Did you know what that was you were sheltering in just then?" says the second mosquito. "What?" "It was an elephant's cunt." (Further roars of laughter, particularly from the women.) "Oh," says the first mosquito, flexing his muscles, "a pity I didn't know that. If I'd realized it was an elephant's cunt I might have done something about it!" (Hysterical laughter, old men clutch their sides, tears course down the faces of the women, food and wine are produced and the teller of the joke is asked for more.)

Now here is a Vietnamese joke; see if you can spot the difference: During the Tet Offensive in 1968, the Vietcong blew up the central span of the main bridge over the Perfume River, and for some time afterward planks were put across, and the bridge was very dangerous. A young and beautiful girl was walking home from the school in which she taught (nods of interest, audience leans forward and is very quiet) when she fell into the water (smiles), which was most unfortunate because she could not swim (smiles disappear). So she started calling out "Help me, help me," and a large crowd gathered on the river bank, but none of the young men wanted to help her (expressions completely disappear). So the girl called out: "If anybody jumps in and saves me, I will marry him." (Smiles) At this point all the young men rushed forward, but every time one of them reached the edge of the water (smiles) another man pulled him back, because everyone wanted to marry the young girl (smiles disappear, anxiety features on faces of young men). And so the girl was very near to drowning when an old man succeeded in getting into the water and saving the girl. At the wedding, he was asked by the press: "How come a weak and ugly old man like you managed to win the girl, when all the young men were trying?" And the old man replied: "Every time a young man tried to get in, he was pulled back by another. But when an old and ugly man like me appeared on the scene, they didn't bother to pull me back. In fact, they pushed me in." (End of joke. Heads nod. There is a little laughter.)

I tried this joke out in Hue, and when I got to the end of the story the effect was striking. First, there was silence. Then I was asked to repeat the punchline. Then all hell broke loose, and I thought for a moment that I might be chucked into the Perfume River myself. After several minutes of animated conversation the company turned back to me. They had two comments on the story. *Primo,* the young men were right in the first place not to jump in— after all, they might have been killed. *Secundo,* the story was not true.

When not collecting jokes or playing Chinese chess I was trying to find out about the war, but this was difficult. Some of the small outposts that were dotted around the mountains—they had names like Bu Prang and Bu Bong—were under attack, and the helicopter squadron was there to give them support. There was a low-level campaign on the part of the Vietcong to wipe out these little impediments, which were used as listening posts along the region of the Ho Chi Minh Trail, and which had been set up largely by the Special Forces in which Sprague had served. It was here that the Special Forces gained their great love of the Montagnard as a soldier. Now the campaign was under the aegis of Saigon, and these outposts were beginning to fall. At one point my chess master produced a hand-drawn map and started to show me what was happening, but he didn't get far before somebody came into the room, and he quickly shoved the map into his pocket. We slept seven or eight to a room, and in the middle of the night I awoke to the sound of rifle fire. There was an extraordinary noise going on, and I suddenly thought Good God! They're attacking Gia Nghia. They're coming into the camp and blowing whistles. Why are they all blowing whistles? They're blowing whistles in order to tell each other where they are, perhaps to create a panic in the camp . . . panic! I got up and went to the window. One of the soldiers burst out laughing. There was no gunfire any more. A soldier had shot at a shadow, perhaps, and the noise of whistles, though it continued, was nothing more than the noise of the jungle.

During this period I often suffered from nightmares. It was as if some great spade was digging through my mind, turning over deep clods of loam. If Saigon was a nightmare by day, it was to Phnom Penh that my thoughts returned at night. It will already be apparent that I was one of those who infinitely preferred Cambodia to Vietnam, but this does not mean that I found the former merely picturesque. I found it deeply alluring, and frightening. In Saigon I was shown some photographs that had come in from Cambodia, which AP had decided were too horrible to use. In one, a smiling soldier was shown eating the liver of a Khmer Rouge, whom he had just killed; from the expression on his face, he could have been eating anything—the liver was obviously delicious. In the next photograph, a human head was being lowered by the hair into a pot of boiling water—but it was not going to be eaten. In the third photograph, decapitated corpses were being dragged along the road behind an APC.

My nightmares were about war and torture and death. I remember one particularly vividly. We were standing—myself and a friend who was a poet—at the edge of a battle. The landscape was hilly, but belonged neither to Cambodia nor to Vietnam; it seemed to be northern European. The soldiers had taken several prisoners, and there were wounded and dead lying all around. Their features were Cambodian. As the prisoners were brought in, it became obvious that they were about to be beaten up and killed. The soldiers gathered around them. The poet began to shout out: "No no, this isn't happening. I'm not here, I'm not here." When the beating-up began, all the bodies of the dead and wounded rose into the air, and began to travel around the sky above the hill. "Look," I said, pointing to the hill, "isn't that interesting. Those figures. They look just like the shepherds in that van der Goes altarpiece in the Uffizi." "I say," said a journalist at my elbow, "that's a rather good image. But I suppose you'll be using it in your story." "Oh no," I replied, "have it by all means. I'm not filing on this one." Here the dream ended.

After a month I was due to go to Laos, and my visa was coming to an end. I paid up at my hotel, and by the time I was through immigration at the airport I had no currency left. I was badly in need of coffee, and I was absolutely terrified that the plane would not come. Suppose I had to stay in Saigon any longer. The neurosis came back alarmingly. I got talking to a Chinese businessman, whom I had helped with his luggage. He bought me coffee and began a lengthy chat about the virtues of South Vietnam as a source of raw materials. Raw materials were very much needed in Hong Kong. He dealt in anything he could find—here was his card—he dealt in timber, scrap iron, swatches. . . . "What are swatches?" I asked. "Rags," he said, "like these," and indicated my clothes. Then he left for Hong Kong. I just did not believe that my plane would go. As it taxied along the runway, a cockroach scuttled along the floor in front of me. I thought, this plane is hopeless, it'll never make the journey. We flew for some way along the Mekong, and the neurosis subsided. But then suddenly I looked out and—What! We were flying over the sea! Something's gone wrong, I thought, the pilot's got lost, he's going to turn back and go to Saigon. It's all going to happen over again. But then I looked down and saw that the sea effect was a mirage. We were indeed flying over Laos, and we were beginning to lose altitude.

KAMPUCHEA
KROM

The Khmer Krom

A year later I was back in Vietnam and made two trips to the Mekong Delta, where I narrowly avoided meeting the Khmer Rouge (to my great relief) and the Vietcong (to my regret). I enlisted the help of a Vietnamese student as interpreter, and we set off by bus from Saigon to Cantho. At the terminal just outside Saigon there were vast crowds of screaming touts, who rushed at you and tried to seize your baggage. Little girls were most insistent that you would need sunglasses for the journey. Every form of food and refreshment was pressed into your hand. The first leg of the journey was by minibus, nonstop to Cantho. We fell in with a couple of Vietnamese who were on their way to Ha Tien, the seaport by the Cambodian border. You must go to Ha Tien, they said, because of the market. Everything is so cheap—cloth, drink, cigarettes—you could buy whatever you wanted at a fraction of the price in Saigon.

It was impossible to go with them at first, because we were working on research into the Cambodian communities of the delta. However, after a couple of days in Ba Xuyen province, where for some reason all the Cambodians appeared to be getting married (it was I suppose the Khmer equivalent of Whitsun) we decided to return to Cantho and rejoin them on their journey. As it happened, our friends were nowhere to be found, so we set off to Ha Tien on one of the large, ancient, boneshaking buses that served on the route. The trick with these buses was not to sit in the back, because it would be full of chicken, ducks, and catfish, and not to sit in the middle, because there was no room for your legs, and not to sit in the front, because it was absolutely terrifying. For the first part of the journey we sat in the back, and every time the bus hit a bump—that is to say, every five minutes—I would hit the roof. Later I sat in the front, and watched a series of near misses. There were two boys on the bus employed to collect the fares and, as we made our rapid progress on the clearer stretches, to hang from the doors screaming at anyone near the road to get out of the way.

Two things held us up. First, there was a series of refreshment pauses as vendors climbed aboard and screamed "Boiled Crab!" or "Shrimp Pancake!" in your ear, or proferred chunks of sugar cane. Some of these pauses had been arranged with the driver. Others had been ingeniously arranged—a sort of commercial ambush. One woman had placed her baby in the path of the bus as if to say "Either you buy my rather indifferent madeira cake or you kill my baby. The choice is yours." The second reason for holdups was the activity of the Vietcong frogmen, who had blown up several bridges along the way. This also added to the expense of the trip since, although Thieu's army had plenty of equipment to meet such emergencies, they considered that they should be paid for their efforts. At one point, as we waited for the bus to be precariously loaded onto the pontoon ferry, I went and talked to the small group of soldiers beside the destroyed bridge. They pointed to a clump of bushes about a hundred and fifty yards away and said that the Vietcong were there. I wasn't sure whether they were telling the truth. It seemed ridiculous that the situation could be tolerated. But in fact it was typical of the delta in those times, and typical indeed of large areas of Vietnam. The *amour propre* of the Saigon government, and the tolerance of the Vietcong, kept roads open through areas that did not belong to Saigon in any way.

By this time it was getting toward evening, and a woman on the bus advised us that it would be better to sit away from the front seats since it was quite likely that we would be stopped either by Vietcong or by bandits. I remembered the golden rule of travel in Indochina: Never be on the roads after dusk. Still, there was nothing to be done, and I was not at all worried about the prospect of meeting the Vietcong. As it became dark, barricades were put on the roads at either end of every village. We would stop; the two boys would rush to the barricades, parley with the guards, and wave us through. The excitement and the hurry mounted. We met more and more Vietnamese Cambodians. One leapt onto the bus and met his mother-in-law. He slapped her so hard on the back that she shrieked. Then he started talking to her with such speed and amusement, holding his head first on one side, then on the other, like some kind of garrulous bird, that he soon had put her into a good mood. The happiness of these two was infectious. My interpreter, who had never traveled in this area before, was completely beguiled. He told me that he had never, never seen such a happy group of people in Vietnam as on this bus.

But at the last village before Ha Tien another bridge had been blown up, and this time it would be impossible to get through before dawn. We decanted from the bus and went to the village café, where the arrival of a white face at such a time of night caused a great stir. The village was poor and there was nothing much to eat, but in a short while the local police chief and military chief had arrived, and we began talking and drinking together. It was a sad conversation, and much of it consisted of questions to myself: What did I think of Thieu? What would the Americans do if there was another offensive? Could Saigon last? I tried to answer these questions, in the way I always tried, with tact and about two-thirds honesty. People imagine that the officers of the Thieu regime were corrupt and vicious to a man. In my experience, many of them were no better and no worse than anybody else in the world. But of course I only knew them when their fortunes were on the wane, and they had every reason to be reflective about the merits of their own side. In this conversation, there was only one point at which my interpreter refused to translate what I was saying; this was when I pointed out that Con Son island was one of the most notorious prisons in the world, and one of the great reasons why the Thieu regime was disliked by so many foreigners.

By about midnight, the rest of the travelers had found a place to sleep, either in the huts of the village or under the coach itself. We were invited to stay the next day in order to go fishing. There was a rare and highly prized species of crab to be found nearby. We accepted, and were given camp beds and mosquito nets in the military compound. There was a gun nearby, an artillery piece, which fired off at regular intervals into the night, and the guards would occasionally fire shots into the river, to ward off any frogmen. I slept well enough, and woke in an area of most unusual beauty. A dramatic limestone crag lay on the other side of the river, which gave into a calm sea dotted with steep white islands and rocks. We said goodbye to the bus, and climbed into a fiberglass military dinghy to go fishing.

Of course, said our friends as we prepared to set out, we could use grenades, but it's so wasteful of stock, don't you think? We agreed solemnly, but I noticed that we had no tackle with us. There were only two blocks of *plastique*, one hand grenade, and a landing net. We sped out among the beautiful islands, passing one on which a white cross stood, marking the cave where the Emperor Gia Long had spent his exile. Once at the fishing grounds, we stuck fuses into the *plastique*, lit the fuses with cigarette ends, threw the *plastique* into the water, and retired to a safe distance. With the first explosion, the sea gave a slight heave and brought up a total of one fish. The second, however, succeeded in stunning about sixty sprats, and one or two larger items. We decided, rather to my relief since I am mortally afraid of them, not to use the grenade. We never found the highly prized species of crab.

On our return, we found that the village was being visited by two senior police officers, who were very keen to discuss the problems of Vietnam. When I told them I worked for the *Washington Post,* they were pretty annoyed. *"Washington Post,"* they said, "the paper that finished President Nixon." So I told them that I also worked for the *New Statesman* which, as far as I know, never finished anybody. "When the Americans were here," they said, indicating the twisted spans of the bridge, "this bridge would have been rebuilt in one day. Now . . ." They shrugged. They said that it was impossible to continue the battle against the Vietcong without more supplies. I questioned this, pointing out that the soldiers had been firing all the previous night against an apparently nonexistent enemy, so they could hardly be that short of stocks.

They said it was very difficult to combat the Vietcong, because they used such crude methods. "Crude?" I asked. "Yes, crude." The word was spoken with a dreadful scowl. "What do you mean, crude?" One of the officers explained. It was these frogmen. They didn't use proper equipment. They just put a clip on their nose, tied a bit of rubber hose to breathe through, attached stones to their feet, and walked along the bottom of the river. They had found from intelligence sources that that was how they had blown up all these bridges. It was impossible to see them coming. It was all very crude. I had to agree with the officer. It did sound pretty crude. But why didn't they do the same thing in return. Why didn't the Saigon troops go walking around on the bottom of the rivers attacking Vietcong positions? The officer looked at me with utter contempt. "That would be quite impossible," he said flatly.

By this time, another bus had arrived and been ferried across the river, so we continued on our way, along a palm-fringed coast, toward Ha Tien and the Cambodian border. We could see the Elephant Mountains and the region of Kampot. Ha Tien itself was an old town, built in the Chinese-French-Portuguese commercial style, with charming, decorated, crumbling-stucco houses, and the filthiest market I had seen so far in Vietnam. Was this what we had come for? After a revolting lunch, during which my spirits sank, we asked about the big market. It turned out that we needed a Honda cart to take us. The market was not in Ha Tien. It was in a village called Prek Chak ("Poke Village"), and Prek Chak was in Cambodia.

I must have been a little thick that day. It was already about two-thirty, and not the best of times to be crossing borders. However, we set out along the road, passing rows of Cambodian refugee settlements on the way. About a hundred yards before the border post on the main road we turned left into a small village and came to a pagoda complex where our driver left us. There was a constant stream of people passing to and fro, their bicycles laden with goods. We walked through the village and, without our asking, people showed us to the unofficial crossing point. There was a double fence of barbed wire, newly erected, and a Vietnamese soldier standing beside it. No, he said, it was impossible to go through. Look at the barbed wire. Yes, I said, it has been cut; all you have to do is roll it back. No, he said, it was only cut because the Vietcong had cut it the night before. It wasn't really supposed to be cut. This was obviously a lie, but there were so many people around that I didn't like to try bribing the man in public. Finally I produced my military travel documents, and with ill grace the man let us through.

We walked across a field toward a collection of straw huts. There was nothing remarkable about them from the distance, but when we came closer we realized the place was very odd indeed. The huts, which were clustered around a shallow muddy creek, were crammed full of merchandise of every kind. There were cartons of cigarettes from Singapore, bales of cloth from Thailand, crates of whiskey, sacks of cement; there were boxes of Chinese razor blades and bottles of Chinese wine. Everything was in bulk. The place was a hypermarket of contraband.

And as we entered the village, people looked up—not in the normal astonished way to which I had grown accustomed in some of the remoter parts of Cambodia, but in a manner that indicated absolute blank incomprehension. They laughed—the Cambodians among them, although the Chinese didn't—but they laughed in a different way. They seemed embarrassed. They seemed as though they had just been caught out, doing something improper. And well they might seem embarrassed. For they were all gambling. Absolutely everybody was gambling. It was like, I suddenly thought, coming into some allegorical town, say in the *Pilgrim's Progress*. In the muddy alleys between the huts, the children were gambling with rubber bands, squatting on their haunches and shrieking as they lost or won. In the smaller huts they were gambling with cards, dice, shells. On the other side of the creek there were larger huts containing full-scale casinos where the really serious stuff was going on. These were run by the Chinese. Numbers or characters were drawn out of a box, and held up to shouts and groans. A vast litter of Vietnamese and Cambodian notes was raked across the tables.

Sitting in one of the many cafés, I got into conversation with some Cambodians who explained part of the history of Prek Chak. It had begun earlier in the year when the Khmer Rouge had attacked Kampot, and taken away its usefulness as a center for smuggling. The Cambodian Navy had cooperated with the Chinese, and the South Vietnamese had not objected. So the village had grown at an enormous rate, and was still growing. As I walked around, I began to attract a crowd of children, who followed cheering and imitating my every gesture. I wanted to see if, in addition to the Saigon soldiers and police who were walking around, there were any Cambodian military. Yes there were, said somebody, down by the sea. We set off to look for them.

At this point, the children suddenly melted away. I was glad at first, but then I suddenly noticed that nobody was talking to us any longer. We became uneasy, and again we asked the way. This time a Vietnamese woman came up to us and hurriedly explained that if we didn't get out at once we would be killed. It was four o'clock, she said, and at this time the Khmer Rouge came into town. Any foreigners would be killed; one stranger had been killed the day before on the very spot where we were standing. She herself, as a recent newcomer, had been in terrible trouble. We must get out at once? But how? The route by which we had come in had now been shut up for the night. If we went out along the main road, via the official customs post, we would be arrested.

There was one other way.

The woman led us through the village, and as she did so people stared at us in a new way. Suddenly I realized why they had been so surprised when we arrived there in the first place. As the woman explained, Prek Chak belonged to Phnom Penh and Saigon by day. By night it belonged to the Khmer Rouge. Every evening they came in, sometimes trading things, but very often simply stealing them. The Vietcong and NVA came in as well, from time to time, but they always payed for their purchases. Prek Chak by day was a paradise for draft dodgers, smugglers, and gamblers. By night it was quite a different kettle of fish.

As we made our way through the fields, we met a line of people coming back from Ha Tien to their homes in Prek Chak. As they passed us, they told my interpreter: "Don't be afraid. Just walk very quickly." But soon we saw that the route by which they were coming involved at least another mile before the border. Then, we were told, there was a creek, but the ferryman on the creek did not have any authorization, and the previous night his boat had been shot at by the Khmer Rouge. Just at this time, as well. There was nothing for it but to go back to the official border post and argue our way through the guards. By now I was really frightened, more frightened than I had ever been before. The prospect of arrest by the South Viet-

namese seemed as nothing in comparison with meeting the Khmer
Rouge. We hurried back to the border post, and were obligingly
arrested. While this was happening, the South Vietnamese began for
some reason to fire shells over our heads into Cambodia, and in Prek
Chak the sound of automatic-rifle fire began.

The trouble with being arrested was that nobody knew what to
do with us. We protested that it had all been a terrible mistake—we
had assumed that Prek Chak was in Vietnam, and anyway there were
thousands of others crossing the border all the time. The soldiers
were sympathetic, but by now they had reported our case, so it was
too late to let us go. In Ha Tien we were passed from office to office.
Statements were taken, and then the men who took the statements
were roundly abused by their seniors for not taking more detailed
statements. More detailed statements were taken. The police chief
was not around. I was exhausted and irritated and by the end of
three hours began to get annoyed. The police station was apparently
open to the whole public, and a small crowd of children had
gathered to watch the fun. I turned to my interpreter: "Will you
please tell the officer," I said in wounded tones, "that in England it is
customary to offer people chairs." From the depths of the ancient
French building, a chair was brought. We were approaching the
final, most dangerous point, the status of my interpreter. "Why
doesn't he have a press card?" they asked. I lied through my clenched
teeth: "Because in Saigon, press cards are *never, never* issued to
interpreters." "Then how do we know he is your interpreter?"
"Look," I said, "if you want proof, I'll write you out a letter of
introduction for him." I was getting somewhat hysterical. An impressive anger began to sweep through my frame. "In fact," I said,
"I'll *type* you a letter for him, and sign it, *with my own signature,* in the
name of the *Washington Post!*" All right, they said, much to my
surprise. "Well where's the typewriter?!!" They led me into the
building. The children milled around. I sat down in the manner of a
man who was about to blow the lid off the Pentagon. *"I'll need some
paper as well, you know!"* They hurried off and found a piece of paper.
By now the interest was tremendous. I put the paper in the machine.
I did it really beautifully. I've since seen Robert Redford do this bit
on film, but he was pathetic in comparison with me. I really gave
that paper hell. My fingers poised over the keys. I looked down. It

was a Vietnamese typewriter, of course, and all the keys were in the wrong positions. Pathetically, I began to look for the W. There didn't seem to be a W. The children started to snigger. It was perfectly obvious that I didn't know how to type. "Will you please get those children out of here?" I said furiously. Then, key by key, I composed the worst-typed letter of introduction ever.

And yet, for some reason, we were let off, and we went and indulged in a celebratory supper. When we got back to our hotel, the manager told us in lugubrious tones that the chief of police had called and would be back in the morning. We went upstairs with heavy hearts. In the room next to ours, a Chinese merchant had laid out his purchases from Prek Chak, and had erected a small altar, with candles, joss sticks, and offerings of fruit. He was praying, he said, for three things: finance, property, and protection from the Khmer Rouge. Soon, there was a knock at the door. It was the police chief, with a couple of his friends. He was profusely apologetic. He had been away all day, otherwise we would never have had all that trouble. His junior officers had not known what to do. How could he make amends? Would we come to breakfast with him the next day? He would take us for the finest Chinese soup in town. At 6:30? Good. The trouble was, he said, that we had been taken through by the military. The military did not know what they were doing. It was very dangerous for a foreigner in Prek Chak. We could have been killed. He was responsible for us. If anything had happened to us he would personally have been very upset. He considered us, you know, he considered us to be his own sons. . . .

After soup the next morning, the police chief put us on the bus for Saigon, instructing the driver not to charge us for the trip. After we left Ha Tien we persuaded the driver, although with some difficulty, to let us pay half fare. As we went toward Saigon, I noted from time to time that bundles of notes were produced and handed over to the military checkpoints. This was the protection money on which the racketeers of the Mekong Delta made their fortunes. What I did not realize until some weeks later, when it was independently confirmed, was that Prek Chak's main function was gun running. Corrupt officials in Kompong Som, together with the Khmer Navy, brought American weapons and ammunition to be sold to the Khmer Rouge. Later still, I was talking about Prek Chak to a soldier in Kompong Som, and he told me that the place had just been attacked by the Khmer Rouge and burnt to the ground. Many of the inhabitants had been killed, the others had fled to South Vietnam where they were continuing their trade. Clearly the place had outlived its usefulness and had fallen under the righteous wrath of the insurgents. It certainly had stood for everything they despised. I said to the soldiers: "They were selling arms to the enemy, weren't they." The soldier looked alarmed. I lowered my voice: "It was well known. The FANK officers were selling their own weapons to the Khmer Rouge." "Yes," said the soldier ruefully, "they *were* selling arms to the enemy. It is true. But they were only *small* arms."

While in Ba Xuyen province on this trip, I had found a Cambodian monastery where we had been received very well, and which I wanted to investigate more carefully. The trouble (and the attraction) was that it was in a contested area—the Vietcong controlled villages only a couple of miles away. I thought that if I stayed there I might be able to cross over to a PRG zone, but it was obviously unfair to try to do so in the company of my interpreter. I therefore set out by myself a few days later on the same sort of minibus, in the direction of Cantho. The driver was fairly careful but the traffic was heavy. At one point, a young girl stepped out from behind a car, and was hit by the bus. We drew to an abrupt halt, and the child was thrown several yards down the road. Then a large proportion of the luggage on the roofrack slipped off and fell into the road in front of us. The child lay twiching in the road, and the driver, in a state of terrible distress, got out, hailed a Honda cart and took the girl off to a hospital. At once, all the passengers on the bus dispersed. Somebody took me gently by the arm, and indicated a large, red, ancient American car, into which we piled. We left the minibus where it had stopped, in the middle of the road.

The miserable aspect of Cantho, with its drug addicts and cripples, has been well described before.* I shall mention just one thing I saw that night. It was a group of legless heroin addicts, sitting in wheelchairs and drinking together on the waterfront. When the time came to pay the bill, an argument broke out among them. Soon the argument developed into a fight—and a vicious fight

---

*See Richard West's *Victory in Vietnam*.

it was. The purpose of the fight was to pull each other out of the wheelchairs. I did not stay to see the result.

The next morning I was dropped from the local bus not far from Wat Champa. As I approached the monastery, walking through the fields, I greeted one of the peasants in Cambodian. At once, he called out to another peasant on the other side of the field, saying that I spoke Khmer. And then I heard the message passed on further, to the adjoining paddies. A sudden surge of happiness came over me, to be walking alone in the countryside, and to be walking into what was, after all, a tiny pocket of Cambodia. The morning was sunny, the occasion propitious. I had never really seen Cambodian village life functioning before, at least not since my trip through Battambang province the year before. Here I got some idea of it, even though the circumstances were peculiar.

The monastery was set in a spacious grove of tall, umbrageous trees, and the main temple was a work of fantastic imagination. At each corner stood concrete statues of animals, brilliantly painted. The other buildings were more modest, some of them made of wood. The abbot was pleased to see me, and asked after my interpreter. Over a cup of tea, I explained that my purpose was to study a little more of the customs of the monks and to learn a little of the Cambodian language. If possible, I should like to spend a few days at the monastery. "Aren't you afraid of the Vietcong," they said. No, I replied, the Vietcong always behaved well toward foreigners. I was only afraid of the Khmer Rouge. The monks explained that the Vietcong were visiting the village every night to collect taxes, but that they never came to the monastery. The abbot would give me some lessons in Khmer if I gave him some lessons in English. Everything seemed fine.

The monks lived what they were perfectly prepared to admit was a very lazy life. They joined the monastery as young men, at their family's request, and they would leave it when it became necessary for them to work at home. Of course, in wartime the temptation to stay on in the monastery was great. They ate two meals a day, breakfast and lunch. After that they survived on tea and cigarettes, although for senior monks there might be special treats. I once found the abbot chewing sugar cane, which he said counted as drinking since one always spat out the fibrous interior. One evening we ate a dish called "fried milk," which consisted of "Longevity Brand" condensed milk, mixed with coconut, and reduced by heat until it reached the consistency of treacle toffee. The day was spent in lessons—Pali and English—trips to the local villages to beg for alms, attendance at religious ceremonies; and the rest of the time sitting by the monastery pool, feeding the two enormous pet turtles, stomachs rumbling as evening came on.

The buildings were full of surprises. In one, surrounded by winking lights, the last abbot was lying in his coffin. He had died a year before, and it would be another two years before he was cremated. The present abbot's house was stuffed with souvenirs and junk. It looked like the bedroom of some sentimental bit-part actress. There were photographs, ornaments, and knick-knacks, and on a loft above our heads there were piles of embroidered cushions and umbrellas stacked away. But this was nothing to the house occupied by the oldest monk in the establishment, to which we were invited one evening in order to watch the television.

This was a great occasion. There was the strangest altar I have ever seen. On the top level was a row of assorted Buddhas, as one might expect. Below these, and partly obscuring them, was a television set and three bottles of pop, flanked by two model Christmas trees with fairy lights, and an illuminated star of Bethlehem. On the next level there was a row of ancient biscuit barrels and a wholesale tin of Maxwell House instant coffee. At the base there was a coffee table cluttered with china frogs, candlesticks, fluffy animals, alarm clocks, and glasses full of old cutlery, all covered with dust.

The old monk also showed me his cupboards, which were full of souvenirs from the seaside, old swords and daggers, and yet more alarm clocks. He had a passion for clocks. He took out one and placed it, with great ceremony, in my hands; it was a traveling alarm, with a cunning, slatted shutter that could be pulled across the clock face. "Are you—um—giving this to me?" I asked, embarrassed. "No!" he said quickly, and snatched it away. Instead, I was given something to eat. By now, the room had filled up with children and adults from the village, the generator had been turned on, the fairy lights and the star of Bethlehem were blinking away, and I was the center of attention for about fifty people. The monks were not eating, of course, so I was going to be the only one.

I looked into the bowl that they put in my hands. It contained crushed rice, coconut, and about three hundred ants swarming all over it. There was nothing to be done. I spooned up the ants, and wolfed them down with appropriate expressions of "Mmmm! Lovely! Delicious!" But I didn't finish them all. I was absolutely terrified that if I did so they would produce another dish. Finally, when I had done what I considered justice to the dish, I set it down, and the children eagerly consumed the rest.

But still, no television. The cover had been left on it, and nobody seemed interested in plugging it in. I had noticed vaguely, while eating the ants, that people had been coming in and going out after whispered consultations with the abbot. Now there were distinctly embarrassed looks. I couldn't understand it, until a little later the abbot explained. The problem was that the Vietcong objected to the monks giving television shows, and had threatened that if they persisted in doing so they would come into the monastery itself and take away the televisions. As it happened, the Vietcong had arrived earlier than usual that night, and were now in the village. They knew perfectly well what was going on, and had sent a message that there was to be no television.

The abbot was desperately worried about losing his televisions. He spoke about them often. He had two, but the one with the twenty-five-inch screen, of which he was particularly fond, was kept in the central pagoda itself, along with the movie projector, which was also a favorite possession. The abbot used to take siestas there in the afternoon, watching the television and wondering whether he dared turn it on. One night, when the coast seemed clear, a group of young monks did turn it on for me. We watched the local Cantho channel, which was pretty grim: a long program of excruciating Vietnamese pop music, sung by hideous stars. I quite saw what the Vietcong objected to. However, we lounged at the foot of the great statue of the Buddha and smoked Capstans through the evening. Leaning back, I was able to examine at leisure the decorations of the temple.

Two years before, as part of an effort to keep the Cambodians sweet, President Thieu had donated about £1,000 to Wat Champa. Much of this had gone to the restoration of the pagoda. The Cambodians had no sense of respect for an old building, particularly an old wooden building. There were very few in Cambodia itself, and concrete was generally preferred. In Wat Champa, the old lacquered pillars had been removed (I found them rotting in the grounds) and replaced by ceramic tessellations of a modernistic design. The lower parts of the walls had also been tiled, and the installation of strip lighting gave the place very much the air of a public convenience. Higher up were the original paintings, depicting scenes from the life of the Buddha. The monks were a trifle vague as to what exactly was represented, but there was one fine picture in which the Buddha appeared to be receiving homage from the ancient Hindu gods of Angkor Wat. The paintings obviously dated from the early days of the French since in one case, where foreigners were begging for relics of the Buddha, a French officer was depicted in nineteenth-century uniform, pith helmet, and carefully observed shoes.

I went with the abbot and the oldest monk to a funeral ceremony for an old man who had died in a village not far away. We walked along the narrow paths between the houses and the fields, and every time we met someone coming in the opposite direction the oldest monk hit him over the head with his umbrella. I was not sure whether this was custom or mere eccentricity. When people called out from the fields, the abbot told them that I was from Phnom Penh—I was an upland Khmer. This caused great mirth since the upland Khmers (Khmer Loeu) were considered savages, wild tribesmen.

When we arrived in the village, the monks went into the house of the dead man and soon settled down to a large meal that had been prepared for them. I sat outside with the villagers drinking *soum-soum,* the local rice spirit. We talked about the Vietnamese, whom they despised. There was nothing political about this. They just hated their guts. After all, the Cambodians of the delta, the Khmer Krom, still considered the whole rich area to be theirs. Saigon itself was nothing more than an old Cambodian village called Prey Nokor. The very watches of the villagers, and the clocks of the monastery, were set to Phnom Penh time. (Saigon time was an invention of Diem: the North Vietnamese, the Vietcong, and the Cambodians were all synchronized.) And although this area paid taxes both to Saigon and to the Vietcong, although the yellow-and-red Saigon flag was painted on their gates, the allegiance was to Cambodia.

But to a Cambodia with a difference. True, there had been very little interbreeding with the Vietnamese. The people retained their dark skins, which they disliked, their square chins and strong features. If you looked at their ears and lips in profile, the resemblance to the sculptures of the Angkor period was striking. And yet proximity with the Vietnamese, subjugation indeed, had forced them to accommodate to Vietnamese customs to a certain extent. Their dress was similar to the Vietnamese and they were all monogamous— "unfortunately," as one old man put it. Politically and socially they were misfits. A tradition of right-wing nationalist politics had survived there, but only in a degenerated form. I met nobody who had a good word to say for Sihanouk, whereas in Phnom Penh it was hard to find anybody who did not look back on his rule with nostalgia. The hero of the Khmer Krom was Son Ngoc Thanh, but he, after a period with the Lon Nol government, had returned to Saigon, where he was reputed to be too old and sick for any political activity.

Son Ngoc Thanh's memory was still kept very much alive by the Khmer Rouge, who referred to him regularly in their broadcasts as a member of the "traitorous clique." He was especially hated by Sihanouk whose book, *My War with the CIA,* laid special blame on him for the overthrow of the royal government. The Khmer Krom had been trained by the CIA in Mike Force (*Mike* = the letter *M* = *Mercenary*). In the summer of 1970, when the Lon Nol regime was struggling for survival, Mike Force troops were sent to Phnom Penh in large numbers. However the reception they got from the Cambodians there was lukewarm at best. They were thought to be more Vietnamese than Khmer. Their superior attitude, their military sophistication and their ruthlessness were resented. They were used as cannon fodder in a series of disastrous campaigns. Eventually they were almost wiped out. You could still find a few of them in Phnom Penh. They were the gung-ho officers with the perfect command of GI slang. But the experience of returning to the mother country had not been a success. They had found out, although they would not admit this, that they were not Cambodians after all. And if they were not Cambodians, and not Vietnamese, what the hell were they?

In these villages, the Khmer Krom had adapted themselves to their situation as best they could. Several of the peasants traveled to work in the PRG-controlled areas during the day. For those who lived under the nominal control of the Saigon regime, the PRG taxes were higher than for those in the liberated zones, and in addition they must pay taxes to Saigon. I asked a large number of them whether there were many Cambodian troops among the Vietcong. Apparently the percentage was not high; and this seemed to reflect the alienation of the Khmer Krom from Vietnamese politics. The only respected authority in the region was that of the monks.

To become a monk, to shave your head and eyebrows, to give up women and drink and all forms of games, might not be everybody's idea of a good life. But it was a way of saying that you were a Cambodian, a way of avoiding the draft and remaining safe for the moment at least. Beyond the monastery gates, the pleasant grove, the turtles and the pond, the chances of dying were high. There was gunfire daily as the peasants crossed the lines to and from work, and that afternoon the gunfire was nearer and louder than before. I asked the abbot what was happening. He explained that one of the territorial soldiers was about to be cremated. I went out to the crematorium ground, and watched the ceremony.

The women sat apart, wailing together in a manner which, as it gathered force, turned into what sounded like a ritual chant. The men lit the pyre with bits of old rubber tires that gave off a foul black smoke. As the fire began, they hacked at the coffin with axes in order to make sure that the flames got through to the body. It was a sad and shabby occasion. The men were mostly drunk on *soum-soum*, which they passed around. A young soldier, I think he was about sixteen, was supposed to fire the salute. But he managed to jam his rifle. So the old men took the gun from him and fired the magazines off themselves. Every time they fired, there was an answering volley, which came, I think, from the house where the dead soldier had lived. I reflected that the old men had fought for the French, their sons had fought for the Americans, and their grandsons were fighting for the Vietnamese.

By now the coffin was beginning to disintegrate. I wanted to stay and see the whole process to the bitter end. But one of the monks came up to me, pointed at the pyre and screwed up his nose. He told me not to wait around any longer. Why not? I asked. Bad dreams, he said, and besides, they were waiting in the monastery for me to give an English lesson. I walked with him to one of the classrooms, where a group of eager, eyebrowless faces sat patiently. The teacher put a copy of *Understanding English* into my hands, and I began to read out loud. It was a book designed for the type of summer language school that exists on the south coast of England. The main characters in the stories were European students, each with his or her engaging little characteristic. It was full of bad puns and coy little jokes, and as I read the stories out, in a clear, slow, solemn voice, I could hear my own voice ringing around the classroom. No doubt I could be heard as far as the cremation ground, and they would think that the monks were furthering their religious education. By the end of the chapter, I realized that nobody—neither the teacher nor the pupils—had been able to follow a single word.

Every evening I would put on a loincloth and go to the wash house, where my ablutions were an object of great interest and mirth. One thing puzzled the monks. Why did I never relieve my bowels? Was I ill? Was I different in some curious respect? Since I had never had a moment of privacy from the time of my arrival, it was clear that something was wrong. On the third day, therefore, I announced that the time had come. Consternation! "No have Kiss Me," said a monk. This remark might have been disconcerting, had I not been aware that "Kiss Me" was a brand of toilet paper. I don't know whether the monks had ever heard the song "Kiss Me Quick," but one could imagine that they would have well appreciated its urgent rhythms. As for the film "Kiss Me Kate" . . . I took my little can of water down the path, which led past a pleasant stream luxuriant with lotus blossom, beside which the secluded closets stood. A great wave of sympathy and pleasure spread through the monastery.

I used to eat not with the monks—that was forbidden—but with the various lay personnel of the establishment. One evening, as I was sitting with the abbot and a few of the monks, the cook brought in his baby daughter to show me. The child was paralyzed from the waist down, and he did not have enough money to get her proper medical attention. In the quietest, most modest way, he asked if I would give him some money, which I was glad to do, since—apart from anything else—I was enjoying the hospitality of the monastery. I gave him as much as I could spare. The man thanked me and left. I overheard the abbot ask the monks how much I had given. It was something like twenty dollars. "A lot," said the abbot, rather as if I had overstepped the mark. A few moments later, the cook came back, this time with his wife and the child. They knelt at my feet and placed the baby in my arms. Then they said that they would like to give me the child, since they would never be able to look after it properly. This may sound as if they were deficient in love for the baby, but in fact it was quite the opposite, and I hated having to refuse them.

On the last night, I had bought a gift of coffee for the monks and we sat up till the early hours, talking about politics, laughing and joking. I was very pleased with the way the trip had gone, and even though my Cambodian was only rudimentary and there were few English or French speakers, I had learnt a lot in the way that I preferred: not using a notebook more than was absolutely necessary, and allowing events to take their own course. I had missed out on the PRG, but you couldn't have everything, and by now my presence in the area was so well known that it would be impossible to slip across the line without incurring the wrath of the Saigon authorities. Besides, I doubted very much if it was wise to go from this dotty little pocket of reaction across to the liberated areas.

There was one monk who was more intelligent, and much shrewder than the rest. Suddenly he said: "Of course, we know why you have been staying with us all this time." I thought he was going to mention the Vietcong, and indeed he did: "You're from the CIA, aren't you?" I laughed. "If I was from the CIA, I would be afraid to stay here. Besides, I'm not American." "That's what you say. But how do we know? This is an interesting area for you. You want to get information about the Vietcong." "I'm a journalist," I said, "and I hate the CIA." "But of course you'd *say* you hated the CIA." He was quite serious, and what he said destroyed, at a stroke, all the pleasure of the last days. Of course that's what they'd think. Why else would a foreigner come and spend such a time with them? What was worst of all was they didn't *mind*. They seemed almost to be used to it. I was an American spy doing my job; they were Cambodian monks, doing theirs. That was the world as they understood it, and it wasn't until I had thrown what almost amounted to a tantrum that they took the allegation back, and we patched up our friendship.

VIETNAM

Conversations in the Dark

"Ask him why he paints his little fingernails."

And it wasn't just the fingernails either. It was the little toenails as well—carefully pedicured and varnished a deep shade of red. This seemed most inappropriate in a professional soldier. What would his officers say on parade? In the British army, I reflected patriotically, the offending nails would have been ceremonially torn out.

As the question was transmitted, I watched his face. A slow and secret smile came over it. He looked down at the table and mumbled inaudibly. The face was like a baby's, it was quite unmarked by the experience of war. It went, in a way, with the painted nails, but not with the ranger's uniform. At all events, he didn't want to answer the question, so I asked him what he thought about the war.

We were sitting in a café in Go Da Hau, a small town near the Cambodian border, on the Saigon–Phnom Penh road. It was long after curfew, and the only people eating in the café were the owners and ourselves. The ranger had desperately wanted to talk, but he found it difficult to do so. Finally, he said that the war was like a guttering candle. Occasionally it would flare up again, but before long it would be entirely extinguished. And what did he think about that? He thought there was nothing now that he could do. He would become a monk, he said. He would never marry. There was no job he could do, and little possibility of earning money except by soldiering. If the war ended, that was that.

I thought how many people like him there must be in South Vietnam. He was an orphan. His father, he told us, had died in Dien Bien Phu, and his mother soon afterward. He had been educated at military school and served in the army ever since. The war had defined the whole of his existence. No wonder he was still prepared to fight. No wonder, despite what people said, the Saigon Army was still prepared to fight. For many of the soldiers there was simply nothing else they could do. The ranger talked sadly late into the night. For the most part, he did not know how to express himself. His features strained with the burden of something very important that he wanted to say. Finally, a couple of Vietcong were sighted just outside town. Gunfire burst out all around us. The family who ran the café gave us shelter in the back. The ranger straightened himself up, put on the look of a professional soldier, and disappeared into the blackness of the street.

Conversations in the dark, sad rambling discussions which always led back to the war; shy officers who told you one thing by night but begged you not to remember it the next day. Conducted to the accompaniment of Chinese chess, the tongues loosened by Vietnamese alcohol, which tasked like meths and probably was. Click-click went the chesspieces as the dead GIs lined up on either side of the board, the tanks crossed the river, and the officer escort moved around the compound—always diagonally—to protect the general. I developed a theory of journalism on which I hoped to build a school. It was to be called the Crepuscular School and the rules were simple: Believe nothing that you are told before dusk. Instead of diplomatic sources, or high-ranking sources, or "usually reliable sources," the crepuscular journalists would refer to "sources interviewed last night," "sources at midnight," or best of all, "sources contacted a few hours before dawn." It would be considered unprofessional to interview the general on the morning of the battle. You would wait till the evening, when he was reviewing the cost. Crepuscular stories would cut out the bravado. Their predominant colorings would be melancholy and gloom. In this they would reflect more accurately the mood of the times.

For the war was not guttering out yet by any means. In a matter of three weeks the equivalent of the population of a small town was killed or wounded, or went missing. District towns fell, remote outposts fell, enormous enemy losses were claimed—little of it was ever seen. If things were going badly the military did not want you around. If well, no interest was shown. It was difficult to locate the war, difficult to get to it. Indeed, most of the journalists in Saigon had given up trying. For the same editor who, when the Americans were fighting, would have insisted on maximum-risk reporting, would now consider such journalism a matter of minority interest. And so the idea grew up that ARVN, the Saigon Army, was simply not fighting, an idea which, as far as I know, was never tested against the reality of the time, although later it received a sort of retrospective justification.

In Saigon, Thieu was facing opposition from what was loosely described as the Third Force. The center of attention at the time was the Redemptorist Church, where two of the main Catholic critics of the president were working. Father Thanh, the right-winger, had his offices on the lefthand side of the church, while Father Tin, the left-winger, had his on the righthand side. In front of the church the pavement was lined with barbers' stalls, from which the secret police would observe the goings-on. I reckoned that they must have the shortest hair in Saigon.

Of the two movements, Father Thanh's was by far the stronger. As a veteran anticommunist, who had been deeply involved in the religious branch of psychological warfare, Thanh could command the attention and respect of a large number of the military, and his movement against corruption had already brought down three of the four corps commanders. Many people felt that Thieu's days were numbered, and Thanh's message—that it was the corruption of the regime that was causing its downfall—got widespread support. When all remaining government positions in Phuoc Long province, including the provincial capital, were lost, Thanh laid the blame on Thieu. But by this time, for the very reason that there was a military crisis, the right-wing Catholics had lost most of their impetus. Thieu could accuse his Catholic critics of playing into communist hands, clamp down on demonstrations, and cause a failure of nerve in the right.

There were many Third Force groups, but none at this time were able to create the same stir as Father Thanh. Members of the entourage of General Minh were always good for a quote, but they had no real power base. Indeed, they threw their power base away, as I was able to observe on one sad occasion. A Special Forces major, who had been a model of valor over the years, decided he wanted to do his bit for the anti-Thieu movement and approached "Big" Minh's group. He hadn't been corrupt, and consequently he hadn't enough money to buy all the ribbons and medals to which he was entitled. Minh's followers bought them for him, and took the major, all spruced up, to make his demonstration in front of the Assembly. He made a statement, and carried a placard on which were written the words: "I have no confidence in President Thieu." Nobody apart from press and police took any notice. The major stood on the steps of the Assembly, where he could not be arrested, looking very erect and rather scared. Those who had put him up to it stood by him, smiling. The police, with their white helmets and sunglasses, lounged opposite in their jeeps, and when the deputies took the major away by car, they moved in behind the car and followed it home. The deputies were immune from arrest, the major was not. I thought that if that was all the Third Force could think of to do when they attracted a new supporter, then Thieu had nothing to fear from them.

At about this time, I asked a soldier to show me the way to the house of Madame Ngo Ba Thanh, the leader of the Women's Movement for the Right to Live. The soldier pointed out the way, but warned me to beware of the secret servicemen at the gate. In fact, the house arrest had been very tactfully arranged, and one might not have noticed the group playing cards down the street. I asked Madame whether we could expect anything much of the Third Force in the near future, and what she said seemed to make a lot of sense. She said that it was only natural that the right-wing Catholic movement had lost impetus in the face of a real military threat to the Saigon regime. As for the left-wing Catholics, although there were sincere men among them, they were basically—like all Catholics—opportunists. They did not represent any real movement in society. As for her own group, she said that they and the Buddhists had failed to get mass support from the people; there had been demonstrations, but nothing large enough to move the Thieu regime. She said that, primarily, they had failed because they could not stand up to the repressions of the Saigon government. For the moment, at least, they had been defeated.

So it was not surprising, she went on, that the PRG had been forced to continue the struggle against Thieu on the military front. It had been made perfectly clear to them, since the Paris Peace Agreement, that there was no other way forward. She did not like this state of affairs, but she recognized that the only force operating at present was the PRG.

I really wanted to meet the PRG. Having failed simply to screw up enough courage and walk out of the monastery at Wat Champa at night, and not having enough time to arrange a trip through the PRG delegation at Camp Davis, I was beginning to think that the chances of "going across" were rather slim. The problem was simply the period of transition—you were likely to be fired at by the Saigonese troops both if you tried to go in and, of course, when you came out. The problem was not to locate the Vietcong areas. It was simply a question of accreditation and opportunity. In the end, I took a long shortcut.

There was a man in Saigon by the name of Jean-Claude, who had been to Vietcong areas several times before, spoke a bit of Vietnamese, and was a sort of Vietcong groupie. He had been educated, he said, at an English borstal, he very much admired the film of *The Loneliness of the Long Distance Runner*, and in 1968 he had played an active part in *les événements*. Now he was a member of the French Communist Party (although he clearly would have preferred a Lao Dong card), and was living as a freelance photographer-cum-reporter-cum-entrepreneur. The emphasis was very much on the entrepreneur. I never knew how much of what he said was sheer fantasy, and how much was true, but the fact remains (to leap ahead) that when he finally left Saigon it was in an official limousine provided by the People's Revolutionary Government of South Vietnam. What was more, he "made things happen."

Our intention was to hire a car and travel from Saigon to Quang Tri and back, taking in every major town on the way and covering a large part of the Central Highlands. At points along the way, we were bound to come across the PRG—indeed, we intended to go through areas they controlled—and to drop in on them as the occasion arose. It was an appropriate time for us to be doing this, since December 22, 1974 was the thirtieth anniversary of the foundation of the Vietnamese People's Army, the army that had defeated the French at Dien Bien Phu. To mark the anniversary, the delegation at Camp Davis gave a party for the press, where we drank North Vietnamese vodka and watched a documentary film of the siege of Dien Bien Phu.

The film was a mixture of genuine newsreel and reenactment. For instance, when the French surrendered, they emerged in an orderly procession waving immaculate white flags. In fact, the French had had no clean linen out of which to make their white flags so, when they surrendered, they were kept waiting around until white flags could be brought from Hanoi. The French claim that they all refused to take part in this staged surrender, so that the North African troops in the camp had to be used instead. I asked a French friend in the bus coming back from Camp Davis whether he remembered Dien Bien Phu. Yes, he said, they had prayed so much for it at his school, he thought Dien Bien Phu was a sort of saint. At this, another Frenchman in the bus exploded. He had been in the siege himself, he said, and the film we had seen was a pack of lies. He then told us an elaborate story of how he had escaped, and led a unit out through the jungle. This story turned out to contain rather more fantasy than the film we had just seen, but I could understand how, as a patriotic Frenchman, one might be provoked into inventing it.

We left Saigon with great relief: The city was in a festive mood, the loudspeakers were blaring "Angels from the Realms of Glory," there were toy Christmas trees, stars of Bethlehem, tanks and machine guns on sale, and the street vendors were being very insistent about the merits of the most hideous "Xmas Greetings" cards. The first item of interest we encountered on our route was a village on the main road that had been napalmed a couple of days before. The Vietcong had come into the village to cut the road. They had been trapped there, along with many of the villagers, by the Saigon troops. Then the village had been destroyed by a force obviously capable of creating enormous heat. I noticed a pile of bananas that had been charred right through, although they preserved their original shape. They looked like something discovered and preserved in Pompeii. The bodies had already been cleared away, however, and some of the houses were being rebuilt.

We went on through landscapes that were as varied as their inhabitants—the coffee plantations near Djiring, for instance, which were worked by a Montagnard race whose language sounded curiously like Italian. We stayed the first night as the guest of an Italian missionary, who had married a Montagnard and was working in agriculture. He told us of the Montagnard resistance movement, Fulro—how it was growing in his area, and how it was maintaining an uneasy, informal liaison with the Vietcong. We met a French planter, whose factor was Vietcong (there was an "arrangement," as in all rural areas). And we gave a lift to a Frenchman known as Requin ("the Shark") who made his living by selling his own brands of French cheeses and Pernod, which he concocted in a small shack nextdoor to the American embassy in Saigon. Requin was on the road distributing his wares to the various Frenchmen dotted around the country, so with him we dropped in to share a rum punch with an old Martiniquan soldier living just south of Dalat, and in Dalat itself went to tea with an extraordinary Frenchwoman who ran a farm.

She was appalled to see us, when the young Montagnard who was on guard at the gate had let us in. She rounded on Requin, who was a foul-mouthed seventy-year-old, perfectly capable of looking after himself, but who looked fairly crestfallen as she poured forth a torrent of venomous abuse. How dare he not warn her he was coming, how dare he bring these people, and what did he think her Montagnards would think if she had three men staying with her? Then she saw that Jean-Claude had a nervous tic. "You have a nervous tic," she said. "In fact," he replied, "I have two tics." Finally she asked if we would like tea. I said no, I was afraid from her manner that we were not welcome. We would leave Requin and go on by ourselves. She melted. She was sorry, she said, but she was unused to meeting people.

In her kitchen there were baskets full of young ducklings and chickens. She seemed to spend most of her time living in outhouses. But when I asked if I could be shown around the house, she was quite pleased. I complimented her on her garden. She said that the

Vietnamese were trying to take all her land away, but she would stop them, she would marry a Montagnard chief and then they would not dare. I could not tell her age exactly, but she had something of the manner of Miss Haversham. Her father had dominated her life—that was him, with the long white beard, in the photograph. Her father had loved animals, she said, and plants and trees, yes, he had loved trees, but—and here she laid a special emphasis—not people. She showed me to her father's room, which she had left exactly as it had been when he was alive, she said. The mosquito net hung from a baldachin over the bed, and the room was piled high with a chaos of papers. The same uninhabited mess prevailed throughout the rest of the house, which clearly had not been touched for decades. Here was a family photograph, father in the center, and these were all her brothers and sisters, brought up in Dalat. Where were they now? I asked. They were all married, she exclaimed, all of them married, they had all married apart from her! As for her, she had failed to do so. I can hear her now, spitting out the words: *"J'ai failli"* But wait, I must see a picture of Michele, her great love. Where was it now? She scampered over the cardboard boxes. She'd lost it, no she hadn't, here it was. Here was Michele, the goat she had kept when she lived in France. She appeared to have been living in a sort of signal box, working as a goatherd. Absolute poverty. Only a goat for company. Whereas here she had land, and her Montagnard staff, and one day she would marry a Montagnard chief, and then she would be secure.

At Dalat we hit the edge of a typhoon. Mist and pouring rain accompanied us as far as the coast and the seaside resort of Nha Trang, where we spent a gloomy Christmas Eve. It would be nice, would it not, to get to the PRG on Christmas Day. "You know, my friend," Jean-Claude would say, crossing his legs as he drove, steering with one hand, lighting a cigarette with another, and giving me what appeared to be the full benefit of his attention. "You know, my friend, we're going to see some great things, for sure. For sure. Yes man." And occasionally, looking out across the paddy fields of the coastal strip, he would say, yes we were getting warm, and then no, we were getting cold. At one point we came to what appeared to have been a large military base, one of the ones that disappeared overnight when the Americans left, torn down by a thousand tiny hands and carted away for building materials. There were large roads and runways beside the dunes, and at the edge of the sea a single standing arch marked Das Schloss. Beside it stood a village, surrounded by a thorn hedge, where our arrival caused something of a stir. "This is it, my friend," said Jean-Claude, "they're here, for sure, I know it." But of the group of elders who came out to meet us nobody seemed willing to talk, and they said there was no food to be had in the village. There were no government soldiers, no Vietcong to be seen, and no flags of any kind. The only notice in the village had come from the military base, and now formed the wall of a house: Rabies Suspect—No Unauthorized Personnel. We left disappointed.

And continued up the coast, and through a steep valley which had been almost entirely defoliated. The mountains were strewn with huge boulders, and the white stumps of the dead trees pointed up out of the returning scrub. Several of the rocks had been decorated with the skull and crossbones, and under these sat groups of soldiers sheltering from the rain. We drove until evening, when the light began to fade, and we were determined to get to Bong Son that night or fail in the attempt. By failing in the attempt, I mean that we might come across a Vietcong checkpoint on the road. No such luck. We passed through several astonished and frightened groups of Saigon soldiers, bivouacked by the bridges, and the road was just closing up altogether for the night when we entered Bong Son. An officer in his jeep, *en tenue libre* for the evening, was chatting up the girls on the main street. He asked us what we were doing, explained that there was no hotel and invited us to spend the night at his headquarters. He turned out to be the district chief, a certain Major Bang.

The major, as his name so painfully suggests, was very keen on artillery. He explained to us, over a deafening supper, how scrupulously he was adhering to the Paris Peace Agreement. He was only firing defensively, and only at known targets. I concluded, by the end of an ear-splitting night, that he must have been very much on the defensive, and that his *Deuxième Bureau* must have been working round the clock to provide him with new coordinates for the known targets. Either that or, as in the majority of such camps, which were supposed to guard strategic bridges and bases, the tactic was simply to loose off enough ordinance to give an impression of strength. We ourselves were not fired at once during the night. Major Bang also told us that the people of the area, after their experience of the Vietcong, loathed and despised the communists. We had a golden opportunity to check up on this statement the next day.

The soldiers told us that three bridges had been destroyed just up the road, and that the flood waters from the typhoon would render repairs impossible for some days. This meant that our plan of driving to Quang Tri, or indeed to Danang or Hue, was spoiled. It was therefore in a mood of some frustration that we drove up to the first bridge to check for ourselves.

There had been a small battle the night before between the Vietcong and the guards beside the bridge, as a result of which one of the Vietcong had been killed. His body lay there. The face had been completely stove in and the whole corpse lacked blood. It looked as though it had been dragged through the water; around its waist there was still a length of rope. As we stood there, a battalion of soldiers arrived by truck, dismounted, and began to climb along the broken bridge. They were about to begin an operation to flush out the Vietcong from the area, and they were in a rather blood-thirsty, hysterical mood. There was also tension among the large crowd of local villagers and travelers who had assembled by the bridge. One of the soldiers took a stick and prized open the mouth of the dead man. "We go kill too many VC," the soldiers said. There was in their manner a mixture of satisfaction and fright.

Jean-Claude was angry enough at the reversal of our plans, but the scene by the bridge roused him to furious action. "You know, my friend," he said, "the VC are all around here, that's for sure." And if we weren't going to get to Quang Tri, we might as well go across at the earliest opportunity. We drove a little way back down the road, and came to a pathway in which we could leave the car fairly inconspicuously. Then we simply started to walk across the fields. We met one peasant from whom Jean-Claude asked the way to the *Giai Phong* (liberators); he gave a vague indication with his hand. When we had crossed a couple of small fields and were still only about a hundred yards from the road, we came to a small stream and a broken bridge. I was just wondering why the bridge had not been repaired when, looking up, I saw a soldier in green peering over the hedge. He beckoned to us to come quickly and pointed to the part where the stream was shallowest. We waded through, and found that we had crossed into the liberated zone.

The soldier carried an American M79 grenade launcher, and wore an American jacket with pouches for the grenades. From his lack of insignia or helmet we took him to be Vietcong, but there was no particular way of telling. He had a transistor radio slung from his belt. Behind where he stood there was a large pond, and beyond the pond another hedgerow. Behind the hedgerow, looking to see what on earth was happening, was a row of green pith helmets. The first soldier indicated that we should be careful as we could still be seen from the road. We hurried through the pond, avoiding the bomb craters which he pointed out to us, and emerged, dripping with mud and sweat and trembling with excitement, where the group in the pith helmets were waiting. During the whole process, nobody had pointed a gun at us and, although we had dropped in unannounced, nobody seemed at a loss as to what to do. They took us into a small hut and gave us a couple of coconuts to drink.

"Fuck me," said Jean-Claude, "we've made it. Didn't I tell you we'd make it, my friend?" It dawned on us that, although we had got so far, we were now in a considerable quandary. After all, we were only about a mile from where the operation was supposed to begin, and only about two miles or so from Major Bang. "You know what, my friend," said Jean-Claude, "we're going to have to leave that car. They'll see it on the road in no time. But you know that, I don't care, man, I don't fucking care. If we have to walk to Hanoi I don't mind. We can't go back to Saigon now, my friend, that's for sure." I was too elated by having actually got across to be much worried by this talk. It was as if we had just stepped through the looking glass.

The first thing I noticed, with slight dismay, was how well-dressed and clean everyone was. If I'd known in advance I'd have put on a tie. Their clothes were for the most part of Chinese cloth, rather well cut. Their watches came from Japan and were set to Hanoi time. The Northerners among them wore pith helmets and Ho Chi Minh badges, but otherwise they were in mufti. Most carried the regulation guerrilla rifle, the AK-47, but one had an American M16. One man unzipped the embroidered pouch in which he kept his transistor, and turned on Radio Hanoi. A solemn voice, which I afterward learned belonged to Miss Elizabeth Hodgkins, said: "I'm a teacher: I-apostrophe-M A T-E-A-C-H-E-R. *You're* a student: Y-O-U-apostrophe. . . ." But the thing that struck me most was the number of ballpoint pens they wore. Rather good ones too, I thought enviously.

I mention the ballpoint pens because they seemed to be a rather important part of everyday life. When they conversed with us, either in English or in Vietnamese (there were no French-speakers among them), they seemed much happier when committing their thoughts to paper. Jean-Claude said that the Vietnamese they wrote was highly elegant and classical. My conversation was rather less satisfactory. It showed, I thought, that their conception of education, or perhaps Miss Hodgkin's conception, might lean a little far on the rigid side. It went like this. First the soldier wrote:

HOW ARE YOU?

Then I wrote:

VERY HAPPY TO BE HERE.

The soldier looked mistrustfully at this for some time. He almost crossed it out, but then he wrote underneath:

FINE THANKS, AND YOU?

Clearly, as an English-speaker, I had failed at the first hurdle.

While we were thus conversing, a meal of chicken and rice was brought by the villagers, who crowded around to watch us eat. There was intense curiosity, but very little noise. Authority seemed to come very easily to the older soldiers, and the children responded to them at once. Several of those who had been at the bridge came back to tell the soldiers what was happening. One boy of about sixteen seemed particularly moved by what he had seen. He sat on the floor and talked about it for some time in a low voice. Everybody spoke quietly, almost as if they might be heard by the Saigon soldiers on the road. Apart from the odd rifle shot, the only noise was that of the military traffic going up to the bridge. One might have been lulled by the confidence in everybody's manner into a sense of total security had the political officer not politely told us after lunch that it would be dangerous to stay any longer.

Thinking of Major Bang's pronouncement the night before,

that the people of the area loathed the communists, I wondered whether I could be competely mistaken in thinking that it was quite false. Two things stayed in my mind. First, the Saigon troops that we had seen that morning were clearly frightened, conscious perhaps that they were in hostile territory. The second was the sight of a small child in the village who wore the uniform of the local school. Every day he must have had to cross the lines in order to be imbued with Saigon propaganda. Crossing the lines was obviously no problem, but did it not argue a certain political confidence on the part of the PRG that the child was allowed to do so?

A little girl showed us an easy path back to the road and we headed toward where we had left the car. There, to our horror, stood a couple of Saigon soldiers. We walked up as calmly as possible. "You," said one of the soldiers, "why you not obey me? You go see VC." We had our excuses prepared. We had wandered innocently in the paddy to take photographs, we said, and we had been stopped by the VC. "Beaucoup VC," we said, spiritedly, "with guns, same-same you." "I no VC." No," we said hurriedly, "you no VC. Hey, we very scared. VC take us, not let us go. We have to talk, many hours." One of the soldiers, a warrant officer, was particularly angry because he had apparently been shouting at us, telling us not to go. Finally we said to him, would he and his friend like a beer? Yes, he said angrily, so we took him to the nearest village, where he made a great scene about buying the drink. Then we took him and the beer back to his friend. I put some money in his hand. "What's this? he said. "English custom," I said, "It's called Boxing Day, give beaucoup money to friends. Look, if you tell Major Bang we go VC, beaucoup trouble for us, maybe trouble for you. You no say nothing, okay?" And we left him standing by the roadside, suspiciously eyeing the money and the beer.

Driving as fast as we dared toward Bong Son, we again came upon the body of the dead Vietcong. It had been dragged down the road and dumped near a small market, no doubt as a warning to the local populace. The rope was still around its waist, but the arms, which previously had been stretched out, were now bent into an attitude suggesting an embrace. I was surprised. I hadn't thought you could do that to a corpse once it was cold. Jean-Claude brought the car to a near halt. "For Christ's sake," I said, "let's just get out of here as quickly as possible." Above all, I did not want to meet Major Bang again, after we had so shamefully abused his hospitality.

And we were, for the most part, hospitably treated. Doubling back on our tracks, we drove up into the Central Highlands to Kontum, a few miles north of which the road was permanently blocked. We stood on the hillside looking down into the valley, where a couple of burnt-out trucks across the road indicated the front line. On our right was one of the pleasantest camps I had ever seen—it looked like a fortified Club Med. There were straw huts and wooden tables and chairs set in the shade, and you hardly noticed the ingenious system of trenches and foxholes leading to the officers' bunkers. Painted faces with plucked eyebrows emerged from the trenches, while from the bunkers came the sound of female laughter and one or two other things. It was widely feared at the time that the Vietcong might attack Kontum. This would be their first obstacle. "You must spend the night with us," said the medical officer, "in order to share something of the life of the soldier." We were happy to accept.

Most of the officers had "wives." The major's wife prepared a meal, which the major modestly described as frugal. After dinner, another of the wives sang a mournful song. Then we all sang songs, apart from the major, who produced a cassette and played us a medley of dreadful Vietnamese tangos. As it grew dark, the soldiers gathered around to watch us, from a respectable distance. You could see their cigarette ends glowing through the trees. Sometimes, as they began to get drunk on rice spirit, they would abruptly disappear from sight, falling into foxholes or disappearing into trenches. When the officers retired underground with their wives, we were invited to drink with the other ranks.

Their drunkenness had an edge of desperation. They shouted a lot and staggered blindly outside the perimeter fence, saying that they were about to go off on an ambush. They leaned forward and were quietly sick. On one occasion a gun went off by mistake, which didn't frighten me nearly so much as the thought that all this noise must be perfectly audible to the Vietcong in the valley below—the shouts, the laughter, the songs, my fearful rendition of "The Water Is Wide" (in the Britten arrangement). Having been on the other side only the day before, I was more conscious than ever of the forces patiently biding their time. Suppose they suddenly decided that the time was ripe? Supposing they came down, or rather up, like a wolf on the fold, what would one, as it were, do?

The soldiers were also conscious of enormous preparations being made on the other side. On most nights, they said, they could hear the NVA tanks and Molotova trucks maneuvering on the road that was being built in the mountains, the road that would link the Ho Chi Minh trail with the coast. But there were other things that made them depressed. Some of them had not seen their families for two years. They didn't get any leave. They didn't find it easy to live on twenty dollars a month. They didn't like having to go out on patrols, from which their comrades often did not return. They didn't like the fact that the local version of malaria can kill a man in two months, and they didn't like the bitterly cold nights. They slept in makeshift bivouacs, with a sack of rice as a pillow, protecting their food from the numerous rats. In contrast to the officers, they were not allowed "wives" (in Cambodia their real wives would have been living with them in the camp), even if they could have afforded them at the going rate of three dollars a night.

The guard on the north gate was a Cambodian from the delta. He had very much liked serving under the American officers in the Special Forces, but said that with ARVN everything was a fuck-up. I sat up with him throughout most of the night, hoping to hear the movement of the tanks and trucks. From time to time, an old man, also Cambodian, came around with a stick to make sure that the guard was awake. This man was in a good mood—in two weeks, after a service of twenty-five years, he was due to retire. As it happened, he came from one of the villages near Wat Champa, which I had just visited. So I was able to tell him that his home was now in a contested area and very likely to be taken over by the Vietcong. He didn't seem at all worried or surprised by this. He was going to retire—and that was that.

But the guard on the north gate was young and had no option to retire. He very much wanted to leave the army. There were so many things he wanted to do, he said, if only he wasn't a soldier. When I asked him exactly what it was he wanted to do, he was at a loss to say. We sat and shivered and talked. The quiet landscape was brilliantly lit by the moon. To our left we could see the mountains through which the Ho Chi Minh Trail used to run, and ahead of us the site of the new road. Although there was no noise of tanks or trucks, there was no particular comfort from the silence. "Sometimes," said the guard, "I think I will go AWOL—I did it before but the military police arrested me." I told him that I thought it would be a very good idea to go AWOL. Some days later, when I was leaving Saigon, I received a visit from him in my hotel room. I was packing. The guard had come to Saigon because he was about to be moved on to some new operation. He didn't know where he was going, and he asked if I had any civilian clothes to spare.

"I want you to write," said the director of the Open Arms program in Kontum, "that the people of Kontum are not afraid of attack by the VC." The idea was very much in the air at the time. In Saigon it was feared that the coming dry season would see a renewal of operations in the Central Highlands, and that Kontum, a well-known city, difficult to defend, would be a tempting target. It is surrounded by mountains and forests. "You see that mountain," said the director, as we drove aimlessly around the city, "you see that mountain? It belongs to us." But precious little else in Kontum belonged to Saigon. The population of the area was predominantly Montagnard, and the allegiances of the Montagnards were eroded. The official view was that, since they were Catholics, they must be anticommunist. The bishop of Kontum, Paul Seitz, was a staunch anticommunist who had been in the North before 1954, and his mission had been hand-in-glove with the efforts of the Americans and the successive Saigon regimes. Yet what they had sold to the Montagnards amounted to a policy of protection—protection from the spirits for the women, who crossed themselves and invoked the name of "Yezuz" when wading through a stream; protection from the depredations of the South Vietnamese.

In one of the villages near Kontum we asked a group of Montagnards what they would like to see happen in Vietnam. We had been invited to a drinking session in one of the huts, and were sitting around a ceremonial jar. We drank the rice wine through a straw in turns, and it was not long before the elders of the village expressed their hatred of the Vietnamese. First of all they said that they would like the French to come back; then that the Americans were very good; and finally, after admitting that neither the French nor the Americans were likely to return, they said that they would welcome the arrival of the Vietminh. At this point we objected. If they really liked the Vietminh, as they said, then they must have changed their minds about the Vietnamese and the French. No, they insisted, the Americans were *tout droit,* and so were the French. The Vietminh had previously been torturers, but now they also were *tout droit.* Happily, one man said, the Vietminh would soon arrive, take the South Vietnamese and smash their faces in.

This was said at evening, and as we came out from the village we met a group of soldiers from the camp where we had spent the previous night. They were being moved around on some operations, and had come to the village to ask for a drink. They had been served with a jar, but only at a certain distance from the huts. Nobody was going near them as they sat there, and nobody had talked to them, although they were being watched from the straw huts and the long shadows.

In the *Deuxième Bureau* in Kontum I noticed a map marked with the Fulro positions around the town, and I asked what the strength of the organization was in the area. Fulro *(Front Unifié pour la Lutte des Races Opprimées)* was the Montagnard separatist movement that had organized a rebellion in the mid-1960s, after which it was half-defeated, half-coopted by the CIA. "There are no Fulro around Kontum," I was told. "None at all?" "No, only people who call themselves Fulro." The formulation was perhaps reasonable enough.

The French and the Americans had always got on well in Vietnam with any race excepting the Vietnamese. The Special Forces had trained Cambodians, Méos in Laos, and Montagnards in the Central Highlands into highly successful mercenary guerrilla groups. They could trust such soldiers, and they could teach them to fight in the way they reckoned the war would have to be fought: a guerrilla war against a guerrilla movement. But when the Americans had left, the South Vietnamese had no use for the Special Forces. They could not command their loyalty, so they disbanded the units and dispersed them among the regular army. The Cambodian guard at the camp we had visited was typical of such soldiers—badly treated by corrupt officers, he knew enough of professional soldiering to despise those who were now leading him.

In Laos at this time a group of Méos who had formerly worked with the CIA had taken over a town in collaboration with the Pathet Lao, and here in the Central Highlands the hills were full of small groups of guerrillas, who probably lacked much by way of leadership, but who called themselves Fulro and earnestly looked forward to the collapse of the Saigon regime, after which they reckoned they would get their lands back and live as before. Neither the Vietcong nor the North Vietnamese would openly support Fulro, but in various unofficial ways they had given them support, caring for their wounded in jungle hospitals, for instance. The Italian missionary had told us that in the Djiring area, the Vietcong had taken great care to learn the language of the local tribes, and that this had impressed them since it was impossible to find a South Vietnamese official who had bothered to do the same. The Vietcong factor on the coffee plantation, when I had met briefly, showed little respect for Fulro as a movement, or indeed for the Montagnards' capacity to understand politics at all. But the groundwork had been laid throughout the Central Highlands for some kind of working relationship between the two movements. All the South Vietnamese could offer in return was an Open Arms program for a movement whose existence and purpose they denied. The director of the program in Kontum particularly wanted me to mention that, on the day after the program had been announced, two Fulro soldiers had turned themselves in.

We drove on south from Kontum through Pleiku to Ban Me Thuot, on a road that was alive with possibilities: We were told to expect bandits, Vietcong, NVA, Fulro, or the South Vietnamese. As the road deteriorated, it passed through thick forests, uplands commanding a panoramic view toward Laos and Cambodia, and the fields where the Montagnards cultivate their rice. There were tracks leading off the road and into the forest, some of them made by lumberjacks' lorries, and some of them by foot. The road was quite free of traffic except at one point for a military convoy of empty trucks, which was guarded by a helicopter. We were at pains to keep our distance from the convoy, not wishing to be ambushed. First we overtook it, then we had a puncture and it passed us by. By the time the wheel was changed, we were quite alone.

(Incidentally, if you are ever in such a place and you find that the gas tank has cracked and your gasoline is pouring out in a narrow jet, and there is no garage for miles, and the area holds every possibility of ambush or worse (as happened to us on another occasion), the Montagnard method of mending the tank is: Take a cake of soap, break off a section and knead it till soft, then spread the soap along the crack—it will last for ages.)

We were alone, but it did not feel as if we were. At regular intervals along the road there were checkpoints, but none of them, on this day, seemed to be manned. Who had built the checkpoints was a matter for conjecture, and it gave one an eerie feeling, to say the least, to wait around at each in order to make sure it was possible to pass. The checkpoints were beautifully constructed bowers, woven out of the tall grasses that grew on the edge of the road, and the ground showed clearly that they had only recently been made, and only recently abandoned. At one point outside the checkpoint, a gleaming new B-41 rocket stood on its tripod. This suggested the presence of Vietcong, and yet it was uncharacteristic for them to leave good ammunition behind. Were they simply unwilling to show their faces? At another point, three stuffed mannequins of Saigon troops, with GI helmets, lay overturned on the road. This suggested magic, some terrible Fulro curse perhaps.

"Fuck me, my friend," said Jean-Claude, "they're here somewhere, you know, that's for sure." Sometimes, when it looked as if a checkpoint was very recent indeed, we would stop the car, get out and call into the forest—in French, in English, in Vietnamese. If the convoy had frightened them off, surely the convoy was now past. If they were listening in the bushes, they must have thought our behavior was most singular.

A little later we came to a group of Montagnard soldiers standing by the road, carrying a flag that we at first thought must be that of the NLF. It wasn't, but we stopped the car and tried to engage them in conversation. They weren't having any. They also, most unusually for soldiers in Indochina, refused cigarettes. When I tried to speak to one of them, he turned his back on me and began to urinate. We took the hint and drove on. (In Saigon, later, I came upon the design of the flag in a booklet about Fulro—it was one of three used during the 1960s campaign.)

Toward Ban Me Thuot, the road improved gradually. The sun began to sink and the villagers were returning from the fields in long columns, carrying sacks of rice on their shoulders. We saw one soldier marching with such a column, but when he saw us, he jumped off the road and scurried behind a hedge. Further on we came to a Montagnard graveyard. We stopped the car. On the other side of a small valley there was a large fortified settlement. The cattle were being brought in for the night and we could hear them lowing in the distance. It was a beautiful sight, in the sunset. One of the villagers recognized Jean-Claude from a year before, when he had been in the military hospital. He told us that after being wounded, and after the South Vietnamese had disbanded the Montagnard units, he had decided to get out. We asked him whether we could spend the night in his settlement. He said no, it was not possible. He was a little shifty about his reasons, but I thought I understood them well enough.

Everything we had seen, everything we had been told, should have made it clear to us that something was about to happen. In Ban Me Thuot itself that night we met an officer from the *Deuxième Bureau* who told us of the latest military disasters in Phuoc Long province. He said that he thought Ban Me Thuot would be attacked next, and that it might last at most three weeks. In Pleiku that morning, at the II Corps headquarters, we had been told at length how reduced the ability of ARVN was, and how they would be unable to withstand any concerted attack, but we were sceptical about such talk. We knew that South Vietnam was calling out urgently for more funds, and therefore that it was convenient to paint as gloomy a picture as possible. It seemed, furthermore, to be highly improbable that with all those soldiers, all that materiel, the air force, the tanks, the trucks, the convoys we had seen, all that expensive equipment—well, it just seemed impossible that the whole show would be over in such a short space of time. In the *end*, yes—but if someone had come up to us and said "The Saigon regime has exactly four months left," we would never have believed him.

As a matter of fact, that was what almost happened to us, on New Year's Eve, the last night of our journey together.

* * *

"Man proposes, God disposes," he said, by way of opening the conversation. We were slightly taken aback. He was a cyclo-driver in Nha Trang, whom we had invited to join us at dinner to celebrate the New Year. "Yes," he had said, accepting our invitation, "if you have the goodness," and he took out his long trousers from under the seat where, as was customary, they were kept ready pressed by the weight of customers. As he put on his trousers and joined us at the table, he seemed to grow in stature before our eyes. The servility left him, and he became garrulous in excellent French. It was as if everything he had ever learned during his French education and his period as a government employee in Tonkin, all the accumulated wisdom of the French, had swelled up inside him and was now bursting out. He had a store of proverbs to meet every situation. When we asked him whether he resented being a *cyclopousse* after having been a *fonctionnaire,* he told us that every man must work in order to repay his debt to society, and that there was no such thing as stupid work, only stupid people.

The evening passed. He recited a poem about the poor in winter, and some verses about a princess weeping under a tree. After every line he would give us a perfect paraphrase, in case the slightest shade of meaning had escaped us. This was useful for me, but the tiniest bit insulting to Jean-Claude. Then he declaimed a poem by Lamartine, whom I at once vowed never to read. He sang a Boy Scout song (he was a keen Boy Scout, or had been) about the life of the matelot and its attendant dangers. Finally, with terrific flourish and style, so that you could almost hear the piano accompaniment, he sang a song called *"Tant qu'il y aura des étoiles"*; though we are only beggars, the song went, and although our life is utterly wretched in every respect, as long as there are the stars we shall be blissfully content with our lot. He seemed at this point to be the paragon of supine virtues. And he had, of course, a thing or two to say about communism: Violence, deception, and lying are the methods employed, he said, by those who wish to attain a classless society. When we asked him, however, what he *thought* about the possibility of a classless society, he affected not to understand. Finally, using a phrase of Ho Chi Minh's which had become a password for Vietnamese communism, Jean-Claude asked him: "Don't you think that nothing is more precious than independence and liberty?"

At this point he underwent his second transformation of the evening. He looked down at the tablecloth and paused dramatically. Then, as he began to speak, his mouth twisted into the most extraordinary snarl. "I think that Vietnam has been a prey," he said, "a prey to foreigners. We could not do anything about it in the past because we were too weak and feeble. But things are changing now. The future, the future will show you"—and here he raised his voice to the climax: *"L'avenir vous montrera. Je ne peux pas dire plus que ça."*

The Fall of Saigon

Boarding the plane for Saigon on April 24, who should I meet but Garth W. Hunt, the field secretary for Asia of Living Bibles International, who was on his way to get his team out of Vietnam. He had a "hard core" of ten to fifteen translators involved in the production of the Vietnamese "Living Bible" plus a "broad base" of reviewers: theological reviewers and stylistic reviewers. Then there were the consultants ("men of stature, recognized in their own field," he said) including literary consultants, exegetical consultants, theological consultants, technical consultants, and editorial consultants. Each of these had a family and dependents and most of them wanted out, so Garth W. Hunt had set himself a difficult task.

Living Bibles International is an evangelical organization with strong, unmistakable political leanings. "God loves the sinner but he hates the sin," said Mr. Hunt, and in this case the sin was communism, whose philosophy God certainly despised. So did Living Bibles International. They had excellent relations with the presidents of Bolivia and Spain, and no problems with the indigenous Catholics in those countries. At the present moment, their powerful transmitters were broadcasting the Chinese translation of the Living Bible *at dictation speed* into the People's Republic. "Some of these international boundaries," said Garth W. Hunt, "can't keep out God's message."

They'd had no luck in North Vietnam, although they had asked to work there. But in the South they had always had tremendous cooperation from the government. The gospel according to Mark, which was the only thing this vast organization had so far completed in Vietnamese, had already sold 120,000 copies. It had been offered by radio, and distributed in camps and refugee centers. An earlier book, produced by a sister organization, had been distributed to every psychological-warfare officer in the country, and also to every Vietnamese embassy and consulate throughout the world. "This book," said Mr. Hunt, "became the most influential book in Vietnam, apart from the word of God himself." It was called *God Still Performs Miracles*.

My reading matter for the journey, in addition to my complimentary copy of *The Living Bible*, was *Time* and *Newsweek*. *Newsweek* contained a story describing Khieu Samphan as he entered Phnom Penh: "When he returned to Phnom Penh last week, Khieu Sampan [*sic*] was dressed in a simple black pajamas suit and *krama*. No one would have guessed from his peasant look that he had spent the last eight years plotting—and carrying out—the overthrow of the Cambodian government." The story was written by Fay Willey in New York with *Newsweek*'s reporter-in-the-field, "Paul Brinkley Rogers in Hong Kong," who may have written the footnote explaining that Samphan's *krama* was a "traditional Cambodian cotton scarf that can be worn as a turban, a towel to protect the neck or as a loin cloth." The thing that puzzled me was where this story came from. No correspondent or news agency had reported seeing Khieu Samphan entering the city, and there was no evidence that he was even there. But somebody in New York must have assumed that he had been, looked up his photo, and written up the story nevertheless. This was an unusually vivid example of a tendency in American magazine journalism to embellish . . . ever so slightly. I think it was six weeks before that *Newsweek* described the Khmer Rouge as prowling through the humid jungles around Phnom Penh. There are no jungles around Phnom Penh. It is likely that, if there had been jungles, they would have been humid, and it is possible that the Khmer Rouge, if anybody had been able to watch them, would have been prowling. So, given the jungles, everything else followed, more or less. Without the jungles, things were a little different.

The two magazines are run in a manner very similar to that

adopted by Living Bibles International—there is an army of researchers and rewrite men who are the key figures, and who stay in the office. They like sending out long lists of questions to their reporters and stringers. The Phnom Penh *Time* stringer once received a questionnaire for that week's story that included the thoughtful query: "Do the homeless, poor, maimed, etc. of Phnom Penh huddle under flimsy straw lean-tos. Know they have these in Saigon, but are they also in Phnom Penh?" You could see the idea forming in the guy's mind and, being a scrupulous journalist, he wanted to make sure that there were some flimsy straw lean-tos for his homeless, poor, maimed, etc. to huddle under. He was guarding against error, but he'd overlooked one point. The weather was very hot. To huddle, under such circumstances, would be asking for trouble.

Journalists working for these magazines on the spot would often be very embarrassed to meet their colleagues after crass errors were inserted into their stories. To avoid such embarrassment, *Newsweek* now makes it perfectly clear that the man on the spot is only *helping* someone in the office, whose name comes first. Occasionally, if a reporter does something rather spectacular, he is allowed to tell the story as he saw it. But this is a great honor. There was one such story in this same copy of *Newsweek*. It was about the fall of Xuan Loc, and pretty nasty stuff it was too. But the author told me that evening that even that story was touched up. He had had a pair of crutches lying in the road. Somebody in New York had decided it would read better as a *forlorn* pair of crutches. The chances that the crutches might have been anything other than forlorn—hilarious, for instance—were remote.

I got my two-week tourist visa without any trouble. They seemed to be giving the things away. Then the customs man asked if I had any foreign newspapers. I gave him my *Time* and *Newsweek* under the impression that he was merely curious to read them. In fact, it had at last become impossible to allow too many Saigonese to see the wretched things. One of the covers had a photo of a Saigon soldier with a target drawn over his heart. It was headlined "Target Saigon." The customs man said "Do you think. . . ?" and made a sign as if to slit his throat. I told him not to worry. Everything was going to be okay, no sweat.

I checked in at the small hotel near the market, where I had been staying before, and went off to dinner at the Continental. The garden was crowded—*tout le monde* was there. *Le Monde* was there. It was a reunion: The Indochina hands were back for the last act. In the view of the American papers, the last act would be the evacuation. The *Washington Post* staff had been ordered, under pain of dismissal, to leave with the embassy. Indeed, they had been almost evacuated some days before. They were a little fed up about this, and it did seem to me unlikely that, if they stayed and produced marvelous stories, the courageous Ben Bradlee would (a) refuse to print the stories, and (b) sack the correspondent who stayed on. The *New York Times* had also ordered its journalists not to stay behind, and the American networks were planning to evacuate. Everyone was talking about the secret password, which would be broadcast when the time came: an announcement that the temperature was 105 and rising, followed by the song "I'm Dreaming of a White Christmas."

I was wakened the next morning by a sharp rap on the door. In came a rather beautiful Vietnamese girl who, without the usual preliminaries, plunged into a passionate speech. She had been a night-club dancer, and now she simply must leave Saigon, and I must help her. It was early in the morning and I was rather gruff. She redoubled her efforts. "How can I live with the communists," she wailed. "I can't spend my money and I can't wear my clothes. I have to wear Vietcong clothes." Then she knelt down on the floor beside my bed and pretended to cry. It was the worst imitation I had ever heard. "Please help me," she whined, "please help me leave Saigon." She was offering 300,000 piastres, a large sum for her, but with the soaring black-market rate at the time it amounted only to £40. All I had to do to earn this money was to say that she was my sister, then the Americans would give her papers. She would go to Hawaii, where she would automatically be given a U.S. passport. She had a house in Singapore, which she could sell for $100,000. In addition, she already had $1,500 in greenbacks. The last figure she mouthed with respect and wonder. I decided that the house in Singapore was probably a fiction, and pointed out that the greenbacks would not last very long in the United States. But she had it worked out. She would live in Hawaii and set up a Vietnamese restaurant. There were so many Vietnamese going to Hawaii. She would be able to sell spring rolls and things like that. President Ford had said that two million Vietnamese could go to America. They could go this month, but after that it would be too late. I gave her a noncommittal reply, and she left the room in great distress.

"Three hundred thousand?" people said scornfully, "oh, *we've* been offered far more than that." Wherever you went Saigon was using its most ingenious methods either to get out or to make money out of those who were leaving. And, according to the stories, it was not just the Vietnamese but Americans as well who were running the rackets. Hopeful young girls would be relieved of their savings and then left stranded. The bars of Tu Do Street had been combed by the talent spotters of the Philippines. An enormous number of people were simply caught up in a craze for leaving. In a friend's hotel I met a youth of about twenty who was rushing around asking for help. He did not know why he wanted to go, but he had suddenly remembered something his father had given him—the torn endpaper of a book on which was written an American name and address. In his other hand he carried the wording of a cable to the same address: "Please send a cable to American embassy Saigon accepting responsibility for. . . ." It seemed highly unlikely that the addressee would have any recollection of either father or son. Nevertheless, we told the boy to send the cable with that wording. He didn't know how to send a cable. He confessed that his head was in a spin. From his manner it seemed as if he had about five minutes to get out, or face the firing squad.

This mad dash for the planes had begun about a week before when it was noticed that the embassy had started rounding up the people they believed to be in danger when the communists took over. The calls had been carefully conducted under cover of darkness, in the manner of a Stalinist arrest. The criteria were broad. As one of the embassy personnel put it, "The kind of people who know us are the kind of people who would be in trouble." But that was only part of the story. The embassy was clearing out everyone in its address book, but to do so they also had to take their wives and families, and the families got larger and larger. The rich Vietnamese also wanted to take their maids. Sometimes this would be questioned at the airport. They would be told that it was not customary in America to have maids. So they would turn around to the maids, and dismiss them with a wave of the hand. Then there was a flood of letters to the embassy from Americans and Vietnamese living in America. Discreet diplomats would pad up the stairs, knock quietly so as not to arouse the neighbors, and deliver the message: "Your son-in-law says you must leave. Can you be ready this time tomorrow night?" "I don't know. I haven't got a suitcase." "Couldn't you buy a suitcase?" "Yes, I think so." "All right then?" "What shall I wear?" And so on.

Sometimes these visits must have been welcome. At other times they shattered a few illusions. There was one man living not far from my hotel who was a member of the local defense force. I sat up late one night with him and the other members of the force, drinking Vietnamese spirit and chatting about what was going to happen. The members of the local defense force were clear about one thing: They would not lift a finger to defend the area from the Vietcong. As soon as the Vietcong arrived, their duties ended. They had seen the writing on the wall as far as the present regime was concerned, and had begun to look on the bright side of things. It was a fascinating conversation. They all talked with admiration for the other side, and there was not a trace of the usual Saigonese intransigence or panic. "Fuck me," said Jean-Claude, who had introduced me to the group, "you know what they're going to do? They're all going to join the other side at the first opportunity!" It seemed true, and the older man, who had expatiated quietly and at some length on the question of Vietnamese politics, seemed to us, if anything, already a Vietcong cadre. And yet a few nights later the Americans came to his flat. He had been in the secret police. The last the neighbors heard of him, he was being led to a jeep, weeping loudly.

The exodus was continuing at a rate of about 10,000 a day. It was estimated at the time that out of each day's departures, about 3,000 had embassy connections, 1,000 were relatives of Americans, and 1,000 were friends or contacts of Americans. What about all the rest? When I went to Tan Son Nhuot airport to watch the processing of the evacuees, I found very few who had a clear notion of why they were leaving the country. Some were North Vietnamese refugees from the 1950s, others were going because they had once worked in PX stores or as ancillary staff on American bases. One woman just did not know why she was going. Her husband had left the North as a young student. Her sister was married to an American who had insisted that the family should leave. She did not want to do so at all. She was leaving so much behind. For instance, her son was very keen on the piano. She had saved up for five years in order to buy him one. It had only just been installed in her home. Another man did know. He claimed to have led the National Revolutionary Movement in the days of Diem. "Obviously," he said, "as a journalist you will know what it means to live under communism. No? Then you should not in that case be a journalist."

There were snack stands at the entrance to Tan Son Nhuot, set up to cater for the waiting crowd of refugees, many of whom slipped past the guards without any papers. Processing was done in the defense attache's office compound, one of the last bits of pure America left in Vietnam. The last hurdle was in the gymnasium, under the basketball net. There were old notices reminding you not to bring in your pets, and not to put your hands on the walls. The forms were filled in by sour-looking GIs in olive drab, with daggers hanging from their belts. The prevailing atmosphere was one of general menace.

While the Americans were removing their friends from Saigon, the Vietcong were, we later discovered, investing the place with their own troops. The operation was, perforce, quite haphazardly handled. The soldiers came in wearing Saigon uniforms, in military trucks that had been acquired during the previous months. But they had no identity cards or fake accreditation, and must have lived continually on the verge of discovery. They went to Cholon, where one group arrested an ARVN soldier well before the fall of Saigon and used him as a guide during the remaining stages. They also went to positions near important installations in order to take control swiftly when the time came. The student groups were also working out what to do in order to help in the takeover, and the Chinese, always the shrewdest businessmen in Saigon, were already manufacturing NLF flags in readiness for a quick sale. There must have been a tremendous run on the haberdashers. Where red, blue, and yellow cloth ran out, they used colored plastic.

Saigon itself had never become accustomed to the immediacy of war. Even during the days of the Vietminh, when the war was going on just across the river, the city had seemed to live in another world. Only once had it been bombed (by the Americans, during the Tet Offensive), and it had been a long time since the center of town had been shelled. Nobody quite knew to what lengths the other side was prepared to go. Obviously, if they wished, they could reduce the place to rubble, but this, so most people said, was quite contrary to their philosophy. They wanted the town intact.

They were not, however, averse to using a little terror. One night I awoke to the sound of three large crashes, and I realized that the rocketing had begun. I went up to the top floor of my hotel, which was empty now but had once been a bar and billiard room designed for GIs. Although the building was a modest affair, it had a good view over the roofs toward where a couple of the rockets had fallen. Already a large fire had begun, fueled no doubt by the gasoline which was often kept in the houses of the poor. Soon it was clear that a whole block was ablaze, and that the fire was spreading. I watched this fire with mixed feelings. On the one hand, it seemed that the Vietcong had announced their proximity to the city. The fire, though distant, spelled an immediate danger. On the other hand, there is a terrible splendor about a city fire, as long as it is far enough away. Against any judgment or imaginative sympathy I might bring to bear, the fire attracted me. The next day I walked around the burnt-out area, a huddled group of jerry-built shacks which appeared to have encroached on an old Catholic graveyard. In the middle of the ruins the graves had been unearthed again. One of them bore the legend Memento Mori. It was said that the fire brigade had refused to put out the blaze until massive bribes had been produced. A large number of poor people's homes had consequently been destroyed. All this I might have guessed at the time, and yet I was excited by the fire. It seemed to be the curtain raiser for the last act.

It was on the afternoon of April 28, however, that the great psychological blow was struck. The morning had been dramatic enough. Driving out to Newport Bridge at about 6:30 A.M., I found that the Vietcong had come to the very outskirts of the city and were interdicting the road on the other side of the bridge. There were, it turned out, only a few of them, but they served their purpose, calling down a massive amount of firepower where they were ensconced. Saigon brought out all its weapons against them. The helicopter gunships blasted away all day, and it was not until evening that the road was cleared of a few brave men. After watching this scene for a time, I went back to my room and was reading a book when something quite extraordinary happened. Without any warning at all, the city became ablaze with rifle fire.

Once again, I went up to the top floor, but this time there was nothing to see. There was simply a noise; a massive, unvaried, unstinting noise. At first I thought, They've come in, it's an insurrection, they've invested the city with their troops and now they're just picking off anything that moves. But the noise was too uniform for that. There would have been direction to it. There would have been grenades, machine guns, more variety. I asked a member of the hotel staff. Perhaps a coup d'état, he said, shrugging. That again was possible. President Minh was making his inaugural speech that afternoon, and it might be that somebody had decided to topple him before he could hand over Saigon to the enemy. But then, as suddenly as it had started, the firing ceased. The opinion in the hotel was Marshal Ky's back.

I walked out into the deserted street. No dead bodies. Nobody much around. On the corner I met a soldier, and gave him a quizzical look. "Sorry 'bout that," he said, and turned away.

It had been a masterly piece of timing. Minh had finished his speech, calling on the Americans to leave, and on the other side to negotiate. The other side announced at once that this was not enough, that there had to be total unconditional surrender. At the same time, for the first and last time in the war, the Vietcong air force was brought into play. The air force had been picked up in the preceding months, as the northern provinces had fallen in disarray. Not it was used—to bomb the Saigon air force. There was no other way in which the Vietcong could ever have used an air force except against an air base. To have done so at that moment was to announce imminent victory, and to make sure that the victory cost them as little blood as possible. As for the firing in Saigon, the troops had been told of enemy planes on the attack. The plane they were firing at was in fact civilian. It got away.

But there was something about the incident that unnerved people. It was a foretaste, we thought. From now on, anything could happen, and happen swiftly. And when something did happen, there would be nothing we could do about it.

I was awakened the next morning by the ancient doorman of

the hotel, who unexpectedly came into my room carrying one loaf of French bread, two large chunks of palm sugar, and a bottle of Coca-Cola. He returned a little later with ice, and insisted I get up and eat. I gathered from a rather complicated conversation that there still was a curfew, and that these were the siege rations. The bread was wrapped in what appeared to be an American embassy report. As I attempted to eat the sugar and the bread, there was another knock. A young man came in, looking for an Amrican who had promised to get him out of the country. He had been planning to leave from Newport the night before, but the place had been under attack. Now his father, a captain in the army, was waiting outside. We talked for a while. The young man had an infinitely sad face. He was not pushing. He probably knew already that he had missed his last chance. He was unclear as to why he wanted to leave Vietnam anyway. I told him that he should not leave, since this was his country, and if he left it now he would never get back. He said wistfully, "I like going to the country. My family always goes to the country for holidays. We go to Rach Gia and Ha Tien." I said that Ha Tien was now in the hands of the Vietcong. He said: "Do you think people are happy in Ha Tien?" I said I thought so. We discussed what would happen to his father, and I tried to reassure him. But he left as sadly as he had come in.

The curfew did not seem to be very strict, so I set out to find the other journalists and see what was happening. Saigon looked beautiful that morning, with its deserted streets. Everyone was smiling. There were families standing in the doorways, smiling. A group of soldiers passed, smiling. A beggar girl in a tattered silk blouse, to whom I gave some money, ran laughing along beside me. She was young, with an idiot look and no teeth. Clearly the curfew did not apply to idiots. There was a Sunday-morning atmosphere. I felt very happy, as if I was in some English town, setting out to buy the Sunday papers. On the way, I met one of my friends from the local popular defense force, who told me that the airport had been attacked during the night. I appeared to have slept through everything.

At the Continental all the journalists were talking about the previous night's fighting at the airport. They had seen planes shot down with Strela missiles and this, coupled with the previous day's panic when the airport had been bombed, convinced several people that they should leave. Others, who had not intended to stay on, were having difficulty making up their minds. I felt very much excited, but did not consider going. The same principle that had taken me from Phnom Penh would keep me in Saigon. I had made my decision in advance. But I can't deny that I felt a certain superiority to those who were rushing around, paying their bills, gathering their stuff together, or dithering. I wanted to remain in my own hotel, but there was a strong move that all the British journalists should stick together. One of them was very keen to acquire a gun. The main worry for those staying on was that the "friendlies" might get nasty. One of the calculations of those leaving was that the Vietcong would certainly be nasty. As a Beaverbrook reporter said to me, "I wouldn't like to be interrogated by them. You know, they have methods. . . ." "I doubt if it would come to that," I said. "Have you ever done any work with the Americans?" he asked. "No, I was never here with the Americans." "Well I can think of things I've done, places I've been and so on, that I find it very difficult to explain away." I never found out exactly what he meant. As the hotel emptied, I looked at the garden and was reminded of Coleridge: "Well, they are gone, and here I must remain,/This lime-tree bower my prison!" I said: "Won't it be nice to have the place to ourselves." This remark was considered incredibly irritating.

I had to get my possessions and bring them to the Continental. As I walked along the street, people asked me why I had not left yet. "Are you French or Australian?" they asked. One small restaurant was open in which a group of lieutenants were sitting eating Chinese chicken and drinking Johnnie Walker Black Label. They invited me to join them, which I did with some diffidence since they were obviously out to get drunk, and might therefore become aggressive. They began by explaining that they would sit there until they were killed. I tried to say that I thought they were wrong, but when I explained why, I saw at once that I had gone too far. Ice formed over the conversation. "How long did you spend with the communists?" they asked. I said I hadn't been with the communists. Hitherto we had been talking in English. Then we switched to French. They were amused, they said, that when I started speaking in French I began to tremble.

I was afraid that I had fallen into the hands of precisely those "friendlies" who were supposed to be about to turn nasty. I reached out for a piece of chicken and nonchalantly picked up the head. I was not the part I had had in mind, but I bit into the eyeballs with great gusto, and sucked out the brains. The ice was finally broken when one of the officers asked in Cambodian whether I spoke Khmer. A little, I said, and we exchanged a few phrases. We also talked about the drawbacks of an officer's life: the way they were given uniforms that didn't fit; that they had to have them specially tailored, and it was their own families who did the ironing and starching. These men belonged to a breed that was just on the verge of extinction—the nattily dressed, well-groomed, gun-toting, sunglass-wearing, American-style, narcissistic junior officer.

The weight of their impending extinction bore down upon them.

Inevitably, the conversation returned to the impending take-over. I asked them why they were afraid. They were well aware, they said, that in Phnom Penh the people had greeted the Khmer Rouge with open arms. But they said that that was just for appearances. Afterward there would be a settling of accounts. They insisted again that they were going to die. I asked what they were going to do about it. One man said "I'm going to do just what De Gaulle did in the Second World War in London." Another man said: "De Gaulle wasn't in London, he was in Paris." The first man did not have the heart to contradict him. I bade them farewell. They repeated that they were going to sit there drinking all day, until they died.

A short time later I became acting bureau chief of the *Washington Post*, and found the keys waiting for me in the office, together with a charming farewell note from the staff. I had a pleasant young Vietnamese assistant, who was good enough to show me how to open the drawer to get at the office petty cash. The office was well equipped, I could have moved in to live there. Nice bathroom, plenty of books, fridge, bottle of Polish vodka in the fridge. I settled down to work, assuming that the evacuation had begun since there was now a fairly large amount of helicopter activity over the city. I had also assumed that the operation would be conducted with similar speed to that in Phnom Penh. But this was not so. A few moments later David Greenway phoned me from the embassy. They were stuck. Nobody had come yet, and embassy staff were getting nervous that the place might be shelled. Oh, and did I want the car keys; they had left the Volkswagen by the embassy gate.

I went round to the embassy. The crowd outside had grown but it had not yet reached the alarming proportions it would later in the day. There were shady Koreans, a few stranded Americans, and several hundred Vietnamese waiting around or attempting to argue with the marines on the gate. ARVN officers in mufti would come up to you and say, "Excuse me," producing an embassy visiting card, "I'm a good friend of Mr. So-and-so. Do you think I could get in?" Greenway appeared on one of the turrets and threw down the car keys, together with the dramatic stories of a couple of colleagues, to file at Reuters. I went to the car but found that I lacked the knack of turning the key in the ignition. It had always been troublesome and I had never driven the thing before. As I tried to start it I became nervous at being so close to the embassy. There was a sound of rifle fire nearby, and around the embassy the police would occasionally shoot in the air when some angry man became too importunate. I decided to abandon the car.

Before too long, the large helicopters—the Jolly Green Giants—began to appear, and as they did so the mood of the city suffered a terrible change. There was no way of disguising this evacuation by sleight-of-hand or, it appeared, of getting it over quickly. The noise of the vast helicopters as they corkscrewed out of the sky, was a fearful incentive to panic. The weather turned bad. It began to rain. And as the evening grew darker, it seemed as if the helicopters themselves were blotting out the light. It must have seemed as if the light would go forever. All the conditions conspired against calm. There were people all over Saigon who had been promised an escape. There were others, like the officers of the morning, who thought that they would definitely die. And there were others still who, for no definite reason, went into a flat spin. Always the beating of the helicopter blades reminded them of what was happening. The accumulated weight of the years of propaganda came crashing down upon a terrified city.

The crowd around the embassy swelled and its desperation increased. It became dangerous to go out on the streets: The looters were out, the cowboys were on their Hondas, and who knew what grudge might be worked out on the white face of a passer-by. The first major looting took place at the Brinks building, which had served as a billet for American officers from the earliest days of U.S. involvement in Indochina. It proved a rich source of booty. To add to the confusion of the city, the electricity cut out at around seven o'clock in the evening. It was then that I had to make my second shift of the day, from the Continental across the square to the Caravelle, where it had finally been decided that we should all stay together for however long it took for order to be restored. A mere matter of lugging a few cases across a small square, but I remember finding it the most arduous and frightening task as the Honda boys drove by shouting "Yankee, go home!" I cursed the embassy for its bungled withdrawal, and began for the first time to admire John Gunther Dean's Cambodian effort. Always the sound of the helicopters, stirring the panic, made things worse. Indoors it was alright. Finishing my work in my new office that evening, I came across a note from my nice Vietnamese assistant. It informed me that the office was more likely to be looted by the soldiers, and that the assistant had therefore taken home the petty cash. This was the last time I saw the man. Well, easy come, easy go, I thought. I went to the refrigerator and broached the Polish vodka. It was water.

The power cut turned out to be a godsend since by the time light was restored the majority of the crowd had gone home and the police had regained control of the streets. As the lights went on in the Caravelle they found our gallant press corps in the best of spirits. We didn't know how long we would be holed up in the hotel, or in what manner the city would fall. Most people I think were envisaging a rather slow and bloody takeover, but this did not spoil the brave mood of the evening. We had a distant view of the war. Toward the airport it appeared that an ammunition dump was exploding. Great flames would rise up and slowly subside. It went on for hours, like some hellish furnace by Hieronymus Bosch. If you went up onto the roof itself you could hear the war from every direction. But the city center had calmed down.

I had one more story to write. In the foyer of the hotel I found a policeman in mufti, and arranged to walk with him to the Reuters office. It was okay at first, but as we approached the dark area around the cathedral we both became more and more apprehensive. Turning left, we walked down the middle of the road, hand in hand, to keep up each other's spirits. We exhibited all the heroism of children in the dark. To any Vietcong agent, watching us from the top branches of the trees, I should say we must have looked too touching to kill.

* * *

Early on the morning of April 30, I went out of my hotel room to be greeted by a hysterical group of Koreans. "The Americans have called off the evacuation," said one. They had been unable to get into the embassy, had waited the whole night and had now given up. Of all the nationalities to fear being stranded in Saigon, the Koreans had the most reason. I went up to breakfast on the top-floor restaurant, and saw that there were still a few Jolly Green Giants landing on the embassy, but that the group on the Alliance Française building appeared to have been abandoned. They were still standing there on the roof, packed tight on a set of steps. Looking up at the sky, they seemed to be taking part in some kind of religious ritual, waiting for a sign. In the Brinks building the looting continued. A lone mattress fell silently from a top floor balcony.

There was one other group at breakfast—an eccentric Frenchman with some Vietnamese children. The Frenchman was explaining to the waiter that there had been some binoculars available the night before, and he wanted to use them again. The waiter explained that the binoculars belonged to one of the hotel guests. "That doesn't matter," said the Frenchman, "bring them to me." The waiter explained that the binoculars were probably in the guest's room. "Well go and get them then!" said the Frenchman. It seemed extraordinary that the Frenchman could be so adamant, and the waiter so patient, under the circumstances. I had orange juice and coffee, and noted that the croissants were not fresh.

Then I went to the American embassy, where the looting had just begun. The typewriters were already on the streets outside, there was a stink of urine from where the crowds had spent the night, and several cars had been ripped apart. I did not bother to check what had happened to mine, but went straight into the embassy with the looters.

The place was packed, and in chaos, Papers, files, brochures, and reports were strewn around. I picked up one letter of application from a young Vietnamese student who wished to become an interpreter. Some people gave me suspicious looks, as if I might be a member of the embassy staff, so I began to do a little looting myself, in order to show that I was entering into the spirit of the thing. Somebody had found a package of razor blades and had removed them all from their plastic wrappers. One man called me over to a wall safe and seemed to be asking if I knew the number of the combination. Another was hacking away at an air conditioner, another was dismantling a refrigerator.

On the first floor there was more room to move. I collected the following items: one copy of *Peace Is Not at Hand* by Sir Robert Thompson, one of the many available copies of *The Road from War* by Robert Shaplen, Barrington Moore's *Social Origins of Dictatorship and Democracy* (which I had been meaning to read for some time), a copy of a pacification report from 1972, and some embassy notepaper. Two things I could not take (by now I was not just pretending to loot—I had become quite involved): a reproduction of an 1873 map of Hanoi, and a framed quotation from Lawrence of Arabia, which read, "Better to let them do it imperfectly than to do it perfectly yourself, for it is their country, their war, and your time is short." Newly I found a smashed portrait of President Ford, and a Stars and Stripes mangled in the dirt.

I found one room that had not yet been touched. There were white chairs around a white table, and on the table the ashtrays were full. I was just thinking how eerie it looked, how recently vacated, when the lights went out. At once a set of emergency lights, photosensitively operated, turned themselves on above each doorway. The building was still partly working; even while it was being torn to pieces, it had a few reflexes left.

From this room, I turned in to a small kitchen where a group of old crones were helping themselves to jars of Pream powdered milk. When they looked up and saw me, they screamed, dropped the powdered milk, and ran. I decided then that it would be better to leave the building. It was filling up so much that it might soon become impossible to get out. What I did not know was that there were still some marines on the roof. As I forced my way out of the building they threw tear-gas down on the crowd and I found myself running hard, in floods of tears. Although the last helicopter had just left, people still thought there were other chances to get out. One man came up to me and asked confidentially if I knew of the alternative evacuation site. He had several plausible reasons why he was entitled to leave. Another man, I remember, could only shout "I'm a professor, I'm a professor," as if the fact of his being a professor would cause the Jolly Green Giants to swoop down and out of the sky and whisk him away.

There was by now a good deal of activity on the streets. Military trucks went to and fro across town bearing loads of rice, and family groups trudged along, bearing their possessions. As I finished writing my embassy story, the sirens wailed three times, indicting that the city itself was under attack. I returned to the hotel roof to see what was happening. The group on the Alliance Française building were still there, still waiting for their sign. Across the river, but not far away, you could see the artillery firing and the battle lines coming closer. Then two flares went up, one red, one white,. Somebody said that the white flare was for surrender. In the restaurant, the waiters sat by the radio. I asked them what was happening. "The war is finished!" said one.

I looked down into the square. Almost at once, a waiter emerged from the Continental and began to hoist a French Tricolor on the flagpole. There were groups of soldiers, apparently front-line troops, sitting down. From the battlefield across the river, the white flares began to go up in great numbers. Big Minh's broadcast had been heard, and in a matter of minutes the war would be well and truly over.

Under such circumstances, what does one do? For the poor of Saigon, the first reaction was to loot as much as possible. For most of the soldiers, it was to give in as quickly as possible, and make oneself scarce. For the victorious troops, for the students and Vietcong sympathizers within the city, it was a question of taking control as quickly as possible. For the reporter, there was a choice: one either went out to see what was happening, or one wrote about it. It was a cruel choice to have to make, but it was clear that the lines would soon either be jammed or go down altogether. For a stringer, the burden of writing is even greater, since it is during such moments that he earns the fat off which he has to live during the lean years. The first two laws of stringing are: (1) The more you file the more you earn; (2) The more you file the less you learn. I mention this because, throughout the remainder of the day and the days that followed, all my reactions were underscored by a worry about getting the thing written up, and not just written up, but sent out—whereas all my instincts were not to write at all. In the end the instincts won, hands down.

I took a lift with the BBC. We went out toward the Newport

Bridge in a large car driven by a Vietnamese. The Union Jack was flying from the aerial, and the BBC sign was clearly displayed. As we drove along past the lines of anxious faces, it became clear to me that I had come with the wrong crew. The soldiers whom we tried to film felt that the BBC had been on the side of the Vietcong. It had been denounced by Thieu, and now, the moment of defeat, was no time to be flying the flag. There was a large amount of military activity on the roads—truckloads of soldiers returned from the front. There was one bulldozer tearing back from the bridge, with a whole platoon sitting in the scoop. The tanks were waiting by the tank traps, many of them with their crew still in position. As we stopped to film them, I noticed one soldier fingering a grenade, weighing it thoughtfully in his hand. In the doors of houses, families waited nervously. By Newport Bridge itself, the looting of the American stores was still going on, a desparate last-minute effort that held up, in parts of the city, the advance of the victorious troops. The first thing the North Vietnamese and Vietcong saw as they came into Saigon was crowds of looters dragging sacks of rice and cartons of luxury goods. It must have justified their view of the degeneracy of the city.

But they had not yet arrived. Walking up to the top of the bridge, we wondered whether to go on to meet them, or to retrace our steps. Then we were called back to the car by the governor of Gia Dinh.

He looked exceedingly angry and unpleasant—he and one of his officers were laden with pistols and grenades, ready perhaps to make their last stand against the encroaching communists. They were fat men with twisted faces, no doubt gripped by the bitterness of betrayal. Where had we been? To the top of the bridge. No, they said, we had come from the Vietcong. We replied that we had been to the bridge because we wanted to film. "I don't want to hear any more," said the governor. "How much did they pay you? How much did the Vietcong pay you?" "Look," said Brian Barron, "I'm not Vietcong. I'm afraid of the Vietcong. When the Vietcong start shooting, I lie down." "Why you lie?" said the governor of Gia Dinh.

I thought, "This is it. He's going to kill us." And apart from the fear of death itself, there seemed to be something particularly bitter and unfair in being killed as a traitor after the defeat. But instead of killing us, the governor told me to remove the Union Jack from the car, and Eric Thirer to take the BBC label off his camera. The Union Jack was stuck to the aerial with elastoplast, and I remember wondering whether my trembling hands would ever get the thing off. The governor ordered that the car should be placed between two tank traps, where it was later found, completely squashed by a tank. We began to walk back in the direction of Saigon.

I wanted to get back to the city center as quickly as possible. I couldn't understand why Barron was taking such a long time. He seemed to be looking for something in the car, and later he told me what it was. A few days before, he had been reading Ho Chi Minh's works, and had shoved them under the back seat, out of sight. Now he was afraid that they would suddenly find the book, and shoot us on the spot. He therefore decided to get the thing out and shove it under his shirt. He went back to the car, put his hands under the seat, and discovered that the book was gone.

By now there was chaos on the streets. The trucks that had passed us in one direction as we were coming out of Saigon appeared to have returned. Clearly, nobody knew where to go. There was gunfire at the crossroads just ahead, and I think that we all felt in great danger, having lost our car. We were saved by a taxi driver who dumped a load of customers and offered to take us back for four thousand piastres. I would have paid whatever I had. We got into the car, put our heads down, and sped back to the city center.

In the Reuters office I was writing an account of what I had just seen when Barron came in again. "I don't know what's happening," he said. "I've just seen a tank with an NLF flag." I went to the door and looked out to the left, the direction of Thieu's palace, and saw the tank. Without thinking, I ran after it and flagged it down just as it turned toward the palace gates. The tank slowed down and a North Vietnamese soldier in green jumped off the back, and went at me with his gun, as if to hit me. In my confusion, I couldn't remember the NLF salute, or how to explain to the soldier that I wanted a ride. I tried everything—a salute, another salute, a clenched fist, a hitchhiker's thumb. Finally (that is to say, after a few nervous seconds) I held out my hand to shake his. He took my hand abruptly, indicated the back of the tank. I remember worrying, as I climbed on, that I might touch something very hot. Then, as the soldier told me to keep my head down, I idiotically produced my passport, which they dismissed scornfully. The tank speeded up, and rammed the left side of the palace gate. Wrought iron flew into the air, but the whole structure refused to give. I nearly fell off. The tank backed again, and I observed a man with a nervous smile opening the center portion of the gate. We drove into the grounds of the palace, and fired a salute.

I had taken a ride on the first tank to reach the palace, but it was not until several weeks later that I realized this was the case. Looking up from my crouching position at the back, I saw another vehicle in the grounds (in fact an ARVN tank). Damn, I thought, I was on the second; still, never mind. I wondered whether I was under arrest. I tried to talk to the soldiers, but I did not notice that some of them were captured ARVN troops who had been coopted in order to show the way. On the top of the tank was an open carton of Winston cigarettes, which struck me as odd. No doubt it had been thrown up from the looting crowd. Another thing I remember noticing was a tank passing behind us on the lawn. Its tracks crushed the verge of a flowerbed, and I remember thinking, That was unnecessary. Also I noticed an extraordinary number of dragonflies in the air.

I was very, very excited. The weight of the moment, the privilege of being a witness, impressed itself at once. Over and above my self-consciousness, and the trivial details which were made all the more interesting by the extraordinary nature of the event, there was the historical grandeur of the scene. Events in history are not supposed to look historical: No eye perceived a battlefield at a glance, no dying leader composed his followers around him in the neoclassical manner; even many of the great war photographs are said to have been rearranged. The victors write, rewrite, or retouch their history. Indeed, in one Western account of these events, I notice that the tank that I have just described knocks the palace gate to the ground "like a wooden twig." The man who opened the gate, a civilian guard who had been specially placed, has been subbed out in this account. The guards themselves have fled. Nothing is allowed to interfere with the symmetry of the scene, or to interrupt the conquest with wild, flailing arms.

And yet the North Vietnamese do not merely touch up history. They also enact it in the heroic manner. This was the first time I had seen their genius for imposing their style upon events, for acting in the manner of their propaganda. The spectacle was tremendous and, as one of their officers realized, not to be missed. He ran up to Neil Davies who was filming the arrival of the tanks, and begged him: "You take film for us? You take film for us?" The tanks rolled onto the lawn, and formed automatically into a semicircle in front of the palace, firing a salute into the air as they did so. Soon the air became full of the sound of saluting guns. Beside the gate, sitting in a row on the lawn, was a group of soldiers, former members of the palace guard. They waved their hands above their heads in terror. An NLF soldier took the flag and, waving it above his head, ran into the palace. A few moments later, he emerged on the terrace, waving the flag round and round. Later still, there he was on the roof. The red and yellow stripes of the Saigon regime were lowered at last.

I thought, I shall know if I'm under arrest when I jump off the tank. There came suddenly to mind a story of a plane that went through an electric storm: When it touched down, all the passengers were electrocuted on contact with the earth. I jumped off, and noticed that I was still alive and free. The palace grounds filled up with soldiers, and trucks were arriving all the time. The broad avenue toward the cathedral became the center for the arriving troops. Their vehicles and helmets were covered with leaves, their uniforms were green. A great wave of greenery swept over the city. It blended into the scenery, the grass and the trees of the avenue. Only the red armbands and the red tags on the guns showed up. Everything had changed in a trice.

For the Westerners present, it was an occasion for overt celebration. I saw Jean-Claude running through the palace gates, his hands over his head, his cameras swinging hectically around his body. Old colleagues greeted each other with delight. We felt bound to congratulate each other, as if we had a right to partake of the victory. For the NLF troops, on the other hand, such satisfaction as they felt was completely suppressed. They sat down and lit up North Vietnamese cigarettes, like men who had simply done a good day's work—they were justified and did not need praise. Sometimes they shook hands with the foreigners, occasionally they smiled; they waved from the trucks—but never once did I see them lose their self-control.

I walked past the cathedral and came upon an NLF soldier in a condition of extreme embarrassment. He was standing facing a wall, secretly looking at something. I thought he was embarrassed to relieve himself in front of a group of interested onlookers, but in fact he was consulting his compass, unsure of where he was supposed to be. The group realized his difficulty and gave him directions. At this moment the fire brigade drove past, lights blazing, horn blaring, waving their hats in the air, in expressions of wild delight. Further down, along Tu Do Street, I met my friend Terzani and we walked together to the Ministry of Defense, which was in the process of surrendering. At these ceremonies a salute was always fired over the building, and so the city must have been full of falling lead, and yet I never heard of anyone being injured from such fallout. This was one of the many curious features of the day.

The most dramatic change that had taken place was the complete disappearance of the Saigon Army. All around the streets one would come across piles of clothes, boots, and weapons. Some of the piles were so complete it looked as if their former occupant had simply melted into his boots. And then, in the doorways, one would see young men in shorts, hanging around with an air of studied indifference, as if to say, Don't look at me, I always dress like this—it's the heat, you know. Where groups of soldiers had been caught and told to surrender, they were made to take off their clothes and sit down. I came across one such group by the town hall.

A historic building (it was from here that the British had expelled the Trotskyists after the Second World War), it looks like a *mairie* in a small, pretentious French town. The Saigon troops were sitting on the pavement opposite, while the NLF were trying to remove the flag from the pole. They had been unable to open the heavy decorative iron gates, and one of them was hopelessly attempting to shoot the flag down with his rifle. I sat down to watch how they would solve the problem. A most odd thing happened. Across the square, whistling ostentatiously and bearing an M16 on his shoulder, came an enormously tall Frenchman. He walked up to the NLF. An angry Vietcong in black told him to put the gun down. He taunted the man: "I know how to use it, you know," he said. A couple of us shouted out to the man to throw the gun away, for God's sake. He did so eventually, with a mad smile, and strolled off again, still whistling. Meanwhile one of the former Saigon soldiers, in bare feet and shorts, was climbing up the baroque facade of the *mairie,* with the NLF flag gripped between his teeth. He lowered the red-and-yellow stripes, for which he had fought, and raised the blue-and-red flag with the yellow star of the NLF.

By now the streets were beginning to fill up again. Occasionally the requisitioned jeeps of the former regime came past, full of cheering youths in gear that was intended to look like Vietcong attire. These new revolutionary enthusiasts were immediately distinguishable in appearance and behavior from the real thing. Some of them were disarmed on the spot. Others were to last several days or weeks before being sorted out, but for the moment they had a great fling, cheering, shouting, and riding around. Most people were still indoors, wondering what would happen to them. The first to appear on the streets and talk to the soldiers were the old men and women, and young children. They brought out tea to the tired NLF troops, and sat with them, firing questions about what would happen next. The reassurance they received spread visibly throughout the suspicious city, and in a short while the areas where the troops were concentrated (around the palace and the port) took on the air of a massive teach-in.

The sort of questions that were being asked were: Would there be revenge? Would those who had left North Vietnam at the time of the division be forced to return? Would the women be forced to cut their hair? Would those with painted nails have them pulled out, *without anesthetic?* Would the women be forcibly married off to the crippled soldiers of the North? To all such questions, the answer was a gentle no. Another question was, What did the North Vietnamese eat? The fact that such a question could be put shows the ignorance of young Saigon about Hanoi, since the answer of course was rice.

I was getting very hungry and thirsty after the exertions of the day, so I wandered down to my old hotel by the market. The manageress was pleased, and rather surprised, to see me. She had obviously assumed that, whatever I said, I would in fact leave with the Americans. I told her what was happening outside. "We are very pleased to welcome the liberation forces," she said through clenched teeth. The night-club dancer, whom I had failed to assist to leave, was also there. She gave me some very sick looks. She had dressed simply, in black pajamas, and had done up her hair in a bun, in what she imagined would be a manner suitable for receiving the forces of liberation. The landlady and the old doorman produced a meal of bread, olives, walnuts, cheese, and beer, from the siege rations. It was the first and last time that the landlady ever let me have anything for free.

A phrase ran through my mind from the time of the arrival of the tanks and on through the day as I wandered around the streets, meeting people I knew, watching the chatting groups, and seeing how the whole place settled down. The phrase was "a permanent and marvelous disgrace." It seemed to me evident, and bitterly ironical, that all the talk of what the North Vietnamese would do when—if—they took Saigon, all of it had been wrong. During the whole of the day I saw only three or four corpses. The NVA were clearly the most disciplined army in the world. They had done nothing out of order, and it could not be that they were just waiting till the foreigners were out of the way before setting about the rape and pillage that many had prophesied. You could not fake the sort of discipline they had shown, nor could the events of the day be depicted (even by the most bigoted critic) as anything other than a triumph—a triumph that had exceeded the expectations of even their warmest, most bigoted admirers. Consequently, when the story was told (by now the lines were down), it would disgrace those who had predicted otherwise. It would be a permanent and marvelous disgrace. The CIA and Pentagon amateurs, a generation of hawks, would be made to stand forever in the corner wearing the dunce's cap. I did not think that Saigon had been liberated in the way that shortly would be made out. I did not think either that there had been an uprising—I had seen no real evidence for such a thing. But the victorious army seemed to have justified itself by its behavior alone. That I will never forget.

Peace had come, more or less. In the afternoon, one desperate pocket had made a last attempt at a firefight right in the center of town, and sometimes in the distance one would hear explosions, for which I never found the reason. In the outskirts of the town the looting continued wherever any wealthy establishment had been abandoned, or wherever the troops had yet to arrive and take control. I went to the Buddhist University, where the students were already organizing the collection of the enormous number of arms that had been abandoned on the streets. Nguyen Huu Thai, the student leader, greeted us and gave us a form of identification that would serve for the next few days. Were we not impressed? he asked. Was it not like the Paris Commune of 1871?

As we drove back, we passed the Taiwanese and Malasian embassies, which were being throughly looted. People were stealing everything, including the chandeliers. The young students who had taken it upon themselves to stop the looting tried to do so by firing into the air. When this did not work, one of them adopted a most terrifying and realistic technique. Holding a rifle in his left hand and a pistol in his right, he pointed the pistol at a looter and fired his rifle into the air.

Back at the Caravelle I watched the landscape settle down in peace. The flares still went up, on and on into the night. The intense excitement of the past days subsided into irritable exhaustion. I had a bitter argument with one of my greatest friends, and went to bed in the worst of spirits. As my head sank into the pillow I burst into tears.

May Day 1975 was probably an occasion for worldwide celebration of the liberation of Saigon. I don't know. In Saigon itself, indeed throughout Vietnam, May Day was not celebrated. It had been canceled by Hanoi, as part of the war effort, and now, the day after the war was over, it was too late to organize. May Day would have to wait.

I went out at dawn on May Day morning. The flares were still going up, and the flags of the National Liberation Front had already appeared on public buildings. NLF washing hung from windows. The soldiers were breakfasting by the parked tanks. They had dug foxholes in the public squares, and slept in Saigon as if in the jungle. The trouserless soldiers of the defeated army wandered around with nothing to do. There were beggars in the doorways, and an old woman asleep and a young girl beside her looking through a work of lurid pornography. There was litter everywhere, military and domestic, and piles of incriminating documents and letters and, in one case, a large stack of 78 rpm records.

There was a pair of nuns on a motorbike, sporting the NLF flag. Sightseers. Saigon was coming out to see the NLF, and the NLF was being conducted around the city in trucks, gazing up at the buildings. It had been told of the poverty of Saigon. It had never seen such wealth. As yet the spivs, beggars, and prostitutes had not come out. But I saw one cripple from the Saigon Army dressed in what he clearly conceived to be the outfit of a guerrilla.

As yet, very few of the guerrillas, the true Vietcong of the South, had appeared. They strolled in in twos and threes, with strangely shaped bombs tied to their belts, and antique weapons. They sometimes had no holsters for their guns, but carried them in their hands or in trouser pockets. Some were barefooted. They wore the same range of cheap manmade fibers in blues and browns. They wore either pith helmets or floppy hats. When I asked them about the difference between these two forms of headgear, they replied that the pith helmets were hard, whereas the floppy hats were—floppy.

I put out my hand to shake that of a Vietcong. He thought I was trying to take the revolver from his hand. Prudently he put the gun behind his back.

Most of the regular troops seemed to come from the North. They arrived in trucks, and all but the officers abandoned their arms. Then they wandered hand in hand through the streets. We rushed down to the port to marvel at the navy in their nineteenth-century suits. At Tan Son Nhuot, the air force arrived, wearing wings and speaking Russian. Near the still-smoldering remains of the DAO compound, these elusive aristocrats of the air could be found drinking Chablis and American beer.

The Saigon bourgeoisie, to meet the occasion, dressed themselves up to the nines and drove around and around the city for days on end, until they were stopped by the price of gasoline. Many cars had been destroyed, and lay at the side of the road. The bourgeoisie then came around and around on Hondas. They were at last admitted to the bar of the Continental Shelf, where they came to be seen. The café crowds came back to their old haunts, and cowboys resumed work, stealing watches and handbags: they thought it good sport to snatch cameras from the necks of NLF soldiers. People were said to have been shot for stealing, but the reports did not deter the criminals.

After a time the beggars returned to their usual patches, and an unusually large number of prostitutes started hanging around the hotels. As Saigon got used to the new soldiers, and realized that their orders were not to intervene, the hopes grew that the city might draw these saints into its aged corruption.

It was easy to pick out the stalls of looted goods. Drink was cheap and, since many embassy wine cellars had been ransacked, the quality was high. It was in liberated Saigon that I learned what happens to aged champagne, how it loses its sparkle and turns to a nutty dessert wine. The French residents of Saigon—there were many—descended on the street markets early and got the best wine home and out of the sun. The journalists—of whom there were not a few—picked off the bottles of genuine spirits: It had been foolish to try to buy whiskey in Saigon before; now the real thing was as cheap as the imitation. Over the next three months the depletion of stocks told you a lot about drinking habits. It was clear, for instance, that since the Americans had left, no one in Saigon could stand tequila, or knew what to do with it. I tried it, and tried to imagine what it would be like with a salted rim. Ten years later the thought still disgusts me.

The chief customers in the market were the NLF. The soldiers had been paid on arrival in Saigon, and with the North Vietnamese *dong* standing at four to five hundred *piastres* (the panic rate) they were richer than they had ever been in their lives. They bought several watches and might wear them all. They bought cigarette lighters with tiny clocks concealed inside them. And the more they acquired, the less they resembled the nineteenth-century army of the early days of liberation. Once they had bought the dark glasses, they had taken on something of the Saigon look.

There were no wounded soldiers. They were not allowed to visit Saigon. The soldiers we met were appealled by what they saw: the beggars, the painted faces of the women, the dishonesty. They spoke of a future in which they would turn Saigon into a beautiful city. They compared it unfavorably with Hanoi.

The soldiers had a mission to perform, but they did not have a missionary's reforming zeal. They knew it was best to take their time, and they had time on their hands. Saigon society slowly returned to abnormal, out of gas and freewheeling downhill. Everyone knew the situation could not last. Nobody knew what would come next.

In those initial days it was possible to travel outside the city since no formal orders had been given. Indeed it was possible to do most things you fancied. But once the regulations were published restricting us to Saigon, life became very dull indeed. The novelty of the street scenes had worn off, and most journalists left at the first opportunity. I, however, had been asked by the *Washington Post* to maintain its presence in Vietnam until a replacement could be brought in. I allowed the journalist's plane to leave without me, then cabled Washington stating my terms, which were based on the fact that I was the only stringer left working for an American paper. The *Post*, on receipt of my terms, sacked me. I had thought I had an exclusive story. What I learned was: Never get yourself into an exclusive *position*. If the *New York Times* had had a man in Saigon, the *Post* would have taken my terms. Because there were no rivals, and precious few Americans, I had what amounted to an exclusive non-story. By now, I was sick of the East, sick of travel, sick of the journalistic life. But I was stuck. I crawled back to the *Post*.

When there was nothing to write about, I described myself, but as this was against house style in an American paper, I had to be thinly disguised: "'It's like a spa at the end of the season,' remarked a dejected Englishman sitting on the empty terrace of the Continental Palace—this abandoned, echoing, colonial hotel. The rains have begun, leaving the air cooler and clearer. Most of the foreigners are preparing to leave." And I went on to record how the old Assembly building had been turned back into an opera house, where a brute of a conductor leaped around in tails, and where the mixed evening always included the same program: a movement of Beethoven's Fifth, some Strauss, and a rendition in Russian of *La Donna è Mobile*, sung by a Vietnamese tenor with an idea of how to smile like an Italian. The NLF soldiers would listen relaxedly, sticking their bare feet over the gallery. It appears to be an idea common among conquerors that what a fallen city needs is a good injection of culture. After the capture of Berlin, every sector was immediately featuring Russian dancing and lectures by T. S. Eliot. Hanoi sent down pretty well everything it could transport; including massed choirs and an archaeological exhibition of a strongly nationalistic bent.

In early June I went to a reception at the presidential palace, to mark the sixth anniversary of the founding of the Provisional Revolutionary Government. Nowadays, I believe, you will find that Vietnam has written the PRG out of history. The process was just beginning then. A particularly frank and cynical guerrilla told me that the talk about the PRG was nonsense. Hanoi called all the shots and it was stupid to believe otherwise. And yet I believe that the members of the southern movement did generally believe in the authority of their own existence. The excitement was, on this occasion, to spot the PRG leaders, such as Huynh Tan Phat, with his face wreathed in smiles, dressed in the kind of khaki suit favored by foreign correspondents in the tropics, but with the addition of a matching khaki tie.

The person we all wanted to meet was General Tran Van Tra, Saigon's military chief. He was in a terrific mood, and laughed and laughed when we reminded him of some of his previous activities. We would ask: "The Americans say you masterminded the Tet Offensive from headquarters in Thu Duc. Is this true?" And he would reply that he couldn't remember. I'd been reading Lucien Bodard's extraordinary *The Quicksand War,* in which Tran features as having organized a patriotic liquidation campaign against the French. Was that true? He said he wouldn't elaborate. All he would say was that he had been in the environs of Saigon since before 1945.

There was a sense that the life work of such men was coming to fruition, that the plan of years could now be implemented. And the implementation could proceed at its own proper pace. The center of Saigon was losing its significance. The shops of Tu Do, dealers in luxury goods, were now also soup stands. But Tu Do itself was deserted. It reminded me of an old French photograph, with a couple of blurred figures in the middle distance, and a cyclo-driver snoozing in the shade.

In the suburbs, by contrast, the mobilization of the youth

groups had got under way. They sat around awkwardly singing revolutionary songs, clapping in unison, and not wearing jeans. They had turned the task of sweeping the streets into a ceremony. They were tearing down the old police posts, but not all the barbed wire, not all the barbed wire by any means.

The major effort was to get people back from urban squats to their homes in the country. A truck would come through the streets bound for Quang Nam, its destination written in large chalk letters along the side, together with the words We drive by night. That was an astonishing novelty. For over twenty years the golden rule in Indochina was not to be on the roads at night.

Something had to be done about crime. Saigon had lived on crime, all kinds, from the petty to the most highly organized. With the fall of Saigon, prisons were opened, all prisoners released, and judiciary suspended. I spoke to one judge, an opponent of Thieu and yet part of his criminal court. He said that after the liberation he and about a hundred other former judges had presented themselves and asked for pardon. The pardon had been given, after they had informed on their fellow judges. Since that time they had gone to their place of work every day, and waited for the arrival of the new minister of justice. Finally he came and looked around the tribunal, delivering himself of one sentence: "Comrades, continue your work." So a hundred judges sat around and waited. In the provinces it was said that they received unwelcome visits from men they had sentenced.

Justice took to the open streets, and in one week the official newspaper (the old papers had been closed down) gave two front-page stories showing robbers executed by the liberation forces. Both accounts emphasized the popular support for the executions. In the first case, a Honda-cowboy was killed trying to escape. Support was *ex post facto*. In the second, the photograph showed a former "puppet soldier" tied to crossed planks in the manner of Spartacus. Public support preceded the action. The man had been caught attempting to steal a watch at gunpoint, had resisted arrest and, not having repented when finally caught, had committed further "savage" actions. So: "In order to protect the tranquil life of the Saigon population and in accordance with the aspirations of the people, the revolutionary law shot the thief Vo Van Ngoc."

In another case, three thousand people assembled in order to judge three thieves. They climbed up on buildings to witness the popular tribunal, which sentenced one of the culprits to death. He was shot "before the joy of the people" whom the newspaper showed in a rather blurred photograph waiting for the event.

That a thief had not repented was a serious point to be held against him. In the judicial and moral climate of the day, repentance was of prime importance, and obstinacy was a political category. Reeducation, *Hoc Tap*, was under way, and everyone was talking about it. It appeared that the private soldier or NCO could go along for the three-day political education session: If he performed well he would be praised, whereas if he was uncooperative he would be told to emulate those singled out for praise. It sounded an absurdly lenient program—perhaps merely a way of filling in the time and keeping idle officers off the street. But later on, the same people who had spoken with modest pride of their good performances in *Hoc Tap* came back to say that *Hoc Tap* was not yet over. It was becoming inexorable; it was impossible to extricate oneself from the guilt of being associated with the Thieu army. In South Vietnam, men of military age had had no choice but to join the army; they were conscripts. And yet they seemed to be asked to share the guilt of Thieu.

It was, in fact, over the question of reeducation that the new regime showed its true character, and it brought to an end the long period in which the Saigonese were prepared perhaps to give their conquerors the benefit of the doubt. One morning my Vietnamese assistant burst into my room. "It's sensational, all the officers have to leave home for a month's course. They're going to be reeducated."

I got back into bed, crossly, and asked why that was so sensational.

"Don't you think it's harsh? They're to be separated from their families for thirty days."

I replied that in the case of the generals I thought the whole thing pretty lenient.

The details of the announcement were extraordinary. You were told exactly how much money you would need for the course, for the purchase of food, and you were advised to bring three kilos of rice as emergency rations. In addition, you needed a change of clothes, blanket, towel, mosquito net, mat, raincoat, pullover, toothpaste, toothbrush, bowl, cigarettes (if a smoker), paper, pen, health card, and medicines. It seemed to indicate a trip to the Central Highlands, and looking at the list I was foolish enough to express the wish that I was going too.

That there was a ten-day course for junior officers seemed to indicate that the duration of the course was seriously meant. The officers put on their raincoats and went off to their departure points, joking that if they tell you to shower and don't provide the soap you are not to go in. They left, and as long as I was there they didn't come back.

The officers had been duped, and you might almost say that the deception was justifiable: There were decades of corruption in an army that was going to be extremely difficult to incorporate into the new society. But the ruse was exacerbated by the way it was reported. In the days of Thieu there had been a press of sorts, and spokesmen of the Provisional Revolutionary Government used to be eloquent in its defense. Then, with the end of the war, they came in and closed the papers down, replacing them with *Giai Phong*.

The new official press hated mentioning disasters of any kind. A friend of mine sent a report abroad concerning a road accident. This was censored, and the rumors began. There was a rumor that two truckloads of former officers had been ambushed, or had hit a minefield, somewhere near Tay Ninh. The rumor grew until I was assured by one woman that two thousand former officers had been killed. The women of Saigon went into shell shock. There were gatherings, real demonstrations in the streets, and slanging matches between the innocent soldiers of the North and the very down-to-earth wives of Saigon. The women wanted to know from General Tran Van Tra what had happened. The soldiers seemed completely unnerved. Worse, there were more officers waiting to leave on similar "courses," and so there was always a group of tearful women waiting behind the post office to learn when their husbands were due to go. I was told that four officers had returned from reeducation in coffins.

* * *

It was becoming impossible for me to work as a journalist. Up to now my stories had all had the theme of life returning to normal, but when the censorship began it was very difficult to describe normality truthfully. I wrote a story about how a fish-net factory had been ordered to stay open with full employment, even though there was no nylon thread for the nets (the implication being that the employer would soon become impoverished). No one questioned the truth of the story, it was that they wanted me to say simply: The factory has been ordered to stay open *despite all the difficulties*. If they could not admit that there was no thread, how could they allow us to say that no one seemed to have returned from the reeducation camps? And if one could not write such a story, how could one justify giving a general impression of normality in other stories? In one I mentioned that a man had committed suicide in the ruins of an old military monument. But the outside world was not allowed to know that there had been a suicide in Saigon.

I began to wonder if there was a code word to explain to my employers on the *Washington Post* that my copy was being censored. The thought, judging from the subjects they asked me to write about, hadn't occurred to them. I had retained from the *Post*'s bureau (before I handed it over to the authorities) a copy of a handbook for the paper's correspondents. I looked up censorship. There was no entry. I looked up Moscow, where the most I learned was that a correspondent should beware of making unflattering personal references to Lenin and to the way Jews were treated in Russia. I decided to solve the censorship problem by stopping writing and applying to leave. It was not a solution, but I could no longer bear Vietnam.

I had a spacious but gloomy old flat in Tu Do Street. If I looked out of my window any time during the day, there would be a bum swinging in the window opposite, which belonged to a body-building club. If I looked down at the street to the corner slightly left, my eye would immediately be caught by a tiny cyclo-driver in a panama hat, who had decided that I was the only generous customer left in the city, and that he might as well specialize. I was under a kind of commercial house arrest, genial enough, but unrelenting. If I told the cyclo-driver I was walking today, I would still have to go past my spastic beggar, the one who was all smiles and whom I was supposed never to let down. But he was generous enough in a way. One day I carefully crossed the street to avoid him on my usual walk. I was studiously pretending not to be anywhere near him when I happened to see he was doubled up in laughter. He knew exactly what pressure he was putting on me every day, and he seemed to think it well within my rights occasionally to refuse.

Early in the morning at, say, 5:30, you would hear the bells ringing in the military billets. Then there was a noise—a great tearing sound—which I thought must belong to some extraordinary contraption for removing the surface from the road. I rose and threw open the mosquito blinds: It was a company of soldiers sprinting along the street in their Ho Chi Minh sandals. The soldiers were relaxed and cheerful at this time of day. They shouted a few slogans, exercised, listened to what sounded like a little pep talk for about ten minutes and then went off to breakfast.

These soldiers—the *bo doi*, as we all now called them—were members of the best army in the world, disciplined in war and extraordinarily well-behaved in peace. But they had no gift for drill—even their gymnastics were uncoordinated—Saigon rooked them·something rotten. The stall holders persuaded the *bo doi*, when they suspected the dud watches they had been sold, that the only foolproof test was to put a watch in your mouth, block your ears, and close your eyes. If you could hear it ticking, it was kosher.

The *bo doi* hated keeping order. They did at one stage execute thieves in the street, but that was at the height of the crime wave in May. Later I saw a robber trying to escape from a pursuing crowd. The *bo doi* were appealed to, but were reluctant to interfere because the *bo doi* had a great deal of sympathy for the poor of Saigon, and all the people they had put out of work by winning. They believed their own propaganda. They *were* heroes. A story was told in the early days after the fall that a *bo doi* had been driving a truck carelessly and had killed a child. His commanding officer said to him: "You have been a good soldier and have sacrificed much for the revolution—the time has come to make the final sacrifice." Whereupon the *bo doi* shot himself. The fact that the Saigonese told these rumors says something for the reputation of the *bo doi*. Even so, they were sometimes stabbed in the back streets, and once or twice one would hear gunfire at night.

If I had been able to talk to the *bo doi*, Saigon would have been the most interesting place in the world. But I mean really talk. They were forbidden to chat to *us*. Once one told me: "I always liked going into battle because the atmosphere was so good. Everybody knew they were going to die. They had no food, and nothing to give in return, you would show him the letter you had just got from your wife. Everybody loved each other, because they all knew they were going to die." But then he became embarrassed at confessing all this to a foreigner.

Part of our admiration for the *bo doi* derived from what, in contrast, we were now learning of the Khmer Rouge after the fall of Phnom Penh. Large numbers of refugees had been making their way from the evacuated Cambodian capital across the border into Vietnam and, in some cases, to Saigon itself. The stories they told made it clear that the Khmer Rouge had not just instigated a bloodbath, they had no plan for the governing of the country they had won. If you could persuade a Vietnamese officer to talk about the Khmer Rouge, the best he would say, with a shudder, would be that they do not respect the laws of Ho Chi Minh. But it was obvious now that the regime was one of unparalleled savagery, and the Vietnamese were shocked by what they knew of it.

What was happening in Cambodia meant far more to me personally than the events I was witnessing in Vietnam, and I spent some time cultivating contacts with those who had escaped the Khmer Rouge regime. In particular, there were nine officers who had been associates of Son Ngoc Thanh, the former Cambodian prime minister and leader of the Khmer Krom (the ethnic Cambodians from South Vietnam). They had now requested asylum in Vietnam, as they were terrified of repatriation. But nobody knew precisely what the relationship between the authorities in Saigon and the Khmer Rouge would be.

The officers were living with their families in a Cambodian pagoda not far from the city center. They were free to go around town. One day, one of them came to see me in the hotel. He asked if he could borrow my spare bed. I asked him why. He explained that over the last few days a particular car had been arriving at the pagoda and taking people away. The pretext was that the officers and the head of the monastery, the Venerable Kim Sang, were to meet with Son Ngoc Thanh himself. Four people went and did not return. Nobody knew if they had been arrested by the Provisional Revolutionary Government, or if Khmer Rouge undercover agents were involved.

I told the officer that he could stay the night, but he would not be able to continue in the hotel for a long time, or he would draw suspicion on both of us. We sat up and talked until late into the night. As it happened I had Sihanouk's memoirs with me, which included a long attack on the CIA and Son Ngoc Thanh for undermining his regime. The officer agreed with much of Sihanouk's account, and admitted to me that he had been involved with the CIA. I asked him a number of times where Son Ngoc Thanh was now. It took a long time before he would say. Finally, he admitted that Son Ngoc Thanh was in Saigon. I said that it seemed very strange, if the man had been an associate of the CIA, that he should have stayed on in Saigon. The officer replied that Ho Chi Minh and Son Ngoc Thanh, both being nationalist leaders, had a respect for each other, and that there was a stipulation in Ho's will that Son Ngoc Thanh must not be harmed in any way. He had nothing to fear from the PRG.

Once his story was out, the officer began to talk about his fears that the Khmer Rouge would catch him. He recounted his escape from Cambodia. He talked about the screams he had heard from the undergrowth when they had taken away suspected officers. He talked about the beatings. He was still pleading for help and he believed that I had influence. I remember his soft voice from the next bed asking if I could imagine what it was like to be put in a cage and left all day in the sun, "like a wild animal, like a wild animal."

That night, every time I fell asleep, there was a loud knocking at the door. I would wake fully, then wait, my heart beating, to see whether the knocking was real. I would doze off again. Then the knocking would resume. The next day the officer left to find a new hiding place.

I was out of my depth entirely, and confided my problem to a colleague who was not only very curious to know who had spent the night in my room and why, but also seemed very well connected. A few days later he came rushing into my room and said that if I could find my lieutenant-colonel, the one who was supposed to have done stuff for the CIA, he couldn't guarantee anything but he just might be able to help him. But it had to be straightaway. I said it was impossible. I couldn't find him. He was in hiding.

Later on, the desperate officer came to see me in my flat. His wife, who was still at the pagoda, had been threatened by the same mysterious men in the car; if her husband did not come with them, they said, she would be beaten up. I think it was on this visit that the officer found something I had not told him I possessed—a copy of the last will and testament of Ho Chi Minh. I had not told him about it because I knew that in the published version at least there was no reference to Son Ngoc Thanh. He flicked through the little pamphlet desperately, and had to agree that unless there was a secret codicil, his hero and mentor was entitled to no special protection from the Vietnamese. And that meant perhaps that his position was even worse than he had thought.

I still do not know what to make of this story. I do not know why Son Ngoc Thanh stayed on in Saigon, or who was causing the disappearance of the Cambodian officers. But the reason I tell the story is this: Those who actually set out to see the fall of a city (as opposed to those to whom this calamity merely happens), or those who choose to go to a front line, are obviuosly asking themselves to what extent they are cowards. But the tests they set themselves— there is a dead body, can you bear to look at it?—are nothing in comparison with the tests that are sprung on them. It is not the obvious tests that matter (do you go to pieces in a mortar attack?) but the unexpected ones (here is a man on the run, seeking your help—can you face him honestly?).

At that time in Saigon there was a craze for a cheap North Vietnamese soup called *bun bo*. All the shops in Tu Do seemed to be serving it in the hope of attracting military customers. Some friends called on me and suggested we should go for lunch in one of these establishments. As we were crossing the road, I bumped into the Cambodian officer, with his pockmarked face and his pleading smile. Something very important has happened, he said, I must talk to you. I told him I was going with some friends for a bowl of *bun bo*. He was welcome to join us. No, he said, this was very urgent; and he added meaningfully that this might be the last time we met. He had hinted at suicide before, and on this occasion my heart hardened. I told him I was going with my friends for a bowl of *bun bo*. The incident was over in the time that it took to cross the road, and I never saw the officer again. But I can remember where I left him standing in the street.

It takes courage to see clearly, and since courage is at issue I know that I am obliged to address myself to the questions raised at the outset of the journey. I went as a supporter of the Vietcong, wanting to see them win. I saw them win. What feeling did that leave me with, and where does it leave me now? I know that by the end of my stay in Saigon I had grown to loathe the *apparatchiks* who were arriving every day with their cardboard suitcases from Hanoi. I know that I loathed their institutional lies and their mockery of political justice.

But as the banners went up in honor of Lenin, Marx, and Stalin, I know too that I had known this was coming. Had we not supported the NLF "without illusions"? Must I not accept that the disappearances, the gagging of the press, the political distortion of reality was all part of a classical Stalinism which nevertheless "had its progressive features"? Why, we supported unconditionally "all genuine movements of national independence." I must be satisfied. Vietnam was independent and united.

In my last days in Saigon I began to feel that it had all been wrong. But when, on a plane between Vientiane and Bangkok, I learned from a magazine that Solzhenitsyn had been saying precisely that, and condemning the Americans for not fighting more ruthlessly, I was forced to admit that I still believed in the right of Vietnam to unity and independence. The French had had no right in Vietnam. The Japanese had had no right in Vietnam. The British had had no right to use Japanese troops to restore French rule in Vietnam. Nor had the Americans had any right to interfere in order to thwart the independence movement that had defeated the French. Many of my bedrock beliefs were and are such as one could share with the most innocent *bo doi*. "Nothing is more precious than independence and liberty"—the slogan of Ho that had driven me wild with boredom in the last few months, broadcast over the p.a. system through the streets, and emblazoned on all those banners— but it is a fine motto.

But the supporters of the Vietnamese opposition to the United States had gone further than that, and so had I. We had been seduced by Ho. My political associates in England were *not* the kind of people who denied that Stalinism existed. We not only knew about it, we were very interested in it. We also opposed it. Why then did we also support it? Or did we?

I was forced to rethink this recently when I read a remark by Paul Foot: "No revolutionary socialist apart from James Fenton was ever under the slightest illusion that Vietnam could produce anything at all after the war, let alone socialism." My first thought was, what about the poor old *bo doi*? Do *they* count as revolutionary socialists? And my second point may be illustrated by an editorial in *New Left Review* ten years ago: "In achieving the necessary combination of national liberation and social revolution the Vietnamese Communists drew on many of the best traditions of the international workers' movement which produced them."

The editorial—written by Robin Blackburn, a Trotskyite as influential as Paul Foot in securing the support of my generation for the liberation struggle of the Vietnamese—never mentions that the victory of the Vietnamese was a victory for *Stalinism,* because to do so would have muddied the issue. The great thing was that the events of ten years ago represented a defeat for American imperialism. The same issue of *New Left Review* quotes Lukács: "The defeat of the U.S.A. in the Vietnamese war is to the 'American Way of Life' as the Lisbon earthquake was to French feudalism. . . . Even if decades were to pass between the Lisbon earthquake and the fall of the Bastille, history can repeat itself." Stirring words, and—look— we don't have to support the Lisbon earthquake in order to support the fall of the Bastille.

Blackburn's editorial ended by saying that the success of a socialist opposition against such odds would have "a special resonance in those many lands where the hopes aroused by the defeat of fascism in the Second World War were to be subsequently frustrated or repressed: in Madrid and Barcelona, Lisbon and Luanda, Milan and Athens, Manila and Seoul." An interesting list of places, and a reminder of the variousness of political change. The example of Madrid, for instance, would, I think, be much more inspiring to anybody in Seoul than the example of Saigon. We seem to have learned that dictatorships can be removed without utter disaster. Is this thanks to the Vietnamese? Maybe in some very complicated and partial way. But Madrid has not yet been "lost to capitalism" like Indochina.

While I was working in Vietnam and Cambodia I thought that I was probably on the right track if my reports, while giving no comfort to my political enemies, were critical enough to upset my friends. I knew something about the 1930s and I absolutely did not believe that one should, as a reporter, invent victories for the comrades. I had the illusion that I was honest, and in many ways I was. What I could not see in myself, but what I realize now is so prevalent on the Left, is the corrupting effect of political opportunism. We saw the tanks arriving and we wanted to associate ourselves, just a little bit with victory. And how much more opportunistic can you get than to hitch a ride on the winning tank, just a few yards before the palace gates?

When the boat people later began leaving Vietnam there was an argument on the Left that this tragic exodus was a further example of the pernicious effects of U.S. foreign policy. Yet it is striking that for three decades after the Second World War such a mass departure did not take place. It is only in the decade since unification that people have been trusting themselves to flimsy vessels in the South China Sea. A recent report described a group of North Vietnamese villagers who acquired a boat and were setting out in the dead of night when they were noticed by another village. The second group said, Let us come too. The first group did not have enough space for safety, but they were afraid that if they did not agree the other villages would raise the alarm. So the boat was impossibly crammed.

The boat people are not merely "obstinate elements" or Chinese comprador capitalists on their way to new markets. They are simply people with no hope.

For two months after the fall there had been no banking facilities in Saigon. Gasoline was expensive and it was not unusual to see students directing the traffic in streets where there was no traffic to be directed. Everything changed when the authorities allowed the withdrawal of small amounts of cash, and when gas prices were reduced. The rich brought out their cars again. The Hondas reappeared. And the whole bourgeoisie went into the café business.

You borrowed an old parachute from a friend. You got hold of a few small stools, brought your crockery from home and you were in business. Every day I walked the length of Tu Do, looking to see if my name had come up on the departures list at the Information Ministry, and one day I counted seventy of these stalls, excluding the allied trades—cake vendors, cigarette stands, booksellers, manufacturers of Ho Chi Minh sandals, and the best example of Obstinate Enterprise, the man who sat outside the reeducation center making plastic covers for the new certificates.

The parachutes were strung between the trees for shade. With their varying colors and billowing shapes, they made the city utterly beautiful. The tables had flowers. The crockery was of the best and the service—inexperienced. It was all an economic nonsense. There was a group of students who ran a bookstall but spent all their time in the café across the street, watching for customers. During the day they might make just enough money for soft drinks. If more, they moved further up the street to join their sorrows in a spirit called *Ba Xi De,* "the old man with the stick." With this they ate dishes of boiled entrails and peanuts which came wrapped in fascinating twists of paper—the index of an English verse anthology, or a confidential document from some shady American organization.

In Gia Long Boulevard, by the tribunal where the judges were twiddling their thumbs, proprietors and clients came from the legal profession. The proprietor of "The Two Taramind Trees" told me she made about a thousand *piastres* a day. Previously she had made two hundred thousand *piastres* a case (755 *piastres* to a dollar). On the street beneath the Caravelle Hotel, there was the Café Air France, known to us as Chez Solange. Solange came from a rich family. She was beautiful. One day she brought two rattan bars and a set of barstools from her house and set up shop. I was one of her first clients, and she told me over a breakfast of beer and beer what it had been like to become a barmaid.

Her elder brothers had told her she was mad to try it. They dropped her off with her things, but would have nothing to do with her. Her younger brothers had been more helpful. But: "This morning when the first customer came for coffee, I was so ashamed that I couldn't serve him. And when I did serve him, I couldn't decide how much to charge him." But once the business was established, the elder brothers relented and were to be seen lounging at the bar most of the day, except during the heat.

Solange had come down in the world. There was a thing called *bia om*, meaning beer and a cuddle, a half-way house to prostitution. The client ordered the beer. With it he paid for the company of an attractive girl. The open-air cafés were not great places for a cuddle, but the suggestion was still there. The new slang term was *caphé om*, coffee and a cuddle, reflecting the diminishing spending power of the bourgeoisie.

The morality of the cafés was attacked in the newspapers, particularly on the grounds that the bourgeoisie were procrastinating. What role were they going to play in the future society? I sometimes asked these people, particularly students, why they didn't try going to the countryside as teachers or in some professional capacity. Of course they were horrified. One man told me that he wanted to stay on in the capital in order to read foreign newspapers (there were no foreign newspapers). Another girl said she couldn't teach in the countryside because peasant children didn't go to school (they did go to school).

The *bo doi* occasionally came along with bullhorns, clearing the cafés away. But a few days later the obstinate economy was back in place. And it was still there when I finally got permission to leave.

The majority of the emigrants at this stage belonged to the French community, and it was obvious at the airport that they had spent their last *piastres* very well. We were going out on a plane provided by the United Nations High Commission for Refugees. You should have seen the kind of refugees we were. I had a Leica and two *Washington Post* typewriters. That was my loot. They, the French, had ransacked the market for hi-fi systems of the very highest quality, and they had snapped up the best of the leather jackets and coats in Tu Do, where for some reason you could get very good calf. Their photographic equipment was luxurious, but the thing that held us all up was the censorship of photographs.

Vietnam had become known throughout the world through photos of a kind which emphasized the grain of squalor. The *bo doi* did not like these photographs, and they weren't fools either: If they found a print of an unacceptable image, say a poor woman squatting, they took the print and insisted on a search for the negative. Everyone's attempts to be better than Don McCullin were confiscated, and the process took a long time. There were more mysterious reasons too. I was told that a *bo doi* confiscated a photo of a flower. When asked why, he explained that there was a kind of powder on the flower; if you enlarged the photo enough, you would see a grain of the powder, and if you enlarged that grain enough—you would see a photograph of the whole of Vietnam.

As I waited for the French to clear their loot, a panic seized me that was just like the panic I had had all those months before. I would never escape from Vietnam. The *bo doi* would never get through all those enormous suitcases. And besides, the runway was absolutely dancing with rain. We would be sent back to Saigon, and then we would be forced through the whole process again. It had happened to others and it could happen to us. I wished those fucking French would get a move on.

And then at last we were let through. The man in front of me had too much hand luggage and I offered to help. I took the French embassy's diplomatic bag from him and we all ran together across the tarmac through the cloudburst. My last memory, as we entered the aircraft, is of the overpowering smell of tropical rain on very expensive new leather.

THE PHILIPPINES

The Snap Election

———

The Project Is Thwarted

———

A man sets light to himself, promising his followers that he will rise again in three hours. When the time has elapsed, the police clear away the remains. Another man has himself crucified every year—he has made a vow to do this until God puts him in touch with his American father. A third unfortunate, who has lost his mother, stands rigid at the gate of his house and has been there, the paper tells us, for the last fourteen years, "gazing into an empty rubber plantation."

I don't know when it was that I began noticing stories like these, or began to think that the Philippines must be a strange and fascinating place. Pirates came from there to attack a city in Borneo. Ships sank with catastrophic losses of lives. People came from all over the world to have psychosurgeons rummage through their guts—their wounds opened and closed in a trice. There was a holy war in Mindanao. There was a communist insurgency. Political dialogue was conducted by murderers. Manila was a brothel.

It was the Cuba of the future. It was going the way of Iran. It was another Nicaragua, another Cambodia, another Vietnam. But all these places, awesome in their histories, are so different from each other that one couldn't help thinking that this kind of talk was a shorthand for confusion. All that was being said was that something was happening in the Philippines. Or more plausibly: A lot of different things were happening in the Philippines. And a lot of people were feeling obliged to speak out about it.

But still, at this stage, although the tantalizing little items were appearing daily in the English press, I had not seen any very ambitious account of what was going on. This fact pleased me. I thought that if I planned well in advance, engineered a decent holiday and went off to Manila, I would have the place to myself, as it were. I would have leisure and space enough to work away at my own pace, not running after a story, not hunting with the pack of journalists. I would watch, and wait, and observe. I would control my project rather than have it control me.

But I had reckoned without the Reagan administration and the whims of a dictator. Washington began sending urgent and rather public envoys to Manila, calling for reforms and declaring that time was running out. There was something suspicious in all this. It looked as if they were trying to fix a deal with Marcos—for if they weren't trying to fix things the alternative view must be that they were destabilizing the dictatorship, and this seemed out of character. Then Marcos went on American television and announced a Snap Election. And this too smelled fishy. I couldn't imagine that he would have made such a move had he not been certain of the outcome. For a while it was uncertain whether the Snap Election could or would be held, for the terms which the dictator offered to his people appeared unconstitutional. The constitution required that Marcos resign before running again for office. But Marcos would not resign. He would offer a postdated resignation letter only, and he would fight the presidential election in his role as president.

In other words, the deal was: Marcos would remain president but would hold a fair election to reassure his American critics that he still had the support of his people; if, by some fluke, it turned out that he did not have this support, the world had his word of honor that he would step down and let somebody else be president. And this somebody else, in all probability, would be the woman who was accusing Marcos of having murdered her husband. So if he stepped down, Marcos would very likely be tried for murder.

It didn't sound as if it was going to be much of an election.

What's more, it was going to wreck my dream of having Manila all to myself. Indeed, my project was already in ruins. By now, everybody in the world seemed to have noticed what an interesting place the Philippines was. There would be a massive press corps running after every politician and diplomat. There would be a deluge of background articles in the press. People would start getting sick of the subject well before I had had the chance to put pen to paper.

I toyed with the idea of ignoring the election altogether. It was a sham and a fake. It would be a "breaking story." If I stuck to my original plan, I would wait till Easter, which is when they normally hold the crucifixions. I wasn't going to be panicked into joining the herd.

Then I panicked and changed all my plans. Contrary to some expectations, the opposition had united behind Corazon Aquino, the widow of the national hero Benigno "Ninoy" Aquino. She was supposedly an unwilling candidate, and supposedly a completely inexperienced politician. But she was immensely popular—unwillingness and inexperience, it appeared, made a refreshing change. The assassination of her husband in 1983, as he stepped off the plane in Manila Airport, was a matter that had never been cleared up. So there was a highly personal, as well as political, clash ahead.

(Not everybody believed, I was to discover, that President Marcos personally authorized the murder. At the time, one is assured, he was having one of his relapses. A man who was involved in the design of the presidential dentures told me, meaningfully, that at the time of Ninoy's death Marcos's gums were very swollen—which was always a sign. And he added, intriguingly, that whenever Marcos's gums were swollen, the gums of General Ver, the chief of staff, swelled up in sympathy. Marcos was in the military hospital at the time, and I have it from someone who knew one of his nurses that, when he heard the news, Marcos threw his food tray at his wife, Imelda. Others say he slapped her, but I prefer the food tray version.)

In addition to the growing opposition to Marcos in the Philippines, there was the discrediting campaign in the United States, which began to come up with some interesting facts and theories. Marcos's vaunted war record had been faked. His medals were fakes. His property holdings overseas were vast. He was shifting huge sums of dollars back to the Philippines to finance the coming campaign. He was seriously ill from lupus erythematosus. He had had two kidney transplants, but whether he still had two kidneys was another matter. His supporters painted slogans around Manila:

WE ♡ FM

His opponents, many of whom had a rough sense of humor, changed these to:

LUPUS ♡ FM

At the outset of the campaign he was obviously very ill. One day his hands were mysteriously bleeding. He had received the stigmata? He was carried into meetings on a chair. Perhaps he would be dead before the campaign was through.

Foreign observers had been invited to see fair play in the elections. There was Senator Lugar and his American team, and there was an international team. Around a thousand journalists arrived, plus other freelance observers. So that when I boarded my plane at Gatwick on January 30, it was with a sense of being stampeded into a story. I had no great hope of the elections. I was going just in case.

A Loyal Marcos Man

There's a special kind of vigilance in the foyer of a press hotel. The star TV correspondents move through, as film stars do, as if waiting to be recognized, spotted. When they come back sweating and covered with the dust of the road, they have a particular look that says: See, I have come back sweating, covered with the dust of the road. When they leave in a hurry on a hot news tip, they have a look that says: What? Me leave in a hurry on a hot news tip? No, I'm just sloping off to dinner. Everyone is alert to any sudden activity— the arrival of a quotable politician, the sudden disappearance of a rival crew, the hearty greetings of the old hands. When the foyer is full, it is like a stock exchange for news. When it is empty, you think: Where *are* they all? What's going on?

I was frisked at the door of the Manila Hotel. It was government owned and nobody was taking any chances. The bellboys came past wheeling massive displays of flowers. In the brown air beneath the chandeliers, obvious agents were keeping track of events. The hotel telephone system was working to capacity, and there was trouble with crossed lines. But I finally got through to Helen, my main contact in Manila, and we agreed to meet in the Taproom.

Here the atmosphere was green from the glass reading lamps on the bar. A pale, shrunken face was knocking back some strong mixture. Hearing me order, the face approached me and made itself unavoidable. "You're English, aren't you? You see? I can always tell. What you doing?"

"I'm a tourist."

That made him laugh. "Tourist? I bet you're M. I. Sixteen." I thought, if he wants me to be M. I. Sixteen, that's fine by me. I stared into my whiskey as if to confirm his analysis. By now he was rather close. I wondered how long it would take Helen to "wash up and finish a few things." My companion ordered another Brandy Alexander. He was going to get very drunk that night, he said, then he would get him a girlfriend.

He was English like me, he said, only he had been deported at the age of eight. Now his Filipina wife had left him, and at midnight it would be his birthday. Could he see my matches? Those were English matches, weren't they? I passed him the box. He was, he said, the only white man to have worn the uniform of Marcos's bodyguard.

Or maybe he said palace guard. He was wearing a *barong tagalog*, the Filipino shirt that you don't tuck in. He'd been at the palace that day—he'd just come from there—and he'd been in big trouble. Hadn't had the right clothes. "Just look," he said, "there are darns in my trousers." His wife had left him and she had taken all his clothes—everything. Now he was going to get drunk, get him a girl, and go home at midnight.

Since it was my turn to talk, I suggested that he find the girl first, then go home.

"It's my *birthday*," he said, staring at his watch under the reading lamp to see how long he had to drink till midnight. He had five hours in hand. His car was parked outside. I suggested he take a taxi home. He told me he had the biggest police car in Manila. I suggested he get a policeman to drive him home. He ordered another Brandy Alexander. The waiters smiled nervously at him and called him colonel. I began to think he might be for real.

He lurched forward confidentially. "I'm a loyal Marcos man," he said, "but this election . . ." He shook his head. "He'll win it," he said, "but it'll be a damn close thing. He'll lose in Metro Manila. Marcos is a great man, but it's the people around him. There's so much corruption at the palace. So many corrupt people . . ."

I didn't want any more of his confidences. I'd been here a couple of hours, and I wasn't going to be drawn. I said: "Tell me about your ring." It was as big as a stud box.

"Oh," he said, "it started off as a piece of jade, then I had my initials put on it, then the setting"—it seemed to include diamonds—"and then the stone fell out and I stuck it back with superglue."

"I thought it must be superglue," I said. In addition to the ring he had a heavy gold watch and an identity bracelet, all gross and sparkling

"The Queen gave me a medal," he said. "And my wife threw it in the trash-can! She threw it away! Look, she tied a knot in the ribbon!"

He fished the medal out of his trouser pocket. "That's a George III medal," he said. "I'm English and proud of it. Anytime I want, I can go back to Cheshire and eat kippers."

Then he said: "Would you do me a favor?"

I panicked a little.

"Those matches," he said, "English matches. Would you give them to me? You see, if I show these at the palace, everyone'll be surprised. They won't know where I got them from. We don't have them here."

I gave him the matches. "What are you doing this evening?" he asked.

"I'm afraid I have a dinner apppointment."

He laughed at these little panics he knew how to create, and told me not to worry. He wasn't going to barge in on my night out.

We returned to the subject of his wife. He produced a letter and told me to read it out loud.

It was very dark in the bar, so we had to huddle together by the reading light. The letter was from the minister of tourism: "Dear _____," I read, "Please remember that ——— is your husband and the father of your two children. Please give him back his clothes so that he can recover his self-respect."

"Read it out," said the colonel, "read it out loud."

Then he told me that Marcos could do nothing to help him. His wife had taken everything, the children, his clothes, the lot. The case was in a civil court and Marcos could do nothing about it.

This was the first time I had heard of a court beyond Marcos's control. I could see what the colonel meant about going back to Cheshire and eating kippers.

Pedro's Party

When Helen arrived the colonel looked startled and impressed. I was impressed too. I hadn't expected Helen to look like Meryl Streep. The colonel shot me a look and I shot one back. He wanted to tell Helen about his wife. "I'm sorry," I said, "but we're late for our meeting." Then I took the surprised Helen and propelled her across the foyer.

"What's going on?" she said. I was just afraid we might be landed with him all evening.

It turned out, though, that there *was* a meeting in hand. That is, one of Helen's friends, Pedro, was giving a party, and if I wanted to go, if I could stay awake after dinner, I was welcome. Pedro's family were squatters, and I noticed—without realizing how customary this was in the Philippines—that at the end of the meal Helen and I had together, she packed up the remains of our food and took it with us for Pedro's children.

I was impressed by Helen; she seemed to know everyone on the street, and most of them by name. People greeted her from the café as we passed, and the cigarette vendors called out to us. We turned down a little alleyway and into a garden beneath a mango tree.

Pedro's hut consisted of a single room with a covered extension. There was a large refrigerator outside, painted green, with a Bad Bananas sticker, and posters advertising a performance of *Antigone* and a concert by an American pianist. Helen disappeared indoors to talk to the women and children, while the rest of us drank beer around a table. There were reporters, photographers, and theater people, and members of the foreign press corps, also friends of Helen. I was beginning to get the idea. We were all friends of Helen. She had a whole society of friends

The great conversation topic was what had just happened in the Manila Hotel. There had been a press conference. As Marcos had been brought in, the *Paris Match* photographer had held his camera in the air to get a shot of him. Two of Marcos's bodyguards had tried to snatch the camera, and the photographer had tried to elbow them away. He had been hustled out of the room and into the hotel kitchen, where the bodyguards had taken turns beating him up. The chef who had been passing was knocked over in the mêlée, and dropped the special cake he had prepared in Marcos's honor.

The party grew, and grew noisy. People taught me the political signs. The Laban sign was an L made with the thumb and first finger. That was the sign for Cory's campaign—"Laban" was Tagalog for "fight." The sign for the KBL, Marcos's party, was a V. If you turned your hand over and rubbed your thumb and fourth finger together, that was the sign for money, the bribe, the greasing of the machine. The boycott sign was an X, two fingers crossed, or two clenched fists across your chest. Many of the people present were solidly, and others liquidly, behind the election boycott. "We're all partisans here!" shouted one guy. He was wearing a red baseball cap with a red star, and an embroidered badge saying Don't shoot journalists. No joke, that. Of the thirty journalists killed worldwide in the previous year, half had been Filipinos. Several of the company were wearing the *tubao,* a purple and yellow kerchief which showed, if you wore it, you had probably been to "the hell of Mindanao," one of the worst areas of the war.

Pedro moved among the guests, and we plundered the crates of San Miguel beer. People tied their kerchiefs over their noses and made fearsome gestures, laughing hugely. A guitar was passed around and songs were sung from the war of independence against the Spanish. Helen sang too. She seemed to improvise a song in Tagalog, and this was doubly surprising because she had been complaining of laryngitis earlier in the evening. Now her voice had woken up for the occasion. It was deep and throaty. She was singing about the Mendiola Bridge, where all the big demonstrations ended up, and where the army or the police used to disperse the crowd with water cannon and tear gas.

There was another song about the Mendiola Bridge, which went simply:

> *Mendiola Bridge is falling down*
> *Falling down*
> *Falling down*
> *Mendiola Bridge is falling down*
> *My First Lady.*

The First Lady being Imelda Marcos. I had heard Imelda was very superstitious, always off to the soothsayer. One day she was told the three things that would happen before the Marcos regime fell: A major earthquake would destroy a church; a piece of earth would erupt after a long silence; and the opposition would cross Mendiola Bridge by force. Since that prophecy had been made, Marcos had spent 2.4 million dollars restoring a church in his native Ilocos Norte for his daughter Irene's wedding. A few weeks after the ceremony there had been an earthquake and the fault had run right through the church. Then the Mayon volcano had erupted after a long silence. As for the third condition, some people said it had already been fulfilled when some opposition people had been allowed across the bridge. But others said no—it must be crossed by force. The bridge was the point of defense along the road to the Malacañang Palace. I imagined that, to have achieved such a significance, it must be a great big handsome bridge. I certainly did not think that I should see the crowds swarm over it. But I was wrong on both counts.

The Americans at the party obviously shared Helen's love for the Filipinos, although they had not been here as long as she had. While I sat there blearily congratulating myself on having arrived and actually *met* people, they were thick in an involvement which I was yet to feel. I could see that they were really delighted to be at

Pedro's house, a piece of somewhat haphazard carpentry. I too felt honored. But I sensed in the Americans a feeling of guilt about the Filipinos, and when I asked one of them what was happening he said: "It's all a sordid and disgusting deal. Marcos has everything on his side—the army, the police, the banking system, the whole apparatus. He's going to fix the election, and Washington is going to go along with it."

Then he gave me a sharp look and said: "You know what you're suffering from. You're suffering from jet-lag denial." It was quite true. Pedro found me a taxi to the hotel.

My hotel, the Philippines Plaza, was a big mistake, perhaps my biggest mistake so far. When people heard I was staying there, they couldn't believe my bad judgment. The thing I couldn't explain to any of them was that I had needed the name of a hotel in order to tell the NPA where they could contact me. By coincidence, a friend from Ethiopia had been staying at this place and had dropped me a note. So now I was stuck in this isolated monstrosity, which I had known only by name, in the vain hope that I would receive some message. In order to deliver the message, the NPA would have to get past the matador at the front door. From what I knew of the NPA, that would be no problem. But what about me? I was a bad case of jet-lag denial. The matador, both of him, saluted and opened the taxi door. I paid my fare and stumbled out, at the height of his frogged breeches.

Among the Boycotters

Harry and Jojo picked me up the next morning. I felt fine, really fine. They, less so. Pedro's party had taken it out of them. Harry asked what I had expected of Manila. I paused. "Probably from abroad you think there are killings going on all the time," said Harry, "but you know . . . they do the killings mostly at night." And he laughed a good deal.

"Why are you laughing, Harry?" I said. "I don't think that's funny at all."

"You don't think it's funny. Europeans never think it's funny if someone's killed. But you know, we Filipinos, sometimes there are demonstrations where two or three people are killed, and immediately afterward people are joking and fooling around. You have to joke in order to keep going. But I've noticed Europeans never joke about these things."

He had been to Europe on business. Photography was only a sideline for him. He wanted me to know that the people we were about to see this morning, the Bayan marchers, were the most important people in the election. "At the end," said Harry, "once the Cory supporters see that it has all been a fix, many of them will join Bayan, or return to its ranks." The marches would go on, up and down the country. That was the important thing, and he insisted on the point throughout the day. Sometimes I would look at Harry and think: "He's as proud of Bayan as if they were his sons and daughters, as if he were living through their achievements. At other times I felt I was being pressed for a response, a confidence. I couldn't reconcile my idea of Harry the owner of the small export business with Harry the admirer of the Left.

Bayan, the umbrella organization for the legal, "cause-oriented" groups in the opposition, was said by some to be nothing but a communist front. Others emphasized the diversity of political opinion within its ranks. I asked many people in subsequent weeks what the truth of the matter was. A communist told me: "It's not a communist front—it *is* the communists." Others strongly rejected this. A Bayan member told me: "It's like this. When the communists speak, we listen to what they say. When Bayan speaks, they listen to us. We are neighbors. I never see my neighbor from one week to the next, but when he is cooking, I know what he'll be having for dinner." It was an open secret, he said, that within four years the NPA would be marching through Manila. When that happened, Bayan would have helped them.

Harry said: "Maybe there'll be some trouble today as the marchers come into the city. Mabye we'll see something."

I said: "I very much hope not." I enjoyed disconcerting Harry with a resolutely anti-good-story line.

Harry said: "You know, photographers—they love it when trouble begins."

I wasn't looking for trouble.

We drove south on the highway, past small businesses, authorized dealers in this and that, scrappy banana palms, pawnshops, factories—some with their own housing estates adjacent—American-style eateries, posh condominiums, and slums. As a first impression it offered nothing very shocking.

Just beyond Muntinlupa we met the marchers, about a thousand of them with banners denouncing the U.S.–Marcos dictatorship. Most of them were masked. They looked young, and I would have thought that they were students, but Harry insisted they were mainly peasants and workers. I was asked to sign a piece of paper explaining who I was. Most journalists, I realized, wore plasticated ID tags around their necks. In the absence of this, you were assumed to be from the American embassy. A masked figure passed me with a megaphone, and shouted: "Down with U.S. imperialism."

"They're very well organized," said Harry. "You'll see. They're ready for anything." And it was true—they had their own first aid team and an ambulance. They quite expected to be shot. If Bayan was the legal arm of the people's struggle it was still organized like an army. The march was divided into units, and when they stopped at the Church of Our Lady you could see how the units stayed close together to avoid infiltration. As the march approached Manila they were expecting trouble from goons. It was clear that they were experienced marchers and knew exactly how to maintain control of their numbers.

The people at the church had not made them welcome, but they took over the building nevertheless. Rice and vegetables were brought from the market, and they ate in groups, or rested in the cool of the building, under the crucified figure of the Black Nazarene, whose wavy brown wig reached down to his waist.

The marchers had seemed hostile at first, and I was in no hurry to talk to them if they didn't want to talk to me. Finally I met Chichoy, who was I suppose in his early twenties, and whose political work, he told me, was in educating peasants and workers toward a state of mind where they did not consider their grievances to be part of an inevitable order of things. It was good work and had produced gratifying results. But, as Chichoy said at one point, "People like me do not live long. We are prepared to die at any time. The point is not to have a long life—a long life would be a good thing—the point is to have a meaningful life." His way of speaking combined a serious firmness of tone with a deep sadness, as if his own death in the cause were something that he had often contemplated, and very much regretted, but there it was.

Not all of the Bayan marchers struck me like this. Some of them seemed to relish the figures they cut, with their red flags and face-masks, and their way of bringing drama onto the streets in the manner of the Peking ballet. Chichoy talked about how a fair election was an impossibility. He was adamant that the intention of the U.S. was to support a dictatorship either way—if not Marcos, an alternative Marcos. If Ninoy Aquino had not been killed, maybe he would have become the alternative dictator. Firmly in his mind was the equation of the U.S. with dictatorship. The Americans had to be overthrown. Their bases had to be closed down. The Philippines would become nonaligned, "and that will be our contribution to world peace."

The march moved off. It was one of a series converging on the city, and it joined with another group under the highway at Muntinlupa. People shouted: "The Snap Election is a fake. So what? We're going to the mountains." There were few police in sight, and nobody tried to stop the teams of girls with paint pots, who scrawled hurried slogans on the curbs and walls. On a house which was decked with Marcos posters, I noticed a window full of boycott placards being waved wildly by unseen people. Bayan had its supporters—over a million of them in the country, it was said. But the crowds did not join in. It was as if these demonstrators were on a dangerous mission of their own. The people watched them and kept their own counsel.

We were marching underneath the raised highway, and the acoustics were tempting. When the firecrackers started exploding, the demonstrators cheered. For my part, I became extremely anxious. We had been expecting trouble, and I couldn't tell whether it was the demonstrators who were lobbing the firecrackers or the crowd. I didn't yet know that this was part of the Bayan style. I asked Harry, "Who's throwing those things?"

"I don't know," he said, clicking away. He hadn't caught the sense of my question.

The Bayan style was to make each demonstration look and sound as dangerous as possible. When the marches converged on

Manila that evening, and the demonstrators sealed off roads by linking arms, the speed and drama with which they operated made it look as if a revolution was in the offing. The defiance of the slogans, the glamour of the torches, the burning tires, the masked faces—it was a spectacular show. But the state was adopting an official policy of Maximum Tolerance, and the demonstrators had the streets to themselves.

The next day they came together and marched toward Malacañang. And so we arrived at the famed Mendiola Bridge, where the barricades were up, a massive press corps stood in waiting, and the military blocked the way. The bridge was insignificant enough—you wouldn't have noticed it if you had not been looking for it. On the side streets, the U.S. embassy men with walkie-talkies were giving up-to-date accounts of the action. "You ought to have a mask," said Helen, "there may be a dispersal." But the tear gas was not used, and the water cannon was only there for display. They burned effigies of Reagan and Marcos at the front of the barricade. Reagan caught alight easily, but Marcos was slow to burn.

Overheard

The telephones in the Manila Hotel were somewhat overloaded. Here is a conversation Helen overheard on a crossed line on Sunday, February 2.

> Voice One: This is the problem, *kumpadre*. We're planning to go to Central Luzon and Tarlac on Monday. I'm sure you understand my position as chairman. I can't just support the campaign for Marcos by words alone. I need the paper.
>
> Voice Two: Yes, yes. Go ahead.
>
> Voice One: We need at least 10,000 pesos deposited by Monday to take care of the people there.
>
> Voice Two: Well, I'll see what I can do.

Voice One: If it's possible, I'd really like to pick up at least part of it this afternoon or early this evening. You know, if I could, I would just go to Malacañang to ask, but I don't want to go ask the president himself at this time. You know what I mean? Do you think it's possible?

Voice Two: OK, come on over.

Voice One: I don't really want to call again. It's difficult on the phone. It's better if I see you. Oh, one more thing, Mr. _____ I've got some news. I've just come back from _____ and the word there is Marcos–Laurel.

Voice Two: Well, anyway, the important thing is that Macoy himself gets back in. If the VP needs to be sacrificed, that doesn't matter. Right? *(They both laugh and say goodbye.)*

The Marcos–Laurel idea was much in the air at the time. Marcos's own vice-presidential candidate was Arturo Tolentino, but the theory was that if a close election was engineered in which Cory lost but her vice-president Doy Laurel won, the Americans might feel that honor had been satisfied. Marcos could say: You see? It is as I told you. The people would not vote for a woman president, let alone a completely inexperienced politician.

Rival Rallies

I never found out whether it was actually true, but people said in a very confident way that Marcos had seeded the clouds in the hope of producing a downpour for Cory's *miting de avance*. If he did, it was another of his miscalculations—like the calling of the Snap Election. The Laban supporters had asked for the grandstand in Luneta Park, just by the Manila Hotel. They weren't allowed it, and were obliged to put up their own platform facing the opposite way. The park filled up. The grandstand itself filled up. The meeting overflowed. People tried to guess how many there were in the crowd—a million, two million. It was impossible to tell. It was the biggest rally I'd ever been in, and one of the friendliest and funniest.

I sat among the crowd just in front of the platform. We were jammed so tight that sitting itself was very difficult. But if we stood we got shouted at by the people behind us, whereas if we shouted at the people in front of us to sit down they literally could not do so. It was very painful, and went on for seven or eight hours. What a relief when the dancing girls came on, or when we all stood for a performance of "Tie a Yellow Ribbon 'Round the Old Oak Tree," Ninoy's old campaign song. The idiom of the rally was distinctly American, with extra-flash gestures, like the priest on the platform who ripped open his soutane to reveal a yellow Cory T-shirt, or Butz Aquino in his Texan hat, or the yellow-ribboned pigeons and the fireworks overhead.

It was not easy for a newcomer to tell the difference between the pop singers and professional crooners on the one hand, and the politicians and their wives and families on the other. Everyone sang—current hits, old favorites, I don't know what. The most electrifying speaker was undoubtedly Doy Laurel, although by the time he came on the anticipation was such that his work was easy. People said Cory was not a professional politician. She was a professional something, though, taking the microphone and singing the Lord's Prayer. After the rabble-rousing of Laurel, the occasion had turned solemn and moving. When the crowd sang *"Bayan Ko,"* the national anthem of the Opposition, you felt all the accumulated laughter and cheering of the day turn into pure emotion. Religion and national feeling were at the heart of what Cory stood for.

The next day, Marcos had to do something about all this. The world's press had seen the great crowds. He had to come up with something equally impressive.

I sat on the balcony of my hotel room, with its view of Manila Bay. Helicopters were passing to and fro across the city. Ships arrived, laden down with people. Army trucks and coaches were busing in the Marcos supporters, who formed up in groups in the hotel forecourt, in order to march down to Luneta.

Helen arrived with Jojo and Bing, another of her gang. They'd come down from Quezon City, where the streets were alive with anger. The Marcos supporters were being stoned as they arrived from the provinces. We went back to have a look.

The taxidriver looked faintly nervous. He was carrying a Marcos flag—all the taxis at the Plaza did the same. He said: "I think we may be stoned."

I said, thinking of something that had happened to me in Saigon: "Wouldn't it be a good idea to remove that flag?" As soon as we were out of sight of the hotel, he did.

Along the road the "noise barrage" had begun—long and short blasts on the horn for *Co-ry*. Groups had gathered at street corners to jeer the buses as they passed. From the car in front of us people were handing out Marcos T-shirts to the other drivers. When a busload of Marcos supporters came past, we found they were all leaning out of the windows making the Laban sign and calling for Cory. Helen asked them what they were up to. "Oh," they said, "we're all Cory supporters here—we're only doing it for the money." And they laughed at us: We were going to have to pay for our taxis, they said, whereas they were being paid to ride in their bus. They all treated the occasion as a tremendous joke. It was worth their while attending a Marcos rally for a couple of dollars. Such sums were not easy to come by.

Bing and I were walking toward the meeting. An enormous number of people in T-shirts were already walking away from it. Bing asked them, straight-faced, "Has Marcos spoken already?" "No," they said. Then why were they leaving the meeting? They looked at him as if he were mad. They'd already had enough.

And now the clouds broke, and people really *had* had enough. As we ran for shelter in the Manila Hotel, the hired supporters (not one of whom would normally have been allowed to set foot in it) realized that they could hardly be turned away in their full Marcos paraphernalia. They stormed the foyer, pushing their way past the security guards and treating the whole occasion as a wonderful joke.

Marcos had been due to speak in the evening, but at this rate there wasn't going to be anybody left. So they brought him forward for an earlier rant.

And afterward, no doubt, they called for the guy who had been told to seed the clouds, and gave him a very nasty time indeed.

Helen on Smoky Mountain

"Within that American body," says Jojo, "there's a Filipino soul struggling to escape." Or another way of putting it was: "Helen is the first victim of Filipino imperialism." She had found herself in another language, and indeed she is in some danger of losing her American identity altogether. Among the circle of friends to whom she introduced me, she speaks English—when she speaks it—with a Filipino accent. Or perhaps it is more a matter of intonation. She will say: "There's going to be vio*lence*." She leans toward the end of the sentence. Instead of saying, "They were *shooting* at me," she says, "They were shooting at *me*." And she has forgotten the meaning of several English words.

English people sometimes find life relaxing in a foreign language if it means that they can lose their class backgrounds. Americans, rather lacking this incentive, don't seem to like to unbend linguistically. Whenever I meet really good American linguists, I always assume they're on a journey away from something. I don't ask Helen very much about her past. It's not that I'm not impertinent. I pride myself on being just as impertinent as the next man. But whenever I garner little details about her past, it's so dramatic that I don't know what to say. If I said, "So what does your little sister do now?" she would be bound to come up with something like, "She was eaten by a school of barracudas." And then I wouldn't know where to look.

She is essentially companionable and generous, and this leads her to do something I've never seen anybody do. She doesn't drink, but she enjoys the company of drinkers and, rather than lag behind as they get drunk, she gets mentally drunk first. One *calamansi* juice and she's slightly squiffy. After a couple of glasses of iced water she's well away.

Another unique feature: She's both a tomboy and a woman's woman. "What do you mean by a woman's woman?" she said one day, bridling. Well, what I meant was that she's the kind of woman women like. She goes into a house and within seconds, it seems, there are fascinating conversations taking place in the kitchen. Then suddenly all the women are going off to the cinema for a soppy movie in Tagalog. Helen has got them organized.

The tomboy side of Helen comes out in her professional life. The Filipino press corps is her gang, and she often says that it was a difficult gang to join, to be accepted by. There were suspicions. There were unkind rumors. She had to prove herself before she was considered one of the group. But by now the group in question is so large that going on a demonstration with Helen is like being taken to an enormous cocktail party which happens, for some reason, to be winding its way through the Manila streets toward the inevitable Mendiola Bridge. Hundreds and hundreds of introductions, slappings on the back, encounters with long-lost friends, wavings across a sea of heads.

Everything turns into a party around Helen. You suggest a working dinner *à deux*. By the evening in question it has turned into a feast *à huit,* with further complications about where to go afterward, because another part of the party is waiting on the other side of the city, a third group is in the offing and there is even a chance that somebody she would like you to meet might turn up at a place which isn't exactly next door to where we are going but. . . .

You have to consider this party as an event which is taking place all over Manila—like a demonstration.

One of the things that makes Helen really angry is the brothel aspect of Manila. The mere act of walking down certain Ermita streets is enough to send her into a passionate rage. She cannot relax among the sleaze—that would be a kind of connivance. If Helen's Filipino friends are rather curious to see the bars (which cater largely, it would appear, for Australians) she cannot follow them. Her rage would stand like a bouncer at the door, blocking her path.

She has a heroic conception of the Filipino people. The opposite conception—of an easy-going, lackadaisical, prostituted, and eventually degraded nation—this she will fight against. You cannot help noticing that the struggle of the Filippino is carried on in the deepest recesses of her mind. Once she was saying, "Anyway, even if Cory Aquino were to become president of the United States of America, that wouldn't change anything—"

"Helen, do you realize what you've just said? Cory isn't standing for president of the United States of America."

"Is that what I said? Oh, so that's really Freudian, *huh?*"

"Yup," The Filipino struggle is the missing radical wing of American politics. This is Helen's discovery.

* * *

The car stops at a red light and the pathetic moaning children beg for money.

"I'm not going to give money to you," says Helen to a boy. "you just give it to the police."

The boy is scandalized and drops the moaning immediately. "How do you know we give money to the police?"

"Everyone knows the police organize you kids. There's been gossip about it for years."

"Well if you spread gossip like that, that means *you're* a gossip," he snaps. Helen laughs. It's obvious that the gossip is true. The police take a cut from the street urchins, just as they get money from the child prostitutes. Another Manila speciality.

Manila is a city of more than eight million, of whom three to four million live in the Tondo slums. And in some of these slums you see people who are barely managing to remain on the brink of existence. Smoky Mountain, one of the main garbage dumps of Metro Manila, is such a place. The people live from scavenging plastic or polyethylene which is then sold to dealers and recycled. The mountain itself provides a living for rival communities who take it in turns to go out and sift the garbage. Sometimes there are quarrels over the shifts, and the scavengers actually fight over the tip. The worst work is by night: It is said that the truck drivers pay no attention to the scavengers and drive over them.

Infant mortality among the scavengers is sixty-five to seventy percent. The people live in huts at the foot of the tip, by the banks of the filthy Pasig River, a sewer in which they wash. It is here, by the bridge, that they sometimes find the mutilated victims of the latest "salvaging."

Coming here with Helen is like trailing in the wake of royalty. Word passes among the huts, the children swarm around her, they all know her by name, and she seems to know a great number of them. She loves making children laugh. She keeps a glove puppet in her camera bag for the purpose.

Up on the burning heap itself, I meet a boy who can say two sentences in English. "I am a scabenger, I am a scabenger," he repeats, and "This is garbage." He makes me feel the top of his head, which has a perfectly round dent three inches across, where he was beaten up, and he opens his shirt to show me a scar running from his neck to his navel, a war wound from one of the scavengers' battles. In his hand he holds a piece of cloth, like a comforter. He is high on solvent.

He tells Helen of his desperation and asks for her help, but she is severe with him. She says she'll only help him if he gives up the solvent. He says he only takes it because life is so desperate. She says she knows all about that. She's been a drug addict herself. But addiction doesn't help any.

Helen is hard on herself. In work, she likes to push herself to the limit. All the day it's go, go, go until the point when she's about to keel over. At that moment, all other expressions leave her face, and what you see is panic. When I catch her pushing herself to this point, I want to boss her about, like some Elder Brother from Outer Space.

But nobody bosses Helen about. She has her own destiny.

Election Eve: Davao

There is a way of seeing without seeming to see. Harry had it to a certain degree. An eyebrow moves. A quiet word alerts your attention to the fact that something is going on. But it is no use expecting to be able to follow the direction of a gaze in order to work out what you are supposed to be taking in. The seer will not give himself away. He is entirely surreptitious.

I noticed it first with Harry among the boycotters in Muntinlupa. We were sitting in the car not far from a peanut stall. What Harry was watching, without seeming to watch, was the behavior of the policemen standing by the stall, keeping an eye on the Bayan rally. Casually, as they talked, they were helping themselves to the peanuts. The stallholder made no protest. He was reading a comic. I suppose he too was seeing without seeming to see.

The policemen moved on. Then a plump figure in civilian clothes wandered past and the stallholder passed him some notes. "What do you think he is?" I murmured to Harry.

"Looks like a gangster," he said. The man had been collecting the protection money. A small sum, no doubt, and it wasn't as if the policemen had been stuffing their faces with the peanuts. It was just that these were the kind of overheads a peanut vendor had to allow for.

Davao was quiet on election eve. It felt almost as if a curfew was in force. The sale of alcohol was prohibited, and there was no life around the market. Our driver had told us that there were salvagings almost every day—meaning that bodies were found and the people knew from the state of their mutilations that this was the work of the military. The driver had his own odd code. He told us that he wouldn't go along a certain street because there were a lot of dogs there and he couldn't stand dogs.

The eating place we found was open to the street, and the positioning of its television meant that the clientele sat facing the outside world, but with their heads tilted upward. There was a video program of Sumo wrestling, with a commentary in Japanese. Even the advertisements were in Japanese. The clientele were drinking soft drinks. Nobody was talking. Everyone was watching the wrestling.

It seemed a hostile sort of place. We chose our food from the counter, but the waitress was slow and indifferent. Behind her, on the wall, was a Marcos sticker and, for good measure, a Cory sticker. I sat with my back to the street. Jojo and Helen were facing outward.

At first I didn't notice that Jojo had seen something. Then I turned around and scrutinized the darkened street. Two jeeps had drawn up. I could see a man with a rifle disappearing into a house. Then a confusion of figures coming back to the vehicles, which drove swiftly off. In short, nothing much.

"They're picking someone up," said Jojo. "There'll probably be a lot of that tonight."

As far as I could tell, nobody else in the eating place had observed the little incident. They were all engrossed in the wrestling. Except I didn't know how many of them had this gift of seeing without seeming to see.

Voting Day in Mindanao

It wasn't hard to tell which areas were going to vote for Marcos and which for Cory. In the Cory areas people were out on the road, cheering and waving and making the Laban sign. In the Marcos areas there was an atmosphere of quiet tension. The crowd, such as it was, did not speak freely. There was a spokesman who explained calmly and simply that Marcos had done so much for this village that there was no support for the opposition. As we could see, the explanation continued, there was no intimidation or harrassment. People were voting according to their own free will. They all supported Marcos.

It was only out of earshot of this spokesman that members of my group were told *sotto voce* that they had been threatened with eviction if they voted the wrong way. Even so, some people said, they were not going to be coerced.

We drove to Tadeco, the huge banana plantation run by Antonio Floirendo, the Banana King, one of the chief Marcos cronies. The Cory campaigners were hoping to get the votes from this area disqualified, as the register apparently featured far more names than Mr. Floirendo employed. He had something like 6,000 workers, many of whom were prisoners. But the register had been wildly padded.

The polling station was at the center of Mr. Floirendo's domain. Rows and rows of trucks were lined up, and a vast crowd was milling around, waiting to vote. At the gates, a couple of disconsolate observers from NAMFREL, the National Movement for a Free Election, complained that they had been excluded from the station on the grounds that their papers lacked the requisite signatures. In fact the signatures were there and in order, but the people on the gate insisted this was not so. A sinister "journalist" began inquiring who I was, and writing down my particulars. "Oh, you come from England," he said menacingly. "Well, that may be useful if we all have to flee the country." Whenever I tried to speak to somebody, this man shoved his microphone under my nose.

We asked to speak to Mr. Floirendo, and to our surprise he appeared, with an angry, wiry little lawyer at his side. The lawyer was trying to explain to us why the NAMFREL people should not be allowed in. He had a sheaf of papers to support his case. We introduced ourselves to Mr. Floirendo, who looked like a character from *Dynasty* or *Dallas*—Texan hat, distinguished white hair, all smiles and public relations. He was a model employer. Everything here was above board. No, the register had not been padded—we could come in and see for ourselves. We asked him why the NAMFREL people had been excluded. He turned to his lawyer and said: "Is this so? Let them in, by all means." The lawyer expostulated and pointed to his sheaf of papers. Mr. Floirendo waved him aside. Of course the NAMFREL people could come in. There was nothing to hide.

(One of the things they might have hidden better, which my companions noticed, was a group of voters lining up with ink on their fingers: They had already been through at least once.)

We asked if we could take Mr. Floirendo's picture. "Oh," he said, "you must photograph my son, Tony-Boy—he's the handsome one." And he called to Tony-Boy, a languid and peculiarly hideous youth. Mr. Floirendo thought that Tony-Boy could be a Hollywood star. I thought not. Mr. Floirendo invited us to lunch. I thought not again. Mr. Floirendo was overwhelming us with his honesty and generosity. He asked the crowd whether he was not a model employer, always available to his workers, and they all agreed that he was indeed a model employer.

In the early afternoon news came over the radio that the KBL had switched candidates, and that Imelda was now stepping in for her husband. "But they can't do that," I said. "Oh yes they can," said the people in the car. For a while we believed the rumor. Jojo giggled helplessly. "If Imelda gets in, there really will be panic buying. Only we've got no money to buy with. We'll just have to panic instead." And he flopped into a panic as he contemplated the awesome prospect.

Now the returns began to be announced over the NAMFREL radio. The idea was to do a quick count, so that the possibilities of tampering would be kept to a minimum. In precinct after precinct the results were showing Cory winning by a landslide. Around Davao alone they had expected her to get seventy percent of the vote. And this indeed seemed possible. It all depended on what went on in the outlying areas such as Mr. Floirendo's fief. NAMFREL could not observe everywhere. They simply didn't have enough people. But if they could monitor enough returns fast enough, they might be able to keep cheating to a minimum.

Davao, which featured in stories as being one of the murder

capitals of the world, had had a quiet day. I think only two people had been killed. The NPA-dominated quarter called Agdao, and nicknamed Nicaragdao, had voted for Cory, although it was plastered with boycott posters, including one that showed the people taking to the mountains.

As the radio continued to announce Cory wins, Jojo came up with an idea. The votes could be converted into different currencies. Cory gets ten million votes, and these are expressed as rupees. Marcos gets five million, but these are dollars. So Marcos wins after all.

Certainly some kind of device was going to be needed.

In the hotel lobby, a desk had been set up to coordinate the results. The blackboard showed Cory with a healthy lead.

On the television, it appeared that far fewer of the results had so far been added up. Marcos was doing okay.

The figures in the lobby came from NAMFREL, which was the citizens' arm of the official tabulating organization, COMELEC. In the end it would be the COMELEC figures that counted. But the sources of both figures were the same certified returns. Something very odd was happening.

The head of NAMFREL was called Joe Concepción. The head of COMELEC was Jaime Opinion. The television told us to trust Mr. Opinion; the radio, Mr. Concepcion.

Late that night, the COMELEC count ground to a complete halt. Something had gone wrong—and it was perfectly obvious what.

The NAMFREL *Struggle*

There were several ways of fixing the election, all of which Marcos tried. The first was to strike names off the electoral register in areas of solid Cory support, and to pad out other registers with fictional names for the flying voters. You could bribe the voters with money and sacks of rice, or, above board and publicly, with election promises. You could intimidate the solid areas. You could bribe the tellers. You could have fake ballot-papers (a franking machine for these had been missing for a whole week before the election). You could put carbon paper under the ballot form, to make sure that an individual had voted the right way before you paid him off. You could print money for his payoff, and if you printed the money with the same serial numbers there would ne no record of how much you had printed. You could force the early closure of polling stations in hostile areas. You could do all these things and you might, if you were Marcos, get away with it.

But what if, after all that, the early returns made it plain that you still hadn't won?

Then you would have to start stealing the ballot boxes, faking the returns, losing the ballots, shaving off a bit here, padding a bit there, and slowing down the returns so that, you hoped, once the initial wave of anger had subsided, you could eventually declare yourself the winner. To explain the delays in the counting of returns, there was a formula that never failed to unconvince. You could say over and over again on Channel Four, the government broadcasting station: "What the foreign observers fail to realize is that the Philippines is a nation comprised of over 7,000 islands. It takes a long time to collect the ballot boxes. Some of them have to be brought by boat or by carabao from very remote areas." But in the meantime votes would be taking a mysteriously long time to find their way from one side of Manila to the other.

This second phase of corruption was now beginning, and the people who stood against it were the NAMFREL volunteers and the Church. There was a great deal of overlap. Outside the town halls where the ballot boxes were kept and counted stood rows of nuns chanting Hail Marys, seminarians grouped under their processional crosses, Jesuits, priests, and lay people. Outside Pasay Town Hall in Manila, the day after the election, I asked a Jesuit whether the whole of his order had taken to the streets in this way. He said that the only ones who hadn't were the foreigners, who didn't feel they could interfere. They were manning the telephones instead.

The Jesuit was a cheerful character. He told me that, in the past, members of his order used to go on retreat with Marcos once a year. He invited them down to a country residence of his in Bataan. They'd been very well catered for—food had come from a posh local restaurant. But Marcos himself had eaten very simply and kept retreat in the most pious manner. He had offered them the chance to go water skiing, but the coastguard had said there were too many jellyfish.

"What would the pope have said," I asked him, "If you'd gone water skiing? Would he have approved?"

"Maybe not," said the Jesuit. "Skiing yes, water skiing perhaps no."

Anyway, these days of retreats with the Marcoses were now over. Not only were the Jesuits out on the streets. There were all kinds of people. At the same place I talked at length to a police cadet who was an ardent NAMFREL supporter. There were poor people and there were extremely elegant ladies—but elegant in the Cory, not the Imelda, style. In the trouble spots, at Makati Town Hall and in the Tondo for instance, they had kept a vigil over the ballot boxes. They linked arms to protect them. They formed human chains to transport them. They all said, and they said it over and over again, that all they could do was protect the vote with their bodies. They were expecting harrassment and they got it. They were expecting to be beaten up. They were expecting martyrdom and they got that too.

The expression, "the sanctity of the ballot," had been injected with real force, real meaning. It had been preached from every pulpit and it had sunk into every Catholic heart. The crony press was full of vituperation against the Church. It abominated Cardinal Sin. The Church that had once supported martial law, and had been courted by the Marcoses (Imelda was always swanning off to the Vatican), was now a public enemy. Paul's Epistle to the Romans was cited by the *Sunday Express* against the Church:

> Everyone must obey state authorities, because no authority exists without God's permission, and the existing authorities have been put there by God. Whoever opposes the existing authority opposes what God has ordered; and anyone who does so will bring judgment on himself.

But they did not continue with the next verse: "For government, a terror to crime, has no terrors for good behavior." Which proves that Paul had not envisaged the Marcos dictatorship.

As the NAMFREL struggle continued, and behind the scenes the

Marcos men were working out the best strategy for cooking the books, Marcos himself gave a press conference at Malacañang. You couldn't get near the palace by taxi. You had to stop at the beginning of a street called J. P. Laurel, then walk down past some old and rather beautiful houses in the Spanish colonial style. As you came through the gate, you found that the lawns had been turned over to the cultivation of vegetables in little parterres. I wondered whether these were siege rations. What were the Marcoses expecting? Beyond the vegetable garden lay a sculpture garden depicting mythological beings in concrete. It looked rather as if some member of the family had had a thing about being a sculptor, and been indulged in her illusions.

A further gate, a body search, and then you came to the grand staircase flanked by carved wooden figures, leading up to an ante-room where several grand ladies, Imelda clones, sat chatting. The room's decorations were heavy. There was an arcaded gallery from which, I suppose, members of the Spanish governor's household would have looked down on the the waiting petitioners. The ante-room led directly into a large and brightly lit hall, got up very much like a throneroom. Here the cameras were all set up, and Marcos was in the process of explaining that the delays of the night before had all been the fault of NAMFREL. They had refused to cooperate with COMELEC in what had been intended as a simultaneous and coordinated tabulation of results. However, that matter had all been cleared up earlier this morning. As far as the stopping of the count had been concerned, there had been no malicious, mischievous, or illegal intent.

Marcos's eyes were lifeless. He could have been blind. Or perhaps he had only just been woken up. His mouth was an example of a thoroughly unattractive orifice.

He had his own set of figures, and he explained at great length how the arithmetic would work out. As he did so, his hand gestures were like those of a child imitating a plane taking off. He conceded he might have lost in Metro Manila. He conceded he had lost in Davao. But by moving his million-and-a-half votes from the Solid North all around the shop, so that you could never tell quite what he had set them off against, he managed to arrive at a "worst possible scenario" where he won by a million-and-a-half votes.

I couldn't follow him. Imelda had slipped in at the side and was watching in admiration. Like any bad actress she had a way of telling you: This is what's going through my mind, this is what I'm feeling. And the message she was putting across that day was: I've just slipped in, inconspicuously, to watch my husband brilliantly rebutting all the awful things that have been said about him by you foreign meddlers; look at him—isn't he wonderful?—*still,* at *his* age; how deeply I love him and how greatly I appreciate him; why is it that you lot can't see things the way I do? Don't look at me. I'm just sitting here admiring my husband, plain little inconspicuous me.

And she shook her head very gently from side to side, unable to believe how great he was, and how lucky she had been.

The COMELEC *Girls at Baclaran*

The next evening I was sitting with some Americans in the foyer of the Manila Hotel, wondering whether perhaps we might not have preferred to be in Haiti. There was after all something gripping about the way the people there had dug up Papa Doc's bones and danced on them. And what would happen to all the dictators in exile? *Rolling Stone* suggested a Dictator Theme Park, where we could all go to visit them in natural surroundings.

A chap came up to our table, hovering about three inches off the floor, his eyes dilated. He had taken some high-quality something. "Listen you guys, nobody move now because the opposition's watching. The COMELEC girls have walked out of the computer count, in protest at the cheating. The whole thing's fucked."

We got up casually, one by one, and paid our bills. The "opposition," the rival networks, were no doubt very far from deceived. At the door I bumped into Helen.

"Helen," I said, "be absolutely casual. Just turn around and come out with me. The COMELEC girls have walked out of the computer count. Let's get down there."

But Helen was bursting for a pee. I swore her to secrecy and told her again to act natural. I knew, as I waited for her, that the chances of Helen crossing the foyer of the Manila Hotel without meeting a friend were zero. I dithered, frantic with casualness, by the door.

Helen kept her word, though, and only told one other journalist.

The COMELEC count was taking place in public, in a large conference center which was one of the Marcoses' notorious extravagances. When we reached the auditorium there was nothing much to see. The girls, around thirty of them, had got up, taking their computer disks with them, and simply walked out of the building before anyone realized what was going on. The remaining operators were still in place but, because the girls who had walked out occupied a crucial part of the whole computer system, nothing could be done until they and their software were replaced.

A seething general, Remigio P. Octavio, was outside the auditorium. Helen asked him what had happened. Nothing had happened. "Well, General, there seem to be quite a lot of operators missing."

Nobody was missing, said Remigio. The girls had needed a rest. People in the gallery had been jeering at them, throwing stones and paper darts, and they'd gone outside for a rest. They were upset. The gallery had been full of communists. And tomorrow, he said, he would make sure there were enough police down here to prevent a recurrence. He would bring in reinforcements.

"As for the girls," said the General, "they will be back again shortly."

Helen wrote all this down on her pad. When she clicks into her reportorial mode and starts firing questions, it's an impressive sight. She laces her sentences with respectful language, and makes a great show of taking down every detail and improbability. But when somebody is lying to her in the way Remigio P. was, the effect of all this is mockery. I wondered whether the general would realize he was being sent up. If I had been him, I would have shot Helen.

The girls had taken refuge in Baclaran Church, and it was there the press corps tracked them down. By now they were said to be very scared at the consequences of their walkout. They needed all the protection the church could give them, but they also perhaps needed the protection of the press. Perhaps. Perhaps not. Members of the official teams of observers arrived. There was a great sense that these girls were in extreme danger.

It was the second time that day that I had been in Baclaran Church. In the afternoon it had been jam-packed as Cardinal Sin celebrated mass. Cory had attended. The crowds had spilled out into the churchyard and the street market nearby. Cardinal Sin had preached a sermon so emphatic in its praise of NAMFREL that he had made its members seem almost saints. Depending on your point of view, they were either heroes or villains. There was no middle ground.

Now the church was about a quarter full. Those who had heard about the walkout had come to express their support. To pass the time they sang *"Bayan Ko,"* and when the girls finally came out in front of the high altar the audience burst into applause.

The cameras had been set up long since and there were masses of photographers angling for a shot. The girls were sobbing and terrified. I could hardly bear to watch the grilling they got. Their spokeswoman said that they would not give their names, and that it was to be understood that what they had done was not political. They were not in fact (although we called them the COMELEC girls) officials of COMELEC. They were computer operators, highly qualified, who had been engaged to perform what they had taken to be a strictly professional job. All had gone well until the night before, when they began to be instructed not to feed in certain figures, so that the tally board giving the overall position was now at odds with what they knew to be the actual total so far.

I remember the word that was used. Discrepancies. Certain discrepancies had crept in, and the girls were worried by them. Finally they had decided that they were being asked to act unprofessionally. They had come out, and they had brought printouts and disks with them, in order to prove their case.

Earlier that evening the international team of observers had given a press conference at which John Hume, from Northern Ireland, had been the spokesman. He had been adamant that there had been cheating on the part of the KBL, but he had purposely left open the question of whether that cheating had been on such a scale as to alter the eventual result of the election. The reason he had done this was that people feared Marcos might declare the election null and void, using the evidence of the foreign observers. Marcos was still president. He hadn't needed to call the Snap Election. If he now annulled it he could, constitutionally, go on as if nothing had happened.

Now the COMELEC girls had come out with the most authoritative evidence of cheating so far. People had been killed for much, much smaller offenses. The Americans could not possibly overlook this evidence, I thought. There would be no getting around it. That was why the girls were in such danger.

One of the American reporters said to the girls that of course they were entitled to withold their names, but that if they did so Marcos would claim they had not come from COMELEC at all, that this was just black propaganda. For their sakes, they should tell us their names.

At which another pressman snapped, "It's not for their sakes. You just want to get a good story."

The press conference drew to a close. I was thinking: So many people have gone so far—they're so exposed—that the Cory campaign must move forward. If it grinds to a halt now, all these people are just going to be killed.

A figure came rushing into the church. It was the Jesuit from Pasay Town Hall, the one who had been so entertained by Marcos. He came up through the press. "It's very important," he said, "it's very important. They *must* give their names. They *must* give their names."

But the conference was already over, and the girls had gone into hiding.

The Narrow Road to the Solid North

The Café at Kilometer Zilch

Marcos was from Ilocos Norte. That and the surrounding provinces were his stronghold, and everyone referred to the area as the Solid North. Everyone, that is, except the communists, who called it Ilocoslovakia. From the electoral point of view, Northern Luzon was cut and dried. From the revolutionary perspective, it was quite different.

Fred, my new guide, had been working there for the last few months. There was too much competition among the photojournalists in Manila. He had to prove himself. He had to get some exclusive stories, and that meant working in the provinces, where the war was. "My only weapons are my courage and my guts," he said. He would work from his home province for the next couple of years, and if all went well he would then move to Manila.

The disadvantage of working from near home was that he wouldn't be able to marry his fiancée yet. It was impossible to do so at home without inviting all their friends and relations, and this they simply could not afford. Whereas a wedding in Manila could be a much more modest affair.

Fred had strong aspirations. Obviously he wanted to see a new social order, but as to the question of how that order was to be achieved he was quite prepared to think things over from scratch. He would not brush aside an inconvenient argument. He would dwell on a doubt. He would brood over it and become enveloped in thought. His fundamental conception of society was dynamic rather than static: History in his view never stops.

Talking about photojournalism one day, he said: "I would like to cover the guerrillas in China."

"What guerrillas?"

"Aren't there guerrillas in China?"

"I've never heard of them. Maybe there are."

"There *must* be guerrillas in China. Thesis—antithesis. If there aren't yet, there must be some soon."

Most of his life has been spent under Marcos's rule, and his habit of thought was to doubt the story as presented in, say, the newspaper, and to try to guess the story behind the story. As we got on the bus to go north, for instance, he suddenly said: "Do you think the Americans have finally decided to dump Marcos?" The day's papers would not, on a superficial reading, have given much hope of that, but there was some detail that made him think he'd seen the light at the end of the tunnel. He was always a step ahead of me, and I was constantly being told: "There, you see, you didn't believe me. Read this." So I fully expect, in the next years, to discover that there are indeed guerrillas in China, and that Fred is on the story.

The bus was air conditioned and took the road at a practiced lick. I slept and froze and clung to my seat as best I could. In the early hours of the morning we reached the Café at Kilometer Zilch, which was run by a friend of Fred's, a former artist named Johnny. Johnny had put his premises at the disposal of the Aquino campaign, and now that the election was over he was exposed and in danger. The local KBL men had been making threats. There were scores to settle, as there were all over the country. The election violence had not stopped. It had already claimed an illustrious name, that of Evelio Javier, the former governor of Antique. In Manila I had seen the corpse of an obscure beautician called Archie, who had been shot by a sniper while on a Cory rally. The bodies of girls who had worked for NAMFREL had been found, raped and beheaded. Thugs had disrupted the demonstrations around the parliament in Quezon

City. In the "solid" provinces, those who had conspicuously campaigned for Cory had every reason to be worried.

Johnny gave us a room. The next day, when I looked out across the paddy fields to the Cordillera, I could see the NPA zone. It would not have been a long walk.

Fred said: "There's been a dialogue. We just missed it."

"What sort of dialogue?"

"The NPA came to a municipal hall not far from here and had a dialogue with the military for about an hour."

It took me some time to realize we were talking about a gunfight. Fred went off to find out more.

I was sitting in the café reading a book. Associates of the Aquino campaign dropped in during the day. One was an engineer whose family were KBL. He told me how during a previous election he had gone to the house of a relative and watched them faking the ballots. Instead of putting their thumbprints on the returns, they had removed their shoes and inked their big toes. The engineer was on a drinking spree. He was angry and becoming desperate. A nun sat with him drinking Coke and offering some calm advice.

Johnny came up to my table. He had a farm as well as the café. He had not painted for some time. Now he had an idea for a painting, in which the Filipino people were depicted as prisoners inside a ballot box. Maybe he would do that.

He was in a deep gloom, and the drink had not relieved it. He was receiving threats. I suggested that he go down to Manila until things cooled off a bit. He said it was impossible. His wife was down there and he had to look after the business. I didn't know what to say. Johnny said: "Well, if they come for me, I shall defend myself." And he lifted his T-shirt to show me the pistol tucked into his waistband.

We sat in silence for a while.

When he moved back to his companions at the other table, I picked up my book, put my elbows on my knees and tried to read. There were black and white tiles on the floor. With great force, as if a memory had taken on the power of a hallucination, I recalled what a drop of blood looked like on a tiled floor, something like an ink blot but more perfectly, regularly pointed. I seemed to be suffering from a mental nosebleed.

Evelio Javier had been gunned down, I seemed to remember in a café. When he ran wounded and locked himself into the toilet, they came after him and finished him off in there. Perhaps Johnny was thinking of that. Javier had been unarmed. He had foreseen his death, and had gone to the lengths of recording a tape, naming the man who was after him. Javier had come back from the States in order to campaign in the election. Presumably he knew there was no point in being armed. If they wanted to get him, they would.

Fred appeared, and we set off by jeep to the scene of the recent "dialogue," leaving the main road and driving in the direction of the Cordillera. The building in question was a military post at the foot of the mountains. Bobby, the commanding officer, was a friend of Fred's. He greeted us and ushered us into the hall, past the marks on the floor and wall where the grenades had exploded.

I felt certain from the moment I saw Bobby, casually dressed and with an easy authority, that he was a very good officer. He was certainly proud of what he had achieved during the dialogue, and he had drawn an elaborate map of the operation. He had heard that the NPA were planning an attack, and had pretended to withdraw some of his troops from the municipal building, taking them down to the other end of the village, and waiting. When the attack had come, he could have taken a direct route back to the municipal building to relieve his men, but reconnaissance by fire told him that ambushes had been set up along that road. So instead (all this beautifully illustrated in different-colored ballpoints) he had brought his men very quickly around the back, and convinced the NPA that they were outnumbered. In fact it was he was he who was outnumbered. He had managed to inflict several casualties on the other side.

His job, it appeared, was to live like this at the edge of the NPA area—that is, at the foot of the mountains—and to prevent the communist infilitration of the villages around. But infiltration went on all the time. (The fact that his feigned retreat from the building we were sitting in had been noticed by the NPA was enough to indicate that news traveled fast in the area.) He had made a list of all the informants and collaborators in the village, had told them he knew exactly who they were and that they were to present themselves to him, admit what they'd been up to and give full details.

"And they did?"

"Sure, they did. They knew I had good intelligence."

"What happened to them afterward?"

"They went back to the village. Nothing happened."

"But they had informed on the NPA. Didn't the NPA do anything about it?"

"No. The NPA just know they can't work here. That's all."

What kind of reality was represented by this story I did not know. On the one hand, the NPA could well have told the villagers to comply with Bobby's instructions. On the other, it might be just as he said. The two sides knew a lot about each other, and knew that, in such a war, that was inevitable. They might win a village, lose it, win it again. They were fighting a political battle, and this was the way such things go.

"I say to my men," said Bobby, "they have to be with the people. They have to be trusted by the people. If not, they're like a fish out of water."

"But that's Mao," we all said at once.

"I know it's Mao, that's why I say it." Bobby's intellectual hero was Hans Morgenthau. I hadn't read any, but he expounded a few ideas, and in his version they sounded a bit like Mao as well. As dusk fell we thought we ought to leave. Bobby said: "Why don't you stay the night? I'm expecting another attack."

As it happened we couldn't, and I was sorry. Bobby was a major and the kind of guy, I imagined, who would support Ramos and the movement for military reform. I would have liked to have gotten him to talk about that as well. He had enough confidence to do so. He seemed also to like his job, which left him, essentially, exposed. The NPA theory was not to attack unless you outnumbered the enemy. Bobby knew that. He had been outnumbered in the last attack and he would be again if anything happened tonight. That was what he was proud of.

That night I returned to my book while Fred read *Granta*. Helen had given him my account of the fall of Saigon, which had been much passed around. I was like a bird of ill omen in the Philippines; people said, "So you've come for the fall of Manila, have you?" And indeed there was something eerie about meeting so many foreign journalists whom I had known from Indochina, and watching the past intertwine with the present, the previous, and the next

*Granta*s coiling like seasnakes. I was very curious to know what Fred would think of my piece, but he needed time to brood.

"It's changed my mind on one thing, though," he said before going to sleep. "I used to think the crucial thing would be the battle for Manila. Now I see the crucial thing is what's going on over there, now, in the mountains."

A Typical Politician's House

Times are hard for business in the Philippines, so the garden of Maximo's house has been converted into a lavatory factory, and as you walk up to the front door you pass rows of freshly cast urinals and toilet bowls. There is also a sideline in concrete balustrades.

The exterior of the building is unspectacular, but when you step inside, and look up, you have to be impressed. The whole thing has been lined with narra wood, the most expensive timber. The design of the paneling imitates brickwork, and there is a heavily carved balcony running around three sides of what I think deserves to be called the atrium.

Below the balcony level nothing has been finished. The stairs are makeshift. The lower walls are frankly breeze-block. The floor is concrete. The focus of the furniture is a gigantic television in a wooden case. There are religious pictures and a glass-fronted case containing encyclopedias and school books. Maximo's office is in a small recess.

He is away. His wife is just about to leave, but she insists that Fred and I stay here and treat the place as our home. I compliment her on it. "It's a typical politician's house," she says. She designed the atrium herself. It had to be large and light because Maximo will have to entertain. He is a councilor, and he is hoping to become mayor at the next elections.

But how did she get so much narra? (Nowadays it is illegal to fell the trees. If you want to buy narra, you have to have friends in the military, who have an interest in illegal logging.) She explains that a former mayor of the town had been a great gambler, and he used to drop around at all hours to borrow money from Maximo. It seemed convenient to pay him back in narra logs, which they saved up over a period of fifteen years until they could build a proper politician's house.

Then came the sugar slump (Maximo is mainly in sugar and toilets) and the inflation. Diversifing into toilets had kept their heads above water, but they hadn't liked to borrow money in order to complete the atrium. There was a little narra left, but somehow they would have to find some more. The next problem would be the floor. She wanted marble, but Maximo had said she would be six feet under before they could afford it. So now she doesn't know. She had been apologizing to a priest about the unfinished state of the place, and he had said: "Don't worry. Rome wasn't built in a day." She says: "We're just a typical middle-income-bracket family. Fortunately my husband is an assiduous worker, so we can educate our children."

Some of her children are in Manila. The oldest is a NAMFREL nun, and all the children in Manila, she says, support Cory. Maximo has been an independent, but now he has just decided to join the ruling KBL.

If you were to say to Maximo, "Isn't this an odd time to join the KBL?" he would say: "The fact that I joined the KBL at this moment proves that I'm not an opportunist." There is some doubt as to whether the KBL will field him as their mayoral candidate. If they don't, Maximo intends to stand as Independent KBL.

There doesn't seem to be great strife in the family over their different political allegiances. I think Maximo takes great pride in his children, although the activities of one of them do cause him to raise an eyebrow. Still, I imagine that if your daughter is a nun you listen to her with respect, and if she is a member of NAMFREL you feel involved in its activities as well. Maximo's view is that the KBL must start introducing thorough reforms. This is likely to be his platform in the forthcoming local elections.

If Maximo stands as mayor, it will be to replace Ultimo, the current incumbent who, just before the presidential election, switched allegiance from KBL to the opposition UNIDO. Ultimo's house is not as grand as Maximo's is going to be, but Ultimo has a luminous picture of the Agony in the Garden, and a parrot trained to shriek "Mayor!" And he has lovely daughters and nieces who also support Cory, and who, I guess, might have influenced his decision.

Ultimo says: "How could I have gone on in the thought that my grandchildren and great-grandchildren would grow up in the knowledge that I had supported such an appalling government? I could not! It was a matter of principle." (He also tells me that, as a KBL candidate, he stood as mayor four times. The principle must have been slow in seeping through.)

Fred asks him whether he will hold a proclamation rally for Cory. Ultimo looks disconcerted. He *would* do so, he says, if he thought the support was there. I don't think Ultimo is going to be very keen to hold a rally for Cory. But he says that if she doesn't win he will resign.

He explains that the KBL produced a great wad of money in the town, just two days before the election: Something like two million pesos arrived, and there was widespread buying of votes. Some of the teachers involved in the counting received a thousand (fifty dollars) apiece. His niece had been offered five thousand and had refused.

Ultimo's review of the matter is simple: UNIDO didn't have the money to outbid the KBL. "The way I would have done it would have been to ask—OK, what are they offering? Fine, we'll double it. Ten pesos a vote? We'll make it twenty, and so on." As he says this, he appears to realize that this was not the way the Cory camp were supposed to be electioneering. He has to justify himself. "Because I think you'll agree," he says, "that the only way to match money is with money. Or with guns. We didn't have the money and we didn't have the guns. What can you do?"

Ultimo could hardly have given me a franker account of the way he likes to run things. Elsewhere I am told that he made himself unpopular recently when he pulled a gun in an argument. The "real" reason why Ultimo resigned from the KBL was that he had gone drinking with a friend and, unusually for him, had taken alcohol. He had spoken out against the government, and this had got him into trouble with the really big guy around here, Defense Minister Juan Ponce Enrile. It had all been a bit more complicated than he had made out. (There is no going against Enrile. And when people hear that Enrile intends to have his son, Jackie, appointed governor of the region, they look really alarmed.)

There is no love lost between Maximo and Ultimo. Maximo's family tells me that the real indicator of Ultimo's low standing is that when he switched sides, his clan did not go with him. His immediate family, maybe, but not his clan. And they say: "Did you see his house? It was amazing how quickly he built it after he became mayor." Whereas Maximo's house—well, Rome wasn't built in a day.

After the Ambush

Filipino English is for the most part very similar to American English. But there are words which have gained an ominous significance and force, whose meaning is not always clear to the foreigner. "There's been a *dialogue*," Fred had said, meaning a firefight. "You ought to have a mask," said Helen, "there may be a *dispersal*." Meaning tear gas and water cannon. A *salvaging* is a murder carried out by the *military* (government soldiers) or by *goons*. A *sparrow unit* (two or three members of the NPA) would call their work a *liquidation*. It would be the settlement perhaps of a *blood debt*. *Hamleting* does not appear necessarily to mean putting people from a disputed area into strategic hamlets or concentration camps. Rather the military simply clear the village in question and move its inhabitants wherever may be convenient. Thus: "Many of the families on Smoky Mountain are victims of *hamleting*." "We've been *pinpointed*," said a member of the human rights group, Task Force Detainees (TFD), meaning something like "We've been fingered," but without the implication of guilt. Pinpointed is a very sinister word.

Fred had heard that there was to be a *fact finding*—that is, some nuns, some workers from TFD, and other human rights people had gone off to the mountains where they had learned that a detainee was being tortured. We hired a jeepney and set off after them. One purpose of a fact finding was to let the military know that somebody else in the world knew that they had a detainee. In this way it was hoped that interrogation would not end in a salvaging. Of course, people who took part in a fact finding ran a risk of being pinpointed. That was simply one of the facts of life.

The hilly ground we had been covering must have been deforested long ago. Today it was a kind of grassy down, except where, in the fold of the hills, a more jungly vegetation thrived. Part of the time I was reminded of Sussex. Then we would hit one of these overgrown valleys, and I would see that this must once have been rainforest. The further we went into the mountains, the more frequently the forest asserted itself. We had already passed the scene of an ambush where a colonel and his companions had been killed in their jeep a month or so before. Now we came upon a group of military walking along the road and looking very scared. There had just been an ambush, they said, and they checked us out with great suspicion.

The soldiers were wearing Adidas sportswear. They were well armed with a variety of weapons, but mostly M16s. Seeing how alarmed they were, I assumed at first that there was a whole NPA unit in the area, but when we reached the nearest military camp and inquired about the incident, it turned out to be rather strange.

The jeepney before ours (had we left one hour earlier we might well have been on it) had been carrying a soldier and his sweetheart. Half a mile back, two of the other passengers had drawn pistols. One had hit the soldier on the head. The sweetheart, we were told, had fought with one of the armed men, while the other shot the soldier. In the scuffle, she had actually picked up one of the pistols, but it had not been loaded. The two men had taken the soldier's weapons and disappeared. The driver had gone with them.

"That's the sweetheart, over there," said the commanding officer. The woman was in shock.

The military said that the incident had been the work of a sparrow unit. Attacks on isolated soldiers had been one of the ways the NPA had been able to arm themselves, and on the face of it this seemed the probable explanation. Except the way the operation had been almost bungled—the detail of the unloaded pistol, for instance—seemed out of character. Possibly it was a case of gangsterism. And why had the driver abandoned his jeepney? Had he been part of the plot, or had he feared he would be blamed by the military?

What was most striking was the continued state of alarm in the camp. The soldiers were obviously badly trained. They didn't know how to hold their weapons, and I watched one of them sticking his rifle barrel into the dirt, until an officer reprimanded him. The soldiers were not pleased to see us, and we soon moved on.

Immediately, the landscape looked more jungly, and full of ideal spots for an ambush.

If you hire a jeepney for your personal use (as opposed to joining the passengers on a wildly overcrowded vehicle), you will quite often find that a couple of passengers come along anyway. They may be friends of the driver, or his partners, or there may be some other explanation. Normally I took it as a part of everyday life. But now a fancy formed in my mind that the two unexplained guys we were carrying might also be a sparrow unit. They had a way, when we stopped at a roadblock, of dismounting, dematerializing, and joining us again when we were through.

The news of the incident had spread along the road—so, too, had the alarm.

We met the members of the fact-finding team coming the other way. They had been refused access to the detainee, and they were sorry we had not been there to boost their numbers. The wife of the detainee had not been allowed to see him, but she had spoken to him through the wall of the hut where he was being held. Among the things he had asked for had been iodine for his wounds. When his wife had asked him how he had been hurt, a soldier replied on her husband's behalf that he had injured himself on a nail the night before. The detainee had sounded very weak.

Two members of the fact finding agreed to accoompany us to show us the way. Another member, a journalist, warned us to watch out for a very drunken group of soldiers who had gone through all their things and had deliberately dropped his camera. We told him the news from Manila. Cory had called for a nationwide campaign of civil disobedience. She had asked for a boycott of the crony newspapers and—this was the bad news—San Miguel beer. The man was covered with the dust of the road. He groaned, "Oh no, oh no. Not San Miguel." He looked as if he could use a beer, and the problem was that there was very little alternative to San Miguel. Crony capitalism was a string of monopolies. The future without San Miguel looked very bleak.

We got back in the jeepney—Helen, Fred, our new companions, and my imagined sparrow unit. Before very long we were flagged down by the military. These were the drunken soldiers we had been warned about. I watched the driver's reaction as they told us to drive them back to the last village. He didn't react at all. He was being immensely careful. One of the soldiers examined my press card. The other said that they were scared and that it was very urgent they get back to the village. They were heavily armed and in uniform. One had a Jesus Saves sticker on his rifle. As they climbed into the back, they said they couldn't see why foreigners like us were allowed to come to places like this. We only caused trouble.

We were all rather worried that, by carrying soldiers, we had now become a target. But it was even more worrying to think what these very scared and drunk soldiers might do next. Fortunately, it was to hail another vehicle after a mile or two, and transfer. We turned back yet again. I abandoned the theory about the sparrow unit. The two guys in our jeepney looked as relieved as we were. Now my apprehensions were all to do with the fact that to the right of the road there was a sheer drop of several hundred feet. One of the NPA ambush techniques in this area, I later learned, was to hurl great rocks down in front of military vehicles. A swerving armored car had, not long before, plunged into the ravine.

My awareness of the military, straggled out along the road into the mountains and at the mercy of attacks by the guerrillas, was vivid. One quiet-spoken officer said that he had served in Mindanao and that this place was worse. He wouldn't tell us why, said it was a military secret. I guessed though, from other things I had heard, that the soldiers here knew that they were outnumbered by the NPA.

From the state of the forest, much of which had been planted with bananas, I could see that the jungle had only recently been cleared. I began to think of the Central Highlands of Vietnam. Every time we came to a bridge, it seemed extraordinary to me that it was not guarded, and as night began to fall I thought of the golden rule in Indochina: Never be on the roads after dark. The drunken military obviously obeyed that rule. They were as demoralized as the South Vietnamese at their worst.

I thought that the guerrilla war would not be very advanced. If it had been, all of these bridges would have been blown up. But later an NPA soldier said to me, "Oh no, we like having the military up there. That way we get more weapons." The whole spectacular landscape was a well-laid trap.

That night the villager with whom we stayed told us what had been going on. The military had arrested a well-known thief from the area. To get out of trouble, he had decided to sing. He claimed to have been an NPA supporter himself and he had pinpointed several villagers as belonging to the guerrillas. And had they? No, said our host, they had all been innocent, but the whole place was terrified now of what the thief might say next. He had got himself into favor with the military and was now living with them.

The villagers were living in the crossfire. Sometimes the NPA came along, and the strong traditions of hospitality meant that you had to entertain them. Then the military came along and the trouble began. There was no justice. The NPA were strong in the area—sometimes you would see a hundred or more of them. The villagers were obviously in a quandary over how to behave toward both sides. A nurse told me they were all suffering from hyperacidity, and I could see why.

That night, when our driver and his friends, who were not after all a sparrow unit, had had a little to drink, they began discussing the future of the Philippines. What would happen if the American bases were closed down? What would become of all the employees? "Oh," said one, "they will all become bandits." Another said, "There's no reason for that, they can pan for gold in the rivers—the rivers of the Philippines are full of gold."

The next morning we watched the local gold panners for a while. They were not doing too badly, but there were few of them. This was not a gold rush area. It was in a section of the village which had been haunted by a wailing woman. Some years before, a pregnant girl had died and been buried there. After the hauntings, they dug her up and found that she had given birth after her burial. They had moved the grave and the hauntings ceased.

The military camp was situated in the schoolgrounds, so that the NPA would be unlikely to attack it by day. At the gate a young officer admitted under some pressure that there was a detainee, but of course we could not see him. He had not been tortured and he was eating the same food that they were. The officer was extremely reluctant to talk. As he did so, I noticed he had a twitching muscle below his right eye. He said that the mission of his men was largely political—it was to win the hearts and minds of the villagers here. We asked him if he was going to hand the detainee over to his superiors. "Oh yes, we will do so," he said, and then sneered, "one of these days."

The detainee's wife said the military had been very angry after yesterday's fact finding. They wanted to know who had sent for these people, and she had simply replied she didn't know. (The nuns had warned her that she might get into trouble for reporting the case.)

What had happened was this. The thief had pinpointed the man who was now detained. The military had come to arrest him and found four other visitors in the house. The military had begun straightaway to torture the detainee, whose father, seeing this, had tried to escape. He had taken his *bolo,* his long knife, and cut a hole in the roof of the hut in order to climb out. There had been a scuffle and one of the soldiers had been slightly wounded. As the father ran away, the soldiers shot him dead. The four visitors had also been arrested, but had since been released. There was nothing on them, not even the word of the thief.

The hut was a sorry affair. These people were obviously very poor. In the darkness sat the widow, the mother of the detainee. She was rigid with grief.

The Crossing

The crossing itself is nothing. That is, you hardly know when it has happened. It's not as if a uniform suddenly bobs up, or there's a roadblock to pass, or a document to be shown. I couldn't tell you where I crossed because I don't know myself. For all I knew, I had crossed and recrossed more than once in the last few days. I didn't know, and wasn't interested in knowing which of my new companions belonged to which sort of organization.

We laughed and joked. Children followed us and had a good look at the plastic bag of food and cigarettes I was carrying. They noticed that the cigarettes were locally made. We went through the porch of a church, then out at a west door, down a road to the water, where a boat was waiting. A well-dressed and handsome woman who had joined the passengers passed Matthew—the contact—a note. I tried not to watch the transaction. The note was written in a minute hand, and folded intricately, like a Japanese paper game. In the shallows, before we came to the beach, a man stood strangely. I wondered if he was mad—his body jerked to and fro. But he was searching for shellfish with his toes. He was just a fisherman.

At the House of Pablo Rosario

"A message is being sent to the NPA," said Matthew. "They'll come soon. Would you like to visit the house of Pablo Rosario?"

We had just seen the place where Pablo Rosario had been shot in the days before the election. He had been in favor of the election boycott. We walked through the village and came to his fine stilted house, with its naturally polished hard-plank floor. A man said, and said proudly, "If Pablo Rosario had not been shot, these foreigners would never have come here." Notebooks and a tape recorder were produced, and I listened to the story of Pablo Rosario's last days. A strange mood had come over me. I knew that I was in the house of a great local figure, among his sons and relatives. I knew that the death of the great man was fresh in their minds. And I could follow the account of the efforts of the local police and politicians—could just follow it—as they had tried to locate him, perhaps tried to intrigue with him, and had then decided to kill him. But I couldn't bear to ask more about the story than I was being told, and so I could not really understand the story. I wish the notebooks and the tape recorder had not been around. But it was too late for that.

Matthew said afterward: "You don't seem like a writer." I asked him what a writer was supposed to be like. Well, I hadn't written anything down. No, I had not, and I had not produced my note-book. I find in such circumstances that producing a notebook has much the same effect as producing a gun.

We walked along a beach and I was asked again about Cambodia. I tried to explain what kind of fighters the Khmer Rouge had been. We were by a narrow river, and I pointed to the opposite bank. "Imagine that we, sitting here, are the military, and the Khmer Rouge are in that field. I saw them once in a place just like this, and they were defending their foxholes. The military on this side had been calling in artillery, so the field opposite was exploding all over the place. Just here beside us there was an APC, and it was mounted with a recoilless rifle. They were trying to shoot the Khmer Rouge out of the foxholes. If they aimed too low, the shells hit the water and bounced off into the air. If they shot too high it was useless. They also had machine guns. There was a fantastic noise.

"On this side of the river there was a great crowd, civilians as well as soldiers. People were laughing and fooling around. Every now and then the Khmer Rouge fired at us with their AKs, and people used to throw themselves on the ground as if it were all a great joke. Our side was giving them everything they'd got. *They'd* clearly got only a few bullets left. And finally, one by one, they got up and tried to run for it. Their nerves had gone. And they would run through the field, zig-zagging like rabbits. Shells were exploding all around them, and I remember one of them had just reached the treeline when it exploded on him.

"All the time this had been happening, the people on this side, where we are sitting now, were shouting out to the soldiers—left a bit, right a bit, there's another one, things like that. Then one Khmer Rouge made a run for it and he was carrying his mortar tube. He was running quite well, but he was so dazed he was going in the wrong direction, and he came right down to the riverbank before he saw his mistake. Most of the people had never seen a Khmer Rouge in their life. But this guy really impressed them, because they knew that none of the military would have bothered to carry a mortar with him when he was running away. But for the Khmer Rouge things like that meant *everything*."

They were the bravest soldiers you could have hoped to have on your side, but the war drove them mad.

I had tried to impress upon Matthew what it would be like if full-scale war erupted in the Philippines, and if you had to fight with small against heavy arms. But he already had a sense of this: He had seen an area where bombing had taken place, although such events were exceptional in Luzon. I still could not banish from my mind, as

I stared at the afternoon landscape, the thought of what it would all look like devastated.

When we got back to the house, the NPA were waiting for us. The women were very friendly, and I was amused to see that one of them was wearing a Mickey Mouse T-shirt. Comrade Nicky appeared shy on first meeting, and he remained in the background, talking to the villagers. There was also an eight-year-old boy, "our youngest comrade."

The conversation was slow at first. Somebody said that I had remarked that the NPA were more sophisticated than the Khmer Rouge. Why was that? asked the girls. "Well, for a start, the Khmer Rouge didn't wear Mickey Mouse T-shirts," I said. They looked puzzled. I *was* a puzzle to them. I was a bit of a puzzle to myself. Why did I want to know about the NPA?

I explained to them that most of the articles written about the Philippines began with the fact that the communists were now increasing in strength, and it was clear that the Americans were worried. To write about the place without having met the NPA would be a great pity. I'd managed to meet all kinds of people so far: I'd met a real crony, some goons, the loyal Marcos man, scavengers, nuns, seminarians, Jesuits, a KBL mayor who had defected to the opposition, and an independent would-be mayor who had just joined the KBL. I'd seen remarkable events, but there was still one thing missing, and I didn't have much time left, unfortunately.

"But what do you want to know about the NPA?"

By now the large living room of the house was filling up with villagers. It was difficult to talk in front of so many people. I said that the things I wanted to know would not be very complicated—the normal details of everyday life would be strange enough to me.

The life of the farmers, for instance?

Indeed, the life of the farmers.

By now an old man had occupied the center of the room, and the discussion instead of being general turned into a rather formal interview. But the formality was rather enjoyable—it seemed to derive from the custom of the village rather than the difficulty of the occasion. The old man had been called upon, I thought, because this was the kind of thing he could and should handle best.

His manner when he began was at odds with his subject matter. "There is no justice," he said resonantly, and a charming smile slid to one side of his face as he thought what to say next. He had worked hard all his life, he said, and now he was old and getting weak. And as he talked about getting weak, he giggled, and the villagers giggled, as if there really were something funny about old age and weakness. He told a story against himself, about how he had been told that some kind of chicken feed was particularly good for giving old men strength, and how he had tried it a while before consulting a doctor, and how the doctor had laughed at him. He giggled again.

Then he gave us his view on doctors: They put you on pills in order to make you ill, before giving you something to cure you. The point was, he concluded, that an old man like him was a fool. He had no education. It had stopped because he had married young. Then he had had—I forget exactly—something like nineteen children. This again seemed funny. And then we got down to the reason why he was in a downward spiral.

His land was going from bad to worse. If he wanted to buy fertilizer, he would have to borrow at the beginning of the season. If he went to the bank, the rates were extortionate enough, but he would also need to pay a whole string of extras such as life insurance and legal fees before the money was forthcoming. If he went for a private loan, the extras were reduced. But the interest was phenomenal. If he borrowed 100 pesos, he would have to pay back 250 at the end of the season say, three or four months later. He was in the grip of usury.

That was why, he said, there was no justice in the world. All one could do was trust in God.

Our host, also an old man, invited us to eat. He had provided a large meal, and it was prefaced with a long grace in Ilocano. During the meal, a very vigorous debate began in which the farmer who had been talking about justice started quoting chapter and verse of the gospels. The family was mulling over the evidence that the Last Signs had already been seen, and that the end of the world was at hand. The farmer turned out to be a convinced and well-educated Jehovah's Witness.

We talked quite a bit after dinner about the end of the world, and the Last Signs. Our host was not a Jehovah's Witness—"I'm just a Christian," he said firmly—but he was a very good sparring partner for the farmer. They obviously knew each other's theology backward. They discussed subjects like the class background of the disciples, how many of them were bourgeois and how many peasants.

"Are you a Christian?" our host said to me suddenly.

"No."

"Do you believe in God?"

I thought I'd better come clean. "No," I said.

"If you don't believe in God then you must believe in science."

"Yes, perhaps."

"Do you believe in Darwin?"

"Yes."

"Darwin said we are descended from monkeys."

"Darwin was right to say so."

The farmer smiled and giggled. Our host said very firmly: "If you don't believe in religion at all, then there is no reason to discuss these things. *You* must now start a new subject and we will talk about that."

There was a noise as if someone was clambering over the roof, and the whole house shook. People looked up momentarily. I asked what was happening. Oh, it's an earthquake, they said.

It was a very small earthquake, and I seemed to be the only person present for whom an earthquake was a novelty.

I tried to think of a good subject for debate.

I said to the farmer: "Well, let me ask you a question. Who were the worst—the Spanish, the Americans, or the Japanese?" The question was translated for the benefit of the pabjdd room.

"The Spanish were the worst," said the farmer, "because they wouldn't let us read the Bible."

Several people insisted that the proper form of the question was: Who were worse—the Spanish, the Americans, the Japanese, or the Filipinos? And more than one of them said: the Filipinos.

"But the Spanish were worse," continued the farmer, "because they killed José Rizal." At which the young men laughed at him.

"The Japanese weren't too bad," he went on, "but they worshipped the sun. They did. I saw them. They worshipped the sun. The Americans were bad because they stole our independence after the Spanish, and they killed a lot of people."

"But the Spanish friars also killed a lot of people. The Church killed a lot of people," I said.

The farmer and our host laughed. It seemed I had secured a good debating point.

Now it was time to leave. Our host said to me: "You can't go without saying what you believe is the answer to the question." But I wasn't sure what the answer was. I realized, however, that it was time for me to make a serious contribution to the debate.

I said: "Well, let me say just this. I think the worst thing the Americans have done recently, but I'm only talking about recently, has been over this election. To push Marcos for reform, to insist on an honest election when he offered one, to watch people go out and risk their lives and actually get killed in an honest election—and then to turn around and pretend nothing has happened—I think that's purely cynical. I think that what Reagan said about their having been cheating on both sides was absolutely wicked."

As we prepared our baggage, one of the old men said: "Where are you going now?"

"To the next barrio," said the NPA.

Our host came up to me. "I am the father of Pablo Rosario," he said simply. There was a silence between us.

"I have heard about your son," I said, "and from what I have heard he was a fine man. He acted according to what he thought right, and that is all we can do. You should be proud of him."

"Yes," said the old man, coming as usual straight to the point, "but he's dead."

Moon and Farm

It was not quite true that we were going to the next barrio. We were instructed not to use our flashlights unless told to, and never to point them upward. There was a full moon, and the trek along the paddy dyke presented no great problems. Nobody spoke. We passed some outlying houses from which there came no sound. Then the path led us into the hills. We followed a stream, and I began to regret that I had worn the rubber soles of my shoes quite smooth. We passed over a piece of open ground, where the NPA feared we might encounter a military patrol, then into the woods.

And now we really began slithering. One of the girls told us we might use our flashlights. The mud was not deep, but it was, well, muddy. I felt a complete fool, and was only cheered when I heard one of my companions falling over the way I had just done. I was carrying a shopping bag full of instant noodles—not a difficult task, one would have thought—and with my other hand I was trying to keep my sombrero on my head. Perhaps the sombrero had been a mistake. It seemed to make a terrific noise, brushing against the undergrowth. Nobody else was making the kind of noise I seemed to be making.

We left the track and scrambled through the undergrowth. We were among thickets of bamboo, handsome plants with stems three inches across. I swung on a few creepers to negotiate the mud. Then I abandoned that little experiment. Now we slithered down and around, and around again. I began to think, In a few moments we will arrive back at the house of Pablo Rosario. They've just laid this on as an adventure holiday.

Now we had come to a new stream with a bed of flat rock. The banks rose steeply on either side. It was quite enclosed. The leaders of the party began to call out in Ilocano: "Moon! Moon!" And a voice called back: "Farm!"

We climbed again, past a bamboo cooking hut of a kind I recognized from Borneo. From here there were steps cut into the mud, but they weren't much help to me. The soldier ahead offered his hand and hauled me up the steepest bits. At the top of the hill stood a smiling figure with a bandoleer and an M16. He was smiling at my exertions. "Congratulations, comrade," he said. We had reached the camp.

In the Forest

It was not a fighting unit, although everyone was armed. This was the propaganda unit's base camp. They spent most of their time in the barrios, and only came up here for periods of paperwork and for special meetings. The bamboo structures were not elaborate; there were no trenches or defensive positions and there was no stockade. The roofs of the huts alone told you something of the level of military activity to be expected in this area. They were made of plastic tablecloths with flowered patterns. There was no attempt at camouflage. The air war had not reached here, I assumed.

"Are you afraid to be here?" asked a soldier.

"Not in the least," I said.

"But what if the military attacked?"

"I assume you know what you are doing and you would be able to look after us."

The soldier considered this. He obviously wanted me to be a bit afraid, so that he could tell me there was no *need* to be afraid. But I wasn't going to give him this opportunity.

"But what if it was a really big attack?"

"I'm never afraid," I said airily, "when I'm among soldiers who know what they're doing. It's when people panic that I start to get nervous. The other day on the road, the military were in a real panic. That made me afraid because I didn't know what was going to happen next. But here, no."

All this was translated back to the soldier. I'd stolen his lines and he didn't know what to say next. Coffee had been doled out and the NPA had made doughnuts in our honor. (It is said that in Mindanao the guerrillas have their own bakeries. Here the catering was modest but good.)

"Are you afraid when you go into battle?" I asked the soldier.

"No," he said. Two could play at this game.

"What do you do, how do you prepare yourself before a really important fight?"

"I think of how what I'm going to do will further the revolution," said the soldier. There was a little laughter among his comrades, as if this was slightly too glib an answer, too heroic.

"Do you say your prayers?"

"No."

"Do you write a letter home?"

He had not seen his family for years.

"Is there some special, personal thing that you like to do before going out to fight?" This question was very difficult to put across.

The soldier was shy anyway, and I could tell that he was trying to think what the correct revolutionary answer would be. Whereas I was trying to ask a question to which there would be no correct answer. I wanted to get him away from the rigmarole. "I'm sure," I said, "that every soldier has some little thing he likes to do before a big fight."

"There isn't time," he said, "there's so much to plan. You have to say to yourself: I must kill and not be killed. There are all the details to think about."

I was so hoping for a small thing, an eccentricity or a superstition that I didn't take him up on the big thing he had mentioned—which was of course the answer to my question. You have to get yourself into a killing frame of mind. Before he went into a fight he said to himself: It's either them or me. But how did he think about *them* in order to make himself really want to kill them?

Before they went on what they called a strategic offensive, the NPA normally had a cultural program—songs, theatricals, speeches, a good meal, and so forth. And after the strategic offensive there was another cultural program, at which one of the important elements was a commemoration of those who had died, and an analysis of why they had died, what purpose their deaths had served.

I could see why they put such emphasis on this. The difference between the NPA and the military was that the NPA gave a meaning to everything in a soldier's life and death. They demanded enormous sacrifices, but if asked the purpose of these sacrifices they would not be short of an answer. You don't have to subscribe to their aims in order to see that an army which has a clear idea of what it's doing is superior to one that doesn't. The military might say: But we're fighting communism. But if you asked them: On behalf of what are you fighting communism?—how many of them would have had an answer? The correct answer, in many parts of the country, would have been: On behalf of warlordism. The private soldier of a warlord does not have a *purpose* as a soldier. He merely has a feudal mentality.

To say that a soldier had an overriding purpose which gave meaning to every action in his life and death was the same as to say he was a fanatic. The NPA I met were not fanatics at all. They were far too empirically minded for that. In many ways they were ignorant of the world, but they knew that. They chafed against their ignorance. They wanted news. They wanted books. They even wanted advice.

I was saying: "I don't see how you're going to manage the next stage. Let's say you manage to capture enough weapons to arm the 50,000 people you are supposed to have ready. In that case, the Americans will step up arms supplies to the military. You are going to need antitank weapons and missiles."

"Yes, we know," they said, "where do you think we should get them?"

I didn't know. "Still," I said, "People achieve amazing things with very little. I heard of a tribesman in Laos who aimed his crossbow at a helicopter and happened to hit the hydraulic system and—"

The soldier guffawed: "Oh, that's just *Rambo*. It's impossible."

"You've seen *Rambo*?"

Sure, they'd *all* seen *Rambo*.

"Where?"

"On the Betamax."

"Betamax!" Somewhere in the mountains they had a Betamax. They'd seen quite a lot of films. *State of Siege* had made a big impression. They had film shows and then discussions afterward.

"So what did you think of *Rambo*?"

"Superincredible," said the soldier. He'd obviously had a good laugh. I was beginning to wish I'd seen *Rambo* too.

One thinks of guerrillas as living thoroughly austere, remote lives. But of course, although these people spent much of their time in the mountains, they had comrades in the cities, and they sometimes went on leave to Manila. Some had their families there. There were facilities for conjugal visits. It wasn't as if there was one world of the jungle, pitched against another world of the wicked city. You had to think of the NPA as the kind of guys you might bump into at the Jollibee Yumburger or the Dunkin' Donuts in Cubao.

"Once in a blue moon," said one of the girls, "we have a party. Once in a blue moon. But then there's everything"—and she reeled off a list of drinks which ended with Gilbey's Gin. Then, she said, they would make their *own* Dunkin' Donuts, and if they forgot the baking powder they called them Tonkin Donuts (no reference to Vietnam—it meant "hard doughnuts" in Ilocano).

I was finding it difficult to adjust my image of the NPA. Suddenly I saw them all, in the remote Cordillera, with their feet up in front of the Betamax, watching *Rambo*, eating Dunkin' Donuts and drinking Gilbey's Gin. It sounded great. But where did ideology come in?

Actually it was rather difficult to pin them down ideologically. Their movement had its roots in Maoism, and much of the talk about the masses was what you'd expect from a Maoist group. But when you asked which authors they studied, the answer was really, or appeared to be, that they studied their own Filipino ideologues. They emphasized a Filipino solution to Filipino problems. Had I spoken to the communists in Manila I might have received an entirely different impression. There was a large element of chance in this. But I was very intrigued to come across one guy who had only the vaguest notion of Ho Chi Minh, but knew all about General Giap. The NPA were an essentially self-financing organization, and they were not beholden to any foreign power. They were not in debt to Russia. They didn't have Cuban or Chinese advisers. The war they had fought so far was quite unlike anything in Indochina, because it was essentially still a guerrilla war, not a conventional war as Giap had fought at Dien Bien Phu. The reason I had asked what the next phase of this war might be was simply that, at the moment the NPA became dependent on some foreign supplier of sophisticated arms, their political character might congeal.

There was a theory that the NPA wouldn't need to enter a conventional phase of war in order to win the Philippines. It went like this. At the beginning of the struggle, the guerrillas had been hampered by the fact that they were spread over so many islands. But as their forces grew, geography would work in their favor. If they managed to develop evenly over the whole archipelago, they would tie up the military on a multitude of fronts. There would then be no possibility of operations on a divisional level. Suddenly there would be a coordinated uprising, in every city, on every island. The war would explode as if out of nowhere.

According to the NPA there was no shortage of volunteers. There were masses of people waiting to join, and it was the proudest day in your life when you were given your first pistol. After that, you might work for a while in a sparrow unit until you had earned or acquired your first rifle—another great day. Most of the rifles were M16s, although any guerrilla would prefer an AK-47. If for any reason you lost your gun, you would be in the doghouse for a year or so. It would be a terrible disgrace.

Every region was supposed to be responsible for arming itself—which was why the NPA really needed to have the military around.

"But isn't there a political problem for you, if you move into the area to recruit the masses and that is immediately followed by the military coming in and committing atrocities?"

"Not at all," they said. "People see the difference between the way they behave and the way we behave."

"What would happen if you captured something really sensational, like an armored car? Would you hand it over to some central authority, or would you automatically keep it in your region?"

They said they would report the capture and they'd probably be told to store it away somewhere safe until such a time as it might be needed.

I said: If they were going to need an army of, say, 100,000 men, and the only way of getting weapons was by killing soldiers, they were going to have to kill an awful lot of their fellow Filipinos before they reached their target. They said: Yes, that was a problem, and that was why they much preferred to conduct raids on camps and depots. Daylight raids of this kind were the only occasions when the NPA wore uniform—they dressed up to look like the military, drove into a camp, were normally respectfully received, and then took the place over.

I asked a man who had been on such raids what they did to the common soldiers. He said that sometimes a private would point out the notorious officers. If they were people with a blood debt, they would be liquidated, but ordinary soldiers were not executed simply for being soldiers.

"So what exactly is a blood debt? If I'm an officer and I've led a successful raid against your camp and I've killed some of your best men—is that a blood debt?"

"No. Killing someone in battle is not a blood debt. Murder or torture of prisoners—that's a blood debt."

"And I understand you also execute cattle rustlers."

"Yes, if the masses want it. If we catch a cattle rustler, he will be tried by the village. If it's serious, he'll be executed."

"Let's say I have stolen two carabao from a farmer. What's going to happen to me? I've been caught and I've confessed."

"Oh, stealing carabao is very serious indeed," said the soldier, and he drew his finger across his throat.

"But it was only *two* carabao!" I realized I had landed myself in big trouble. In this part of the country carabao were considered a part of the family.

"If you stole a farmer's carabao, the farmer himself would probably hack you." Meaning, he would get to carry out the sentence.

"I want a defense lawyer," I said.

"The NPA would defend you."

"I don't want to be defended by the NPA!"

The soldier smiled.

I said: "OK, I'm going to conduct my own defense. It's true I stole two carabao. I admit it and I apologize for it. But I'm a poor man and my life is desperate. My village was hamleted last year. I lost everything. I have no money, no land, nothing. That's why I took to crime."

"That's easy," said the soldier. "If your village has been hamleted, that must mean that we were in the region. So you tell us the name of your village and we will find out whether what you have said is true, whether you were an honest farmer or whether you were just a thief."

Shit! I thought. I clearly didn't believe my own defense.

I asked about justice. Everyone had talked about justice, but it seemed to me that if you considered the legal and illegal opposition to Marcos as part of a united movement, they were having it both ways. On the one hand there was the demand for bourgeois justice in the courts—with habeas corpus and all the traditional rights of defense and an independent judiciary. On the other hand there was what we had just been talking about—revolutionary justice, village justice, based on a quite different set of criteria.

The soldier with whom I was speaking at the time could not see the problem, and the conversation turned uneasy—as indeed it did whenever we strayed into an area where there might be a real difference of position, or where a person was feeling inadequately briefed. The longest discussion in the two days I spent in the camp was over the American bases. I wanted to know precisely what the objections to the bases were. It seemed the crucial question for the future, and it seemed obvious to me that if there were any way for the Philippines to avoid a direct confrontation with the Americans in the future, it should be tried.

If the objection to the bases was that they guaranteed American interference in internal politics, would it not be possible, I asked, to negotiate a deal whereby the U.S. presence was greatly reduced but not abandoned altogether? The Americans would still have their bases, would still be, as it were, denying them to the Russians. But they would be a token presence, and the size of the U.S. embassy staff would be severely restricted. What were the insuperable objections to such a scheme?

One of the big objections was that the American presence made the Philippines a nuclear target—and this was hard to deny. The ancillary objections were that the bases could be used in operations against other People's Movements in Southeast Asia.

"What other People's Movements?"

The uneasiness began. "In Malaysia, Indonesia, Thailand . . ."

I said that if they thought there was any chance for a communist movement in Thailand, after what had happened in Indochina, they were mistaken. It would be absurd for the NPA to risk battle with the Americans on behalf of communist movements which really didn't exist.

"Well," they said, looking somewhat dismayed, "they might start up again. And anyway it's not just communists. . . ." I tried to say that anything was better than full-scale war. The NPA might take on the Americans, might even win against them, but the cost would be so prohibitively high that it would surely be better to decide precisely what was so unacceptable about U.S. involvement in their country, and what would be—by way of compromise—a working relationship.

It was at moments like this that our conversation was least happy. A knowledgeable friend said afterward: "Well, you were asking the wrong people. The NPA would like to find any way to avoid a direct confrontation with the Americans, but this is not the time for them to put forward a compromise formula, because nobody's asking their opinion on the matter."

The NPA in the camp said, "The matter is being discussed by the Central Committee."

"Well," I said, "that's the answer to my question."

Strong winds and heavy rain had kept us confined to our shelters, where we slept wrapped up in banners left over from a demonstration against the killing of Pablo Rosario. One of the villagers came up, bringing vegetables. We were safe from attack, because if the military had appeared in any of the nearby barrios a messenger would have been sent to warn us. The soldiers talked about the amount they had learned from the villagers. They were always trying to learn from them. When the early recruits had come from Manila, the first thing they had had to do was learn Ilocano. Now they enjoyed talking to the old men about their experiences fighting the Japanese. There were a lot of old *bolo*-men in the barrios, they said.

Comrade Nicky, whom I had guessed to be the senior member of the group, had spent the last day reading *Granta* 15. It was only just before I left that we struck up a conversation. Not only was he shy. He had not had a chance to use his English for several years. "Excuse me," he said, "what is your class background?"

"Bourgeois," I said, "and you?"

"Upper petit-bourgeois," he said.

It was always hard for me to understand the NPA conception of class. A soldier had claimed to be lower petit-bourgeois—his father had been a truckdriver.

"Did he own his truck?"

"No."

In Comrade Nicky's case the term upper petit-bourgeois meant that his father had been a government official who was also a businessman, now retired and gone to live in Canada. "My parents know what I am doing, and they accept it."

Comrade Nicky and I had a friend in common, who had once worked in the same cell as he. They had been captured, tortured, and imprisoned. I was to send her Comrade Nicky's greetings—they hadn't met for years. After his release he had been arrested a second time, but his false papers had saved him. His news to her was that he was married now. Conditions had been so hard for Comrade Nicky's wife in the mountains that she had had two miscarriages. Now she had a son, with whom she lived in Manila. They saw each other from time to time—she came up here, he went down to Manila. One of the things he missed was books. In Manila he had a book on Nicaragua, but he wanted to read anything about what was going on in the world. He pointed to the issue of *Granta* and said: "Those people in Vietnam and Cambodia—do you think they have a better life now?"

It was a point on which I could give him no reassurance at all. He shook his head and said: "It's the Russians."

Comrade Nicky was not the kind of man who blocks his ears to bad news. I thought he had a very clear idea of what he valued in life, and a strong sense of the difficulty of achieving it. He spoke very simply of his own sufferings, and without bitterness. And as for the future, it held no glib solution.

One More Thing

Fred and Helen and I were about to split up. I had an errand in Baguio. After that, back to work in London.

"You look troubled," said Fred.

"Wasn't the trip good?" asked Helen.

"Oh, the trip was good," said Fred, reading my thoughts. "If you've had something to think about—that's good. If you're troubled it's good."

We'd just heard the news that a congressional panel had voted to cut off military aid to Marcos. But there had been no planes from Manila that day and we couldn't get hold of the latest papers. I knew that there was enough military aid in the pipeline to last for a little while, but I knew too that the military would eventually have to ditch Macoy. I was sorry to be leaving. But Fred was quite right that I was also troubled.

He himself had a lot to think about. That evening as we were lying on our beds he said: "I seem to have got ahead of my schedule.

174

I thought I'd be here a couple of years. But I've proved I've got courage and guts. I've proved I can do it. Maybe now I'll go and try to work in Manila."

It was obviously a good idea. He might even be able to marry.

"Do you have enough for your article?" he asked. "You said you'd have enough if only you got to see the NPA."

"Yes, I've got plenty to describe," I said, putting the bottle of Andy Player to my lips and mentally holding my nose (for it is a truly awful drink). "I'd just like one more thing."

"One more thing?" said Fred. "What sort of thing?"

"That's it. I don't know. Just one more thing to round it off."

The Snap Revolution

Marcos Detects a Plot

When it happens, it happens so fast you can't believe it's happening, and only afterward can you truly catch up with your perceptions and your emotions. It began on a Saturday and ended the next Tuesday, and I doubt that there was anybody in the Philippines who really felt abreast of events. I wasn't. I was in Baguio when the minister of defense, Juan Ponce Enrile, and the chief of national police, General Fidel Ramos, having supposedly learned that they were about to be arrested, took refuge in the Ministry of Defense at Camp Aguinaldo. And even the next morning I wasn't quite sure what to make of the news. "You see what I was saying last night," said a friend, "Enrile could be the next president." We wondered whether Philip Habib, Reagan's latest envoy to the country, had tipped him the wink.

But if it looked like a coup it also looked ominously abortive. Ramos and Enrile were holed up with a small number of men. It sounded as if they were scared as well as cornered. Ramos had said: "I am calling on the people of the world to help us restore decency, justice, freedom, and democracy in this land. There is no justice, no decency, no real freedom, much less democracy in this helpless land.

Nobody has indicated any help to us. We are going to help ourselves even with our bare hands." He had fought for his country, he said: "I don't have plenty of medals but the hour of reckoning is here and now for me. When you serve your country you have to take risks. Anyway, if I die tonight or tomorrow, Mr. Marcos will also die some day. He has no immortality, but at least my heart is clean."

Enrile has spoken about a hit list which had been drawn up at Malacañang—a list which, according to a report in the London *Times*, featured 3,000 people. The opposition was going to be arrested and liquidated. In withdrawing his support from Marcos, Enrile claimed that in his own region, Cagayan Valley, the KBL had cheated by some 350,000 votes. When asked whether Marcos might reimpose martial law, Enrile had said bitterly that martial law had never been abolished. This was all very striking, coming from the administrator of martial law himself.

But it did seem as if very small numbers of soldiers were as yet involved, and it seemed unpromising that it was only *after* rebelling that the two men had begun to bring arms into the Ministry of Defense.

Also unpromising was the fact that I was due to leave the next day.

I took a taxi to Manila, and the driver insisted on bringing a friend. This man had served in the army, and he knew the military along the first stretch of road. With him in the car, we were less likely to have to bribe our way. These back-handers to the military had nothing to do with the immediate political situation. The problem was simply that the soldiers were in the habit of stopping a long-distance driver and demanding to see his license. If money was not forthcoming, the soldier would claim some irregularity in the documents and inform the driver that he could pick them up by reporting at such-and-such a place on such-and-such a day. It had happened to me on the way up to Baguio, and it happened again on the way back. You could see why the military were held in such low esteem. For the commercial traffic taking vegetables down from the highlands, bribery was also a fact of everyday life. The farmers who grew the vegetables knew that supplies of fertilizer were in the hands of a monopoly, which kept the price artificially high. The network of bribery was much like the old system in the Mekong Delta. This was how the military earned their perks.

On Sunday evening, when I got back to my room, Marcos was giving a press conference on television. Rows and rows of generals and officers were lined up behind him, demonstrating their loyalty, while Marcos was explaining there had been a plot against his and Imelda's lives. A young colonel, Marcelino Malahacan, was presented before the press, and stutteringly explained that his intention had been not to kill the president but to hold him. The belief of the conspiring officers had been that "this is the only option left to save the republic from bloody confrontation."

The colonel blinked and stammered through his confession. I supposed he must have been tortured. What he was actually saying, though, in front of Marcos and in view of the whole nation, seemed immensely brave, because it was surely what vast numbers of people believed. Whereas all Marcos was saying, by putting him on display, was: If you try to rebel against me, this is what will happen to you.

I phoned England and arranged to postpone my return. Then Helen came on the line. She had spent the night at Camp Aguinaldo. Cardinal Sin had called the people out on the streets to form a human barrier to protect the rebel troops, and the crowd had responded with enthusiasm. Now there were tanks waiting to attack, and there was artillery in place and—hold it, she had to go, the tanks were just about to attack again. "Helen, where *are* you?" I pleaded. She gave me instructions and rushed off to the fray.

By the time I reached the scene, there were no tanks and no attacking troops. Camp Aguinaldo and Camp Crame lay on either side of Epifanio de los Santos Avenue—known as EDSA. This was the major urban motorway in Manila, and now it was blocked off by the crowd, which had already swelled to hundreds of thousands. It was really impossible to judge. The Church was out in force. The Cory supporters were there, as were Bayan's—for by now the two had a common purpose. The soldiers manning the perimeter walls of the camps said that all was calm. They were in good spirits. People had brought them food and cigarettes. There were barricades of singing nuns, statues of the Virgin and the Santo Niño, hot dog stalls, but no soft drinks to be had for love or money. It was a festive vigil. To see the soldiers treated as the heroes of the crowd was a novelty for me, and obviously something of a novelty for them.

Late that night Marcos came on the television again, and whereas in the previous press conference he had maintained a gelid calm, now he was angry and almost out of control. It was now clear, he said, that there had been an attempted coup on the part of Enrile and Ramos, and we were not to imagine this was in order to make Cory president. This was a military grab for power which was to eliminate both him and the opposition.

Now Marcos was ranting. "Some people say the president is incapable of enforcing the law. Let them say that once more and I will set the tanks on them. If they think I am sick I may even want to lead the troops myself to wipe out the Enrile–Ramos group. They may say I'm sick, but I am just like an old warhorse, smelling powder and getting stronger. I have all the power in my hands to eliminate this rebellion at any time we think enough is enough. I am not bluffing. I am telling Enrile and Ramos, if you do not listen to my pleas for discussion let the blood fall on you." At another moment he said that Cardinal Sin was "spouting all kinds of sedition" but "we'll attend to that later on."

He looked very angry indeed. Whether he looked dangerous I wasn't quite sure.

Maximum Tolerance

"Marcos," said the taxi-driver the next morning, "is in Guam."

"Bullshit," I replied. "I saw him on the television late last night. About one-thirty. He can't be already in Guam."

"It was probably a recording," said the taxi man. He was the type I would normally have assumed to be working for the secret service.

"So where did you get this information?"

"Oh," he said conspiratorially, "military sources."

He tuned in to the rebel radio. Unconfirmed reports, said a voice, have it that Marcos has been seen arriving in Guam.

"I think we'd better go to Malacañang as quickly as possible," I said.

The radio was exhorting the people at Mendiola Bridge to be patient. Somebody would be sent as soon as possible to negotiate the removal of the barricades. "We've waited for this twenty years," said the voice, "we can wait another twenty minutes."

All the cars were sounding their horns in celebration. I thought: "Maybe it *was* a recording—it was in a studio, no identifying features. The noise barrage increased. The taxi driver was in a good mood. He was right and I was wrong. We reached the point on J. P. Laurel Street where you had to walk to get to the palace.

The soldiers at the gates were wearing white arm-bands. Journalists had been asking them what these were for, but the soldiers weren't talking. Everyone looked faintly shifty. I met an old colleague I'd last seen in Korea. "You've heard of course," he said, "Marcos is already in Guam." He had some more convincing details. We asked the commanding officer if we could come in. By now a small crowd had gathered and the soldiers were getting nervous. They moved us gently back down the street as a couple of limousines came in through the gates.

Then a very confident journalist arrived and said to the commanding officer: "General Ramos has called us to a press conference here. Perhaps you will let us through." The man let us through and through we rushed.

"What was that?" we asked this fine man.

"Oh," he said, "I made it up. I was just bullshitting him."

Something very odd was happening. Where the vegetable garden had been (it had been planted on Imelda's instructions, as part of some pet scheme), they were now laying a lawn. And the sculpture garden too—all the concrete statues were being smashed and carried away. The workers watched us as we passed. There were tanks by the next gate, and the security check was still in operation. "It's extraordinary, isn't it," someone said, "the way they keep going on as if nothing had happened. That platform—they must have been told to put it up for the inauguration. Now Marcos has gone and they're still putting it up."

As we came through security, a voice began to speak over the public address. It was giving instructions to the military to confine itself to the use of small arms in dealing with attacks. It was outlining Marcos's supposed policy of the whole election campaign—Maximum Tolerance.

"Whose voice is that?" I asked.

"It's Marcos. It must be a recording."

We ran up the grand staircase and turned right into the anteroom. And there sat Marcos himself, with Imelda and the family all around him, and three or four generals to the right. They had chosen the anteroom rather than the main hall, for there were only a few journalists and cameramen, and yesterday's great array of military men was nowhere to be seen. I looked very closely at Marcos and thought: It isn't him. It looked like ectoplasm. Like the Mighty Mekon. It was talking in a precise and legalistic way, which contrived to sound both lucid and utterly nonsensical. It had its left hand under the table, and I watched the hand for a while to see whether it was being deliberately concealed. But it wasn't.

So Marcos was still hanging on. Indeed he was back in his calm, lawyer's frame of mind. I remember somebody asking him whether he was going to go ahead with his inauguration the next day, as planned. Marcos replied that it was his duty to do so, as laid down by the constitution. The inauguration had to take place ten days after the proclamation by the National Assembly. If he'd been pressed any further in the matter he would have started quoting acts and statues. That part of his brain was functioning perfectly. The bit that wasn't functioning, it appeared, was the bit that should have told him the game was up.

At first I felt embarrassed, as if I had been caught red-handed by Marcos, trespassing in the palace. Then I felt embarrassed because, there being so few pressmen around, I might be expected to ask the president a question. And I couldn't think of a thing to ask. People hovered around the microphone, and whispered to each other, "D'you want to go next?" Very few people did. One journalist actually went to the side of the room, sat down, and buried his head in his hands, as if overwhelmed by the irreality of the occasion.

General Ver was quivering and in an evident panic. I wondered whether his gums had swollen. He stepped forward and asked for permission to bomb Camp Crame. There were two government F-5 jets circling over it, he said. (Just outside the palace someone had told me that the crowd at Camp Crame appeared to think that these jets were on their side, for they cheered every time the aircraft came over.) Marcos told Ver they were not to be used. Ver's panic increased.

"The air force, sir, is ready to attack were the civilians to leave the vicinity of Camp Crame immediately, Mr. President. That's why I come here on your orders so we can immediately strike them. We have to immobilize the helicopters that they got." (Marcos had sent helicopter gunships against the camp, but the pilots had come out waving white flags and joined the rebels.)

Marcos broke in with tired impatience, as if this had been going on all through the night and he was sick and tired of Ver. "My order is not to attack. No, no, no. Hold on; not to attack."

Ver was going wild. "Our negotiations and our prior dialogue have not succeeded, Mr. President."

Marcos: "All I can say is that we may have to reach the point we may have to employ heavy weapons, but you will use the small weapons in hand or shoulder weapons in the meantime."

Ver said: "Our attack forces are being delayed."

The *Christian Science Monitor,* at my elbow, said: "This is absurd. It's a Mutt-and-Jeff act."

Ver said: "There are many civilians near our troops, and we cannot keep on withdrawing. We cannot withdraw all the time. Mr. President."

All this was being broadcast live on Channel Four, which Marcos could see on a monitor. Ver finally saluted, stepped backward and left with the other officers. I forget who they were, just as Marcos, when he introduced them to us, had forgotten all their names and needed prompting. Now the family withdrew as well.

An incident then occurred, the significance of which I didn't appreciate at the time. The television began to emit white noise. A soldier stepped forward and fiddled with the knobs. The other channels were working, but Channel Four had been knocked off the air. The rebels had taken the government station, which Marcos must have realized. But he hardly batted an eyelid. It was as if the incident were some trivial disturbance, as if the television were simply on the blink.

For me, the most sinister moment of the morning had been

when Marcos said that if the rebels continued they would "be chewed up by our roaming bands of loyal troops."

Someone asked why the troops at the gate were wearing white arm-bands. They had said, he told Marcos, that it meant they would surrender to the rebels.

Marcos explained that this was not so. The arm-bands were a countersign.

A soldier in the audience said that the countersign was red, white, and blue.

The questioner then said, "No, these were plain white arm-bands."

Marcos said, a trifle quickly. "The colors are changed every day."

Somebody asked him whether he was going to leave the country. "No," he said, "as you can see, we are all still here." And as he said these words he turned around to discover that there was absolutely nobody standing behind him.

I thought, Kapuściński has scripted this. I looked around for him. It was like his account of the fall of Haile Selassie, only speeded up so that what had taken a year or so—a gradual elimination of the court—seemed to be happening in seconds. There were soldiers in the audience, but they seemed unusually pensive. Imelda was now standing at the side, talking quietly to some journalists. I went over, but again, when I reached her. I was completely stuck for a question. When asked about when she would leave, she looked in the direction of her husband and said: "You'd better ask him." One of my colleagues must have spent the last two nights at Camp Aguinaldo. He stank of old clothes, and I noticed the moment when Imelda smelled him, turned up her nose, and decided enough was enough; she was going to leave the room.

I met up with Bing, who had been photographing the whole occasion. We walked out together in a daze. It was the first time Bing had seen the inside of Malacañang, and it was all too much to take in. The disappointment that Marcos had not yet left, coupled with the gradual realization that the rebels were on the offensive, made the moment extremely hard to comprehend. We tried to solve the mystery of the countersign and the allegiances of the palace guard, but the man we spoke to was simply close to tears. From the gate, a broad, empty avenue led down toward Mendiola Bridge. There were soldiers there, and water cannon. Beyond the barricade stood the crowd.

The soldiers started firing into the air. Bing threw up his hands, waved at the soldiers, and shouted, "Hey, you guys, wait for me! Wait for me!" And he ran down the center of the avenue toward the gunfire. I followed him at a more leisurely pace, sticking to the side of the street. When we were at the barricade, and order had been restored among the crowd, I heard behind me, from the direction of the palace, a kind of popping sound that seemed familiar.

It was a helicopter gunship taking a pot-shot at the presidential quarters.

People's Power

"So it's true," said Helen, somberly.

"I swear it."

"Did you actually get to see him?"

"I was practically within spitting distance. And Imelda was there too. I was so close I could even tell you what perfume she was wearing."

Now I could hear Helen at the other end of the line, telling Jojo the bad news. Up in Quezon City they had all thought the press conference had been a fake. We agreed to meet up at Camp Crame in the afternoon.

I put down the phone. "So what does she wear?" said the receptionist.

"I'm sorry?"

"You said you could tell what kind of perfume Imelda wears."

It was true. I had been lying. "Guerlain," I said, and then kicked myself. I should have said Poison.

Helen and Jojo were sitting on top of the camp gates. I was hoisted up to them by the crowd. So much had happened since I had last seen Jojo that we hardly knew where to begin. "I've got something to tell you, Jojo: There's been a revolution."

This seemed to me rather a witty remark at the time. As far as you could see, EDSA was jammed with people. They were all listening to the rebel radio for the latest news. Everyone had been called out onto the avenue, and it had taken me hours to get up here through the traffic. It was said that four miles of broad motorway were crammed full of people, and I could well believe it. How many people were involved? Four million? Five million? Ten percent of the population of the Philippines? Or more?

Helen had had no sleep. "I'm revolutioned out," she said. She seemed miles and miles and miles away.

Jojo pointed out that the soldiers were wearing their shoulder patches upside-down, which was the sign for revolution. We wondered where we should be next. Cory had said that she would come to Camp Crame, but there was also talk of fresh Marcos troops advancing from a place called Guadalupe. Perhaps General Ver was still trying to get through the crowd to kill the rebels.

We went out the back of the camp and found a taxi. As we drove off to Guadalupe, Jojo pointed to a small building in the camp and said, "That's where I was tortured." I didn't say anything. The remark had been very off-hand.

The roads from Camp Crame were by now so well barricaded with nuns that it was almost impossible to get out, but eventually we found our way down to a stretch of the avenue where the attacking soldiers were supposed to be.

Their vehicles were pointed in the wrong direction and they were well and truly stuck in the crowd. I went up to the officer in the first jeep and asked him what was happening. He was rather tight-lipped. All they wanted to do, he said, was go back to their base at Fort Bonifacio. But the people wouldn't let them. As he said this, the soldiers in the back seat were making Laban signs at me. The crowd had given them bags of bread rolls.

The officer seemed to think the people were being thoroughly unreasonable. But what could a mere four truckloads of them do against all these millions? People were coming up and cheering them and saying: "You are our brothers. You're Filipinos like us." Jojo asked one soldier whom he supported.

"I don't know," he said. "I'm confused. We have two commanders, Ramos and Ver. We don't know which to support."

We went to the next truck. Jojo asked a soldier: "Are you confused? You seem to have two commanders."

The soldier said: "No, I am not confused. We have only one commander."

Jojo said: "So which is your commander—Ramos or Ver?"

"I don't know," the soldier said.

These men had been brought in from Mindanao, and they were supposed to be pretty ruthless types. One of them said: "I just want to go back to Zambo." (Zamboanga.) They were absolutely loaded down with bandoleers of bullets. They had machine guns—they had everything—and they were entirely nonplussed. At the back of the stranded convoy sat one such soldier, visibly teetering on the edge of defection. A man came up to him and said, "Here, take my watch, take it as a souvenir. Please, go on. We are all Filipinos and we shouldn't kill each other." The soldier was terribly embarrassed. It was a gold watch and the man had tears in his eyes. Only yesterday I had seen my taxi driver bribing a soldier just like this one. This gesture of the man's was like an honest bribe. It was half sordid, half heroic. The crowd told the soldier to take the watch, but the soldier could only shake his head. If he was going to come over to the people, he couldn't come over on a bribe. The gesture was a rebuke to him. It said so much about the relationship between the military and the people.

And it was part of the genius of the Filipino revolution that it moved forward on simple gestures like this. It was essentially a confrontation between a cynical and a heroic view of the national character. Marcos had opted quite openly for cynicism. Filipinos, he had said, both before and after polling day, were great ones for joining bandwagons. And he had calculated that the right expenditure would achieve this effect. There was really nothing covert about his operation—everyone had known what the deal he was offering amounted to.

Opposed to Marcos were the people wearing T-shirts with Ninoy Aquino's slogan: "The Filipino is worth dying for." Their approach was essentially idealistic. If Marcos said, "But Cory is a completely inexperienced politician," this cut no ice at all, because

Marcos had already defined what a politician is. Nobody wanted a politician any more. They wanted heroism. Marcos had always said that he had been a hero. But nobody believed that story any more either. They were fed up with brothel politics.

Marcos was terminally out of touch. That evening, in another weird press conference delivered over the radio and (without pictures) on one of the remaining crony television channels, Marcos was asked whether there would be a curfew. "Now you come to mention it," said the dictator, who had already declared a state of emergency, "I hereby declare a curfew." It was to last from 6:00 P.M. to 6:00 A.M. "But what about night workers?" asked the crony interviewer. "Oh, they would be OK, as long as they could explain themselves."

I have never seen a curfew more blithely defied. This was the kind of curfew where you have dancing in the streets; the kind of curfew where people camp out rather than obey the curfew. More people were out and about during that curfew than on any other night of the revolution.

We returned to Camp Crame, having heard that 2,000 marines were on their way up a certain street, with bayonets fixed. Helen was now completely zonked. Jojo and I left her in the car and went to investigate. In order to get past the human barricade you had to walk along a tricky wall with a deep drop on one side, and it was typical of the organization of these barricades that there were people with flashlights in place to make sure that no one fell and was injured. We reached the relevant place, but discovered that the news, like much else that day, had been an exaggeration. Some marines had been along, been turned back and had *threatened* to return with 2,000 men with fixed bayonets. That was all. I no longer believed in these famous marines.

Further down the road, a mere fifty yards, was a military camp of engineers. We went to the gate and asked for the commanding officer, who told us that their instructions were to remain in the base and do nothing. That was what the general had said. But whom, we asked, did the general support? The officer could not say. He wished us well and bade us goodnight.

It wasn't hard to see what was happening. You only had to turn to the liberated Channel Four, where news of the defections was being relayed by Enrile and Ramos. You could see soldiers arriving in the studio and announcing they had joined the rebels. They gave their names, ranks, and class year. This business about class years was very important. It was as if you were watching Sandhurst or West Point changing sides, in the intimacy of your hotel room. The great news was that the Philippines Military Academy *itself* had gone over, and this was considered the most significant event of the day.

It was very fascinating but I was very tired. I left the revolution running, and flopped onto the bed.

Rival Victors

At 4:30 A.M. on February 25, June Keithley, whose efforts on the rebel radio had earned her the complimentary title of General, came on Channel Four to tell us to get up, say our prayers, and go out on the streets to prevent dawn raids on Camp Crame or Channel Four itself. "Remember," she kept saying, "the darkest hour is before dawn."

I wasn't sure that I believed in these notional dawn raids, but it seemed wise to check. I roused a sleeping taxi driver and set forth on the rounds.

Nothing at Mendiola Bridge. At J. P. Laurel Street, where the marines had fired over the heads of the crowd during the night (slightly wounding two people), all was calm again. Channel Four appeared well-protected by the crowd, although I think some tanks had been turned away. The nuns' barricade by Camp Crame was still perfectly in place, candles burning. One of the defenders told me how a car full of goods had tried to pass, and he had spoken to them and convinced them to turn around. "Nice guys to talk to," he said, *"with your balls in your throat."*

Manila was quiet. The 2,000 marines with their fixed bayonets had not materialized. The crowds had been able to sleep on EDSA, among the litter and the stench of urine. At six o'clock they all stood up and prayers were broadcast from the loudspeaker vans. Everyone remained rigidly at attention, and at the end of the service we all raised our hands in the Laban sign and sang *"Bayan Ko"* once again. By now I almost knew the words, but I had only the vaguest idea what they meant. Strange then that there was one particular line that always brought tears to my eyes. I had been utterly gripped by the mood of national aspiration.

After the service came the by-now routine announcements on the radio about the deployment of nuns and seminarians around the city, an appeal for wine and large hosts in one quarter, paper cups in another. Today Cory was to be inaugurated as president. And today also, although the radio did not bother to mention it, Marcos would be sworn in at the palace. Ideally I should have liked to cover both ceremonies.

Cory had chosen to hold her inauguration at the Club Filipino in Greenhills, apparently a place with nationalist associations, but also symbolic to most people of the rich exclusive society to which she belonged. The rebel military, it was said, had wanted her to hold it at Camp Crame, which for many would have acknowledged her debt to the crowd, but for others, might have made it look as if Enrile and Ramos had taken over her movement. It was important to emphasize that she had won the election first, and that they had finally acknowledged this.

So Enrile and Ramos came to the club, along with the elder statesmen and the architects of her victory, and a multitude of Cory clones in elegant but simple dresses and simply short hairdos. There were two kinds of hairdo among the ladies of standing in Manila. There was Cory style and there was Imelda style. Looking around the room, I noticed that only one Imelda clone had secured an invitation to this exclusive gathering.

I suddenly thought: This is absurd, I'm in the wrong place. What on earth is the point of standing behind a bank of cameramen listening to the ceremony, when I shall be able to hear it on every car radio in the street? I had to phone Helen and get down to the palace.

I left the ballroom and found a phone by the poolside. As I was dialing, a voice came through. "Mr. Lopez here. I want to know whether I can have lunch."

"I'm sorry, Mr. Lopez. I can't help you."

"Give me the receptionist."

"She's not here."

"I want to check my lunch reservation."

The place was swarming with rebel soldiers.

"Mr. Lopez," I said, "could you call back in an hour?"

"Give me a waiter," said Mr. Lopez. I was getting desperate. Helen had said she would await my call.

I replaced the receiver and tried to dial again. But Mr. Lopez kept coming through. His telephone technique was obviously better than mine. "What's happening there?" he asked crossly.

"Oh, there's a revolution, Mr. Lopez. I wonder if you could—"

"My lunch."

He had every right to his lunch, and I had no right to use the phone. So we fought.

Back at J. P. Laurel Street, the road one normally took to Malacañang, the marines were under orders not to let any journalists into the palace. A crowd of street urchins had gathered to taunt the "sip-sip" brigade (the ass lickers or cocksuckers—translations were various) who were being brought in by jeepney for the inauguration. The limousines were arriving as well, ferrying in the loyal elements of the upper military echelons.

The journalists were disconsolate. We pleaded with the commanding officer to let us through. Around us the crowd was managing to turn away several of the vans full of Marcos supporters, and when anyone came out from the direction of the palace they were jostled and jeered at mercilessly. This was not a nice sort of crowd to be on the wrong side of.

A few moments later we were let through. Along J. P. Laurel Street, there were dumpy ladies with Marcos badges, who were saying things like: "No one paid us to come. We are real Marcos supporters. It's you foreign press who have ruined everything, meddling in our country." People were in tears and very angry.

Then someone with a radio said: "Imelda's started to speak." And we ran, as somebody shouted from the pavement: "CIA."

When I got through the palace gates I saw that the new-laid lawn was already dry and shriveled. Lunch boxes were being unloaded from trucks. People had planted their Marcos flags in the lawn in festive clusters. We ran down past the sculpture garden, which had been almost completely dismantled, and through the gates to where the crowd had assembled.

As I moved among them, people nudged each other and pointed to the fact that I was carrying the radical opposition paper, *Malaya*. It was one of a bundle, but there was no way of concealing it now. If I was seen concealing it, that would make matters worse. I could hear the scandalized reaction of the crowd. Many people came up to me, saying that no one had paid them to attend—this was for real. I suppose there were 5,000 of them, and where there was not anger there was a frightening mixture of levity and menace. People offered me flags to wave or badges to wear. I couldn't stand the thought of taking them. So I kept laughing back at them, as if the occasion was indeed all part of a great joke.

On the platform stood a very fat, short fellow with a loud-hailer. He was singing snatches of song, apparently anything that occurred to him, and then shouting a few slogans or making jokes, whipping up the crowd. For his rally Marcos could still get a small crowd of T-shirted supporters, but he couldn't lay his hands on any pop stars. Instead there was simply this grotesque, possibly mad, individual, trying to raise a good noise for the aging dictator, whipping through "My Way" at triple speed. Who was he? The palace cook? A torturer? An expert ballot stuffer?*

I and the other journalists had made our way to the platform, and now we were ordered to sit on one side. Great, I thought, I can sit on *Malaya* and somehow lose it. Then we were told to move further back, and as soon as we had done so they made us get up and move to the other side. Back and forth, up and down we went, obeying the insane instructions with as much good humor as we could manage to feign. A friend said to me: "It feels like being a hostage in Iran." I wished he hadn't said it. We were issued with Marcos badges in a very meaningful way. I thought: If I throw *Malaya* away, they'll see that I read the *Inquirer*. If I throw the *Inquirer* away, they'll see that I read the *Manila Times*. I hadn't got a single crony newspaper.

---

*He was, it turned out, a much-loved figure from children's television.

The people in the crowd had been at pains to point out that no one had paid them to attend, and yet, when they saw the chicken dinners being handed out at the other end of the grounds, whole sections of them detached themselves and ran off. Maybe they were not all such convinced fascists.

"Martial law!" they shouted, when Marcos appeared on the balcony with Imelda and Bongbong and the rest. "Martial law!" "Catch the snakes!" was another slogan, meaning, Get Enrile and Ramos. But the strangest of their cries, to English ears, repeated over and over, was "Give us back Channel Four!" We didn't then know that, while the Marcos inauguration was just beginning to be broadcast and as the commentator from inside Malacañang was saying, "And now ladies and gentlemen, the moment you have all been waiting for," the rebels had knocked them off the one remaining television channel available. Marcos had no broadcasting facility left. He had only the balcony and the crowd. And he must have known this as he came out to us. We were his last audience.

He looked somewhat puffy and less unactual than the day before, less like the Mighty Mekon. He could still rant—and he did so—but there was less power in the baritone voice. You felt that the members of the audience were carrying him along, rather than he exerting his power over them, and this sense of a man faltering in his performance was underlined by Imelda at his side. She was acting out her emotions again, as she had done the first time I saw her, and today's emotion seemed to be: Look what they've done to him, the dear, great old man. Had they no pity? Had they no loyalty? Had they no memory of his greatness?

Marcos's idea had apparently been that this would be his answer to People's Power. People's Power, he said, was for the rich, but he had always been the champion of the poor. Imelda's idea was much the same. It was said that one of the forbidden topics in Malacañang was *Evita*. To William Deedes, who had once made the comparison, she had said: "Well at least I was never a prostitute." But here she was in her long white dress, the figure of glamour, the focus, she always felt, of the aspirations of the poor. And when she gave her speech, and the audience began to sing her song, she languidly took the microphone off the stand and led the final encore. The song was called "Because of You." For the Marcoses and their faction it was the second national anthem. When they came to the final bars, Marcos himself joined in, froglike, for a few notes. The conjugal dictatorship embraced before the crowd.

Imelda's dress had a slit up the back, and, somewhat inelegantly from our point of view, she reached into this slit for a handkerchief. She dabbed her eyes. She blew her nose (rather too loudly). She looked again at the crowd with a look that said: My *people,* oh my *people,* you are the ones who have always supported us, you are the ones who have always understood. Marcos was gently helped from the balcony, but Imelda gave a version of not being able to bear the thought of leaving the crowd. She came back to the microphone and said words to the effect that at least there was still some spirit among the Filipino people and she would never forget them.

People had indeed been weeping. Valediction was in the air. As for the press, I think we all thought the sooner we got out of this place, the better. We were the enemy as much as Ramos and Enrile, the CIA, the NPA and the rest. As we walked back to the barricades along J. P. Laurel Street, the limousines and jeepneys were leaving the palace, and when we reached the crowd outside it had grown appreciably nastier. Before, they had banged the cars with their hands. Now they began stoning them. Those who left Malacañang on foot were really made to run the gauntlet, which they did defiantly and in a furious temper. The dumpy, angry ladies; the aged goons; the young bloods—they were all in for a bad time. But they kept their badges on and they were ready for a fistfight if provoked.

In the crowd, people seemed to be working themselves up to that point where they could kill a Marcos supporter. There was much the same mad jocularity as there had been at the inauguration.

A boy who had been threatening one of the departing goons turned to me and said: "He—he—he very very bad man."

"Who is he?" I said.

"I don't know. Just very very very bad." As he said this, a shiver ran down his body that was so strong it lifted him in the air. I'd never seen anything quite like it. He took off from the pavement on a little rocket of disgust.

"We've Beaten Poland!"

Fred and I were trying to think what the next thing would be. As far as we could tell, the only thing left was Malacañang. The rebels were going to have to move in and take it at some stage, and it seemed extraordinary that nothing had been done about it so far. We were in my studio at Boulevard Mansion, not far from the U.S. embassy. It was dark. Helicopters came over. "That's the Americans taking Marcos," said Fred. I didn't think so. A kind of slack wisdom told me to say: "Have a look if they're twin-bladed. If they're Jolly Green Giants, it's the Americans." (I was back in Saigon.)

So Fred ran to the end of the corridor to look from the fire escape, and then I thought I'd better do the same, and the fire door swung shut behind me and we were trapped on the stairs. By now I was beginning to think Fred might be right again. The helicopters were definitely coming from the direction of the U.S. embassy. But it took a few minutes to get us back into the building.

Jojo was on the phone from nearby. He had heard that the marines at Malacañang had suddenly said there was no point hanging around any more and they were going back to barracks. We'd better get round there quickly, before the crowd moved in. I phoned Helen at home in Quezon City. It would take her half an hour to get down, and I told her we'd meet her in J. P. Laurel Street.

The noise barrage was on again. Everyone must have suspected that this time Marcos was really gone. We cursed the taxi driver for his slowness and argued about the best way to the palace. There were two ways of approaching J. P. Laurel Street, and Jojo had chosen the nearer end. Then as we crossed the river, Fred saw a helicopter coming from the palace toward the embassy, and he wanted to photograph it. "Oh Fred it's not a photograph. It's just a tiny fucking helicopter in the moonlight." I doubt if Fred will ever forgive me for losing him that shot.

Jojo led us down some darkened streets, past a few youths with sticks on their way to the palace. He was right. We got right to the gates very quickly, but we soon realized that we were in the wrong crowd. It was the Marcos crowd. The remainder of the thugs who had attended the inauguration were now, in the absence of soldiers, manning the gates. We knew that some of them had guns. Others were carrying great lengths of wood for clubs. A journalist at the gate asked to be let in and was told fiercely, No, that it was foreign press who were to blame. Nobody knew what was happening. We explained to the bystanders that Marcos had left by helicopter and the marines had gone home. "Let's get into the palace," said one youth, "there might be some money."

The thugs were panicking. I could see it in their eyes, and I could see Jojo seeing it as well. These people were angry and scared and they were very likely to take it out on us. Some of them thought they were going to be killed, and indeed as we stood there a horribly battered body was brought through the gates. Others apparently believed that Marcos had left the palace and its treasure for them, and their job was to defend it. Others no doubt just could not believe that Marcos had walked out on them, and I feared their disappointment very much. I knew from what I had seen earlier that day that the Cory crowd fighting their way along J. P. Laurel Street were not pacifists of EDSA and Camp Aguinaldo, but street urchins, the rabble. If we were to go in with the rabble, I wanted to be with the friendly, not the hostile rabble.

Jojo agreed, but it was very hard to convince Fred. His courage and his guts were on the line. To go away now, even in order to come back right away, seemed unthinkable. "Listen Robert Capa," I said furiously, "if you want to take great photographs you've got to stay alive. Just for a bit." He smiled.

There was a terrified young man who said: "Look, I'm neutral. I don't support either side. Can you get me out of here? I only came today because they said there was going to be food." He'd been after those chicken dinners.

"Come with me," I said.

"And my friends? Can they come?"

"How many friends do you have?" I said, drawing a breath.

His friends emerged from the shadows, boys and girls, five or six of them. We agreed to stick together. We walked down the middle of the road toward Mendiola Bridge, where a large crowd was waiting but was held in check by the nuns and seminarians praying at the front. I could see the barricades were by now almost denuded of their barbed wire. No one was manning them. We slipped down a side street and ushered the chicken-dinner brigade to safety.

By now Fred was going wild with frustration, but we finally made our way to the other end of J. P. Laurel Street, which the marines had indeed abandoned. And now the crowd was moving down toward Malacañang. Here too people were carrying sticks, and some of them held bits of plywood over their heads. You could see the stones flying at the front of the crowd. Fred made a bee-line for the action. Jojo told me, if we were pushed back, to jump into a front yard and stay out of the way. Then he too was off.

I had no interest in being stoned. There were gunshots too, and plenty of firecrackers. The eerie thing about the front of the crowd was the way it was marked by flashing lights. It took me some time to realize that this was where the photographers were concentrated with their flashes. It looked like an electric storm, but with the wrong soundtrack. After a while we were halted. The Marcos men were holding their ground very well. Indeed we were being forced slightly back.

I took shelter in a side street with a few others. As I did so, I heard a voice in my skull saying: *He made the classic mistake, during a street fight, of taking refuge in a cul-de-sac; then he was cut off and hacked to death by enraged thugs.* Where had this belated wisdom come from? People leaned out of an upstairs window and shouted to us to wait. The rebel army was sending some soldiers to establish order. I examined the gates in the street for one I might climb in a hurry. The crowd on J. P. Laurel Street were still being pushed back. The side street had a left turn, but when I investigated it people said: "It's a dead end." They didn't want me to go down near their houses.

Then a man who lived at the dead end told me there was a wounded KBL supporter who needed help. We went down together. The street ended at a small canal, pretty much a sewer. The man showed me where he had seen the KBL guy being beaten up by the crowd. He had called out to him to wade across the canal, which he had done with difficulty. The man had helped wash him and had put alcohol on his wounds, but he had nasty gashes on his head and back.

I told the KBL guy that I would try to get him out. He emerged with difficulty from the house, saying "No ID," by which I presumed he meant that he was not wearing any Marcos paraphernalia. His possessions were in a plastic bag, which I took. He was clutching a walkie-talkie and holding his head with his other hand. He had obviously been very badly mauled.

We walked to the turning, where I immediately saw that what I had feared had happened. The Marcos thugs had beaten back the crowd, and we were cut off. We could see them throwing stones and wielding their clubs. I was back on the wrong side of the action.

A gate opened to my left and someone stepped out for a look. I pushed the wounded guy into the front garden, and followed him, to hear a voice saying: "Close the gate. Oh, you stupid! Look! You, get out!"

"This man is badly wounded," I said. "He needs help."

The man resisted for a moment, and then said crossly: "All right, it's a humanitarian act." So we got indoors, which was nice.

Nicer still, there was a doctor in the house. Nicer than that, there was a beer for me. We sat in a hall at the foot of the stairs, while the doctor gave first aid, tying the man's hair in little knots over the wounds so that they would close up. I was impressed by the determination with which the man held onto his walkie-talkie. The owner of the house said: "Hmm, a Motorola, the most expensive. What do you need that for?"

"To talk to my friends," said the wounded man. We gradually realized that what we had here was a goon, but a goon in such sorry shape that it seemed unfair to ask him point-blank: Are you a goon?

Then the houseowner saw the plastic bag and said: "Who brought that in?"

"I did," I said, "It's his possessions." He looked at the bag as if it was about to explode.

"It's probably loot," he said.

"I think it's just his clothes." It was only then I wondered whether the bag contained a gun.

Shots were fired outside, then the battle had subsided. It was obvious the soldiers had arrived and taken control. I thought: And now I *have* missed it. Fred would be in the palace with Jojo and Helen and all the gang, and I'd miss it. And when they said: But what *happened* to you? I'd have to say I was looking after a goon.

The houseowner and I went out into the street. All was quiet again. He had a glass of whiskey in his hand. He had been celebrating. "You don't realize," he said, "how deep this goes. Nobody will call us cowards again. We've done it. We've had a peaceful revolution. We've beaten Poland."

I thought at first he was talking about football. Then I realized he was the first guy who had drawn the comparison which had been regularly in my mind for the last few days. The nationalism, the Catholicism, the spontaneous organization, the sheer power of aspiration—that's what Poland must have been like.

The goon was all patched up and the houseowner gave him his taxi fare. When we got back onto J. P. Laurel Street we found the statue of the Virgin in place in the road, and a barricade of praying nuns. I tapped a nun on the shoulder and handed over the goon. As we said goodbye he smiled for the first time.

Back to Malacañang

Well, I thought, if I've missed it all, I've missed it. That's that.

I turned back and walked down the center of the road to Malacañang, my feet crunching broken glass and stones. I asked a policeman whether he thought it safe to proceed. Yes, he said, there were a few Marcos men hiding in the side streets, but the fighting had all stopped. A child came running past me and called out, "Hey Joe, what's the problem?" but didn't wait for an answer.

As I came within view of the palace I saw that people were climbing over the railings, and just as I caught up with them a gate flew open. Everyone was pouring in and making straight for the old Budget Office. It suddenly occurred to me that very few of them knew where the palace itself was. Documents were flying out of the office and the crowd was making whoopee. I began to run.

One of the columnists had written a couple of days before that he had once asked his grandmother about the Revolution of 1896. What had it been like? She had replied: "A lot of running." So in his family they had always referred to those days as the Time of Running. It seemed only appropriate that, for the second time that day, I should be running through Imelda's old vegetable patch. The turf looked sorrier than ever. We ran over the polystyrene boxes that had once contained the chicken dinners, past the sculpture garden, past where people were jumping up and down on the armored cars, and up onto the platform from where we had watched Marcos on the balcony. Everyone stamped on the planks and I was amazed the whole structure didn't collapse.

We came to a side entrance and as we crowded in I felt a hand reach into my back pocket. I pulled the hand out and slapped it. The thief scurried away.

Bing was just behind me, looking seraphically happy, with his cameras bobbing around his neck. We pushed our way through to a kind of hall, where an armed civilian told us we could go no further. The journalists crowded around him, pleading to be allowed a look. The man had been sent by the rebel troops. He had given his word of honor, he said. He couldn't let anybody past. But it was all, I'm afraid, too exciting. One of the Filipino photographers just walked past the guard, then another followed, then Bing went past; and finally I was the only one left.

I thought: Oh well, he hasn't shot them, he won't shoot me. I scuttled past him in that way people do when they expect to be kicked up the backside. "Hey, man, stop," said the guard, but as he followed me around the corner we both saw he had been standing in the wrong place: The people in the crowd had come around another way and were now going through boxes and packing cases to see what they could find. There were no takers for the Evian water. But everything else was disappearing. I caught up with Bing, who was looking through the remains of a box of monogrammed towels. We realized they had Imelda's initials. There were a couple left. They were irresistable.

I couldn't believe I would be able to find the actual Marcos apartments, and I knew there was no point in asking. We went up some servants' stairs, at the foot of which I remember seeing an opened crate with two large green jade plates. They were so large as to be vulgar. On the first floor a door opened, and we found ourselves in the great hall where the press conferences had been held. This was the one bit of the palace the crowd would recognize, as it had so often watched Marcos being televised from here. People ran and sat on his throne and began giving mock press conferences, issuing orders in his deep voice, falling about with laughter or just gaping at the splendor of the room. It was fully lit. Nobody had bothered, as they left, to turn out the lights.

I remembered that the first time I had been here, the day after the election, Imelda had slipped in and sat at the side. She must have come from that direction. I went to investigate.

And now, for a short while, I was away from the crowd with just one other person, a shy and absolutely thunderstruck Filipino. We had found our way, we realized, into the Marcoses' private rooms. There was a library, and my companion gazed in wonder at the leather-bound volumes while I admired the collection of art books all carefully catalogued and with their numbers on the spines. This was the reference library for Imelda's world-wide collection of treasures. She must have thumbed through them thinking: *I'd like one of them,* or *I've got a couple of them in New York,* or *That's in our London House.* And then there was the blue drawing room with its twin portraits of the Marcoses, where I simply remember standing with my companion and saying, "It's beautiful, isn't it." It wasn't that it *was* beautiful. It looked as if it had been purchased at Harrods. It was just that, after all the crowds and the riots, we had landed up in this peaceful, luxurious den. My companion had never seen anything like it. He didn't take anything. He hardly dared touch the furnishings and trinkets. We both simply could not believe that we were there and the Marcoses weren't.

I wish I could remember it all better. For instance, it seemed to me that in every room I saw, practically on every available surface, there was a signed photograph of Nancy Reagan. But this can hardly be literally true. It just felt as if there was a lot of Nancy in evidence.

Another of the rooms had a grand piano. I sat down.

"Can you play?" said my companion.

"A little," I exaggerated. I can play Bach's Prelude in C, and this is what I proceeded to do, but my companion had obviously hoped for something more racy. Beside the piano stood a framed photograph of Pham Van Dong, and beside the photograph lay a letter. It was a petition from members of a village, asking for property rights to the land they lived on. It was dated well before the Snap

Election. Someone (Marcos himself? the letter was addressed to him) must have opened it, seen it was a petition, popped it back in the envelope and sat down to play a tune. The keys were stiff. I wondered if the piano was brand new.

A soldier came in, carrying a rifle. "Please cooperate," he said. The soldier looked just as overawed by the place as we were. We cooperated.

When I returned down the service stairs, I noticed that the green jade plates had gone, but there was still some Evian water to be had. I was very thirsty, as it happened. But the revolution has asked me to cooperate. So I did.

Outside, the awe had communicated itself to several members of the crowd. They stood by the fountain looking down at the colored lights beneath the water, not saying anything. I went to the parapet and looked across the river. I thought Somebody's still fighting; there are still some loyal troops. Then I thought That's crazy—they can't have started fighting now. I realized that I was back in Saigon yet again. *There,* indeed, there had been fighting on the other side of the river. But here it was fireworks. The whole city was celebrating.

Bing emerged from the palace. We decided we must see the crowds coming over the Mendiola Bridge. The experience would not be complete without that. And besides, we were both hungry. Somewhere must still be open.

We had grown used to the sight of millions of people on the streets, but there was something wonderful about this crowd, noisy but not mad, pouring across the forbidden bridge. Imelda's soothsayer had got it slightly wrong. He should have said: When the crowds pour over the Mendiola Bridge, that will mean the regime *has already* fallen, not that it is about to fall. Still, that error was minor. The man had been right in broad outline. Many members of the crowd were wearing crowns of barbed wire. Bing snapped out of his dream. "And now," he said, "now they will begin to crack down on the communists. Now there'll be a real crackdown."

We went down a dark, quiet street in the university area, found some food and started chatting to others who had been at the palace. They had taken boxes and boxes of ammunition. We sat out on the pavement. I said to one guy: "Congratulations. You've just had a real bourgeois revolution. They don't happen very often nowadays. You should be pleased."

He said: "If it's a bourgeois revolution, it's supposed to bring in socialism."

I said: "You read Marx?"

He said: "No! I read Lenin!" Then he laughed, and said he was only joking. But I didn't think he was joking, actually. He said: "Cory's a rich woman and a landowner. These people aren't the good guys. You come back for the next revolution. The next revolution it'll be the NPA. The next revolution it'll be the Reds!"

Bing took me to find a taxi, and we said goodbye. He couldn't resist it: He had to go back to the palace. The taxi driver had a linguistic habit I had never come across before. He could survive without any personal pronouns except I, me, and my. "Well James," he said, as I got in, "have I been to Malacañang?"

I thought for a moment.

"Have I been to Malacañang, James?" he repeated.

"Yes," I said. "I have been to Malacañang."

"Has Marcos gone?"

Yes, this time he really had gone.

"Marcos is a good man, James," said the driver, "but my wife is very bad. Yes, James. Marcos is a good man. But my wife is very bad."

"Yes," I said, finally understanding the rules, "my wife is very bad indeed."

That Morning-After Feeling

"How did you get on last night, Helen? I heard you'd had a nasty experience."

"It was horrible, all those thugs—did you *see* the way they beat up the Marcos guy? They weren't Cory supporters. They were just— and the way they were shouting 'We're free, we're free.' That wasn't free*dom*. That wasn't a liberation. Nothing's happ*ened*. Nothing's changed. It was brutal. I hated it. And I hate this job. It's not human."

Helen had indeed had a nasty experience, and she was still having it now, in the foyer of the Manila Hotel. The look of blank panic had returned to her eyes. She had come looking for us along J. P. Laurel Street and had reached the front of the crowd. Then somehow in the course of the fighting she had got among the Marcos thugs. When things had got really dangerous, she had hidden in a kind of shed, but the thugs had spotted her and knew she was inside. They thought she was a Filipino and a Cory supporter. They thought she was a man. And because her voice is deep and she was calling out in perfect Tagalog, the more she protested, the less they believed her. "They were firing at *me!*" she said. "They were firing at *me!*"

Finally, to convince them she was a photographer and not a rioter, she had thrown her camera out of the shed. They told her to come out, and as she did so they began grabbing at her and feeling her up. After that she detested everything she saw, and the friends she met up with were disgusted too. They had seen only idiocy on the rampage. At the old Budget Office, for instance, people had been burning papers, and one man was shouting: "These are precious documents about Marcos. You're destroying precious evidence."

One thing at least had changed, however, and we could see it from where we were sitting. The body searches at the hotel front door had been stopped.

Sitting at our table was a politician who had supported the Aquino campaign and who was now fuming: There had been no consultation with the UNIDO members of the Assembly about the formation of the new cabinet. He himself, he said, had told the Aquino supporters that he did not want a job. But they would find that they needed the cooperation of the Assembly to establish the legitimacy of their new government. The Assembly had proclaimed Marcos president. The Assembly would therefore have to un-proclaim him before Cory could be *de jure* as well as *de facto* head of state. She could have a revolutionary, *de facto* government if she wanted. But in that case her power was dependent on the military. She would be vulnerable. The politician was haunted by the fear that corrupt figures would again be put in key positions, and that the whole thing would turn out to have been some kind of sordid switch. The television announcers were congratulating the nation on the success of People's Power. But all three of us at the table were wondering how real People's Power was.

The previous night, Enrile had made a most extraordinary speech on the television. It had come in the form of a crude amateur video. It looked, in a way, like the plea of some kidnap victim, as if he were being forced to speak at gunpoint. And what he had said was so strange that now, the morning after, I wondered whether I had dreamed it. So far I'd not met anyone else who had seen the broadcast. Enrile had begun, as far as I remember, by saying that Marcos was now in exile, and that he, Enrile, was sorry. He had not intended things to turn out this way. But he wanted to thank the president (he still called him the president) for not attacking the rebel soldiers when they first went to Camp Aguinaldo. At that time (and here I am referring to a partial text of the speech) "the military under his control, or the portion of the military under his control, had the firepower to inflict heavy damage on us." But it did not do so. "And for that alone, I would like to express my gratitude to the president. As officers and men of the armed forces of the Philippines, we want to salute him for that act of compassion and kindness that he extended to us all."

I asked Helen and the politician whether they had heard this, and they hadn't. By coincidence, at that very moment, the television in the foyer broadcast an extract from the speech. The politician was shocked. "He's only been gone a few hours, and already the rehabilitation has begun.

I then tried out my theory on the others. When I had woken that morning, the theory was there, fully formed, in my head. In a way I had been quite startled to find it there, so complete and horrible. The theory went like this. We had all assumed that Marcos was losing touch with reality. In fact he had not lost his marbles at all. He had seen that he had to go, and that the only way out for a dictator of his kind was exile. The point was to secure the succession. It could not go to General Ver, but Marcos was under an obligation to Ver, and therefore he could not hand over the presidency to anybody else. In some way, whether explicitly or by a nod and a wink, he had told Enrile and Ramos: You may succeed me if you dare, but in order to do so you must overthrow me and Ver. You must rebel. If you do so, the bargain between us will be: I protect you from Ver, and you protect me; if you let me go with my family after my inauguration, I will permit you to rebel. Marcos was writing his legend again, and the legend was: He was the greatest president the Philippines had ever known. Then his most trusted son, Enrile, rebelled; Marcos could easily have put down the rebellion, *but he still loved his son, he loved the Filipino people, and he could not bear to shed their blood.* It was a tragic and dignified conclusion.

The theory explained why Marcos had shown himself, on the television, overruling Ver. It explained why there had been so little actual fighting. And it explained the striking fact that no rebel troops had been brought anywhere near the palace until after Marcos had left.

I asked the politician what he thought, and his first reaction was: "It's too clever." But then you could see the theory, with all its ramifications, getting a grip on him, until he said: "My God, I hope you're wrong." Helen was prepared to believe the theory. When I put it to Fred, he brooded over it darkly. His own theory that day was slightly different. "It was scripted," he said, "the whole thing was scripted by social scientists." His idea was that this was a copybook peaceful revolution designed to be held up to other countries all around the world in order to dissuade people from taking up armed struggle.

One way or another, the people I met the day after Marcos left were incapable of trusting the reality of the events they had witnessed. Not all of them believed the theory, but very few of them could muster a concrete argument against it. It was absolutely possible to believe that, instead of joining the revolution, Enrile and Ramos had hijacked it. And everyone was clearly still in the habit of believing in the genius of Marcos, however much they hated him.

Intramuros

I realized I still hadn't the slightest idea of historic Manila. I hadn't looked at anything old. I hadn't done the sights. Instead of beginning with history and working forward, as one might expect to do, I'd gone straight into the thick of things. My feet had hardly touched ground. And now, like Helen, I was revolutioned out.

The taxi driver offered to show me around Fort Santiago, the Spanish bastion defending the old citadel of Intramuros. He must have been a bit revolutioned out himself, for he didn't talk much, and I appreciated his silences. He said that the waterlilies in the moat were beautiful. I agreed with him. Then he pointed toward the river and said something about shooting. Since I hadn't heard any shots, I thought he was talking about somebody making a film.

We climbed the walls. On a quay by the river below us, a small crowd was gathered. "There," said my driver, "you see the body." A ferry was coming in to land, dragging a corpse beside it through the water. Somebody called to ask whether it was a salvaging, but it turned out that some gangsters had knifed a security man before pushing him into the river. Criminal life was back to normal, as was the stock exchange. The peso had rallied. The banks were functioning.

The driver pointed to a warehouse which he said belonged to one of the richest men in the Philippines. I wondered where *he* was today. The richest man I had met here, Mr. Floirendo, was reported to have done a bunk.* We looked over the parapet. Children were sniffing glue. On a stretch of waste ground, beside a packing-case house, a man was soaping himself. To the north lay Tondo, beyond view, and Smoky Mountain. But there were scavengers everywhere around town.

Fort Santiago was where the poet, novelist, and national hero José Rizal was imprisoned before his execution in 1896. I wondered whether numerologically minded Filipinos had noticed that it was now 1986. Marcos's lucky number was seven. He had chosen the seventh for the election, and the twenty-fifth (two plus five) for the inauguration. But the Cory–Doy ticket had seven letters too. He had been out-sevened.

"The Spanish were the worst. They killed José Rizal," the farmer had said. And people had laughed at him. I walked around the little museum to the poet's memory, with its touching exhibition of the clothes he had worn in Europe. It was in Europe first, not in

---

*He later paid the government a large sum, and returned to his estates.

America, that the Filipinos had sought the ideas on which they founded their claim to nationhood and independence. It was from reading Voltaire and Schiller and Victor Hugo. I'd just been reading as much in the newspapers. They may quote you Jefferson or Abraham Lincoln, the article had said, but really it is to Europe that they look. There *was* something thoroughly romantic about the Filipinos. I thought of Chichoy saying: "People like me do not live long. . . ." I hoped on that point he would now be able to change his mind.

Another famous prisoner of Intramuros was Ferdinand Marcos. Or so a little placard claimed. He had been put here in a dungeon by the Japanese.

I wondered whether that was true. And how long the placard would remain in place.

Granta *Gives a Beach Party*

"I'm fine," said Helen, "I was just a bit shaken up yesterday."

"You'd had a nasty experience. You should realize that. These things take some getting over. Bing had this idea we should all go to the sea for a couple of days. Have a rest. I thought *Granta* might throw a beach party."

The reaction at the end of the phone was good. Helen's thoughts were racing. A friend of hers from California had a round hut on a beach up north. It was empty, and we were welcome to use it any time. "There's just this strip of beach, and the fishermen come up and sell you fish in the evening," said Helen. Everything started shaping up wonderfully. Helen's old roommates, Esperanza and Caridad, would join us, plus Bing, Fred, and Jojo. "And don't forget Pedro." I said. "Remember you took me to his party the first night." Then Jojo's mother suggested that she might come along to do the cooking, and if she came Jojo's aunty might come to keep her company, and then—if this was all right—there might be . . . I was beginning to get lost in the intricacies of Helen's friends and relations. There was a man with a jeep nearby who had offered it for a bargain price for the weekend. Everything was set.

Alas, when the jeep arrived to pick me up, Bing was missing. After a sleepless week, he had dosed himself with Valium and was now catching up on his dreams. Fred too had been mysteriously called away. But then it turned out that Helen's old roommate Esperanza had to bring a bodyguard. She had a Chinese lover who didn't know she smoked; *he* couldn't accompany us yet, because he would be gambling in Manila; but if he sent his bodyguard with her, he would know she was not getting up to anything wrong. The Chinese lover would arrive with his other bodyguards later, and all would be well.

We drove off in what I, by now, knew was the wrong direction. Helen's old roommate Caridad had another roommate to whom she had lent some money, but who had not paid up, and Caridad had been obliged to pawn her jewelry. This she had to redeem at once, or all would be lost. We drove to the pawnshop, then back along EDSA, where it was difficult to believe that there had once been barricades. By the time we arrived to pick up Helen, she was triumphant: It was so late. It seemed so out of character for *me*. Eventually the fifteen of us set off for the north.

I felt a bit guilty as we stumbled over the dunes late at night, and woke up the caretaker of the hut. We were unannounced. He was asleep and his wife was pregnant. But later I learned that the caretaker did not enjoy his solitude. The hut had a balcony running all around it, and he told us that quite often the ghosts came and wandered round and round. They were always hearing this wailing woman. Once the caretaker had established that we were not ghosts, we were welcome.

In the meanwhile, Bentot, the driver, had had a secret quarrel with Esperanza. He wanted to be paid extra if he was going to take Esperanza to meet her Chinese lover when he returned from gambling. So Esperanza gave Bentot the slip, and Bentot panicked. He naturally assumed that she had been kidnapped by the military and raped, or this is what he led us to believe. Then Bentot had an idea: He would take Caridad with him to look for Esperanza. Caridad was scandalized. If she went off in the dark with Bentot, her reputation would be ruined. *Ruined.* She appealed to me. I said that if she wanted to go off with Bentot none of us would think the worse of her. Bentot was by now so preoccupied with luring Caridad away that I guessed he didn't really think that Esperanza had been raped. He pleaded with Caridad before the company. He told her it didn't matter if they went off together because his wife was old and ugly. Every time Bentot made a remark like this, Caridad gave him a scandalized riposte and then flashed her dentures in my direction. I knew she wore dentures because I had found her washing them over a sink full of edible seaweed. I told her I thought Bentot was a man of honor—which was not what I thought, and not what she thought I thought either. Caridad took all this in good part.

When Esperanza's Chinese lover eventually arrived on the second morning of the beach party, with two more bodyguards and the look of a man who expected the world to arrange itself around him, Esperanza produced the bundle of live crabs she had set aside in his honor and boiled them up. Helen, disgusted, went off to the sea.

Esperanza was a strange girl. She came from a rich family but lived with Caridad at the YWCA. She was a trained nurse, but unlike Caridad she wasn't working any more. In the old days, when a patient had died in the hospital, the two girls would note the number of the patient's bed, then rush down to the *jai alai* and bet on it. Her lover, being of a rather grand Chinese family, was unable to marry her. But he had bought her a house and installed two servants. Esperanza had refused the deal. She continued living in the YWCA, sending out for food at midday, reading comics, coming alive in the evening and then hitting the gambling dens with her lover. Her parents were supposed to know nothing about all this, but she was beautiful and had refused many suitors and the parents must have guessed something. You can see that her friend Helen and she were rather different types.

Esperanza laid the cooked crabs before her lover, who sat with his three burly chums away from the rest of us. I was called over to join them. After the crabs, the lover snoozed, with Esperanza draped over him.

Helen returned; she loved the breakers, but pronounced them to be dangerous. She loved the sun, but it was harsh on her skin. On the first day she stayed out too long, doing her TM, which she never had a chance to do in Manila. That night she had sunstroke. The next day she stayed out too long again. "I had a fev-*er*," she said.

."I know you had a fever, Helen. You gave yourself sunstroke. But I've decided by now not to get between you and your self-destructiveness."

"So I'm the one who is self-destruct-*ive*?" said Helen. But she smiled as if she quite liked the idea.

Caridad was slicing pork for the barbecue, and mixing it in the marinade of soy and *calamansi* juice. There was a seaweed salad. There would be tuna and *lapu-lapu* and all good things. We had two crates of San Miguel beer, and we genuinely believed the boycott was over. Jojo's relations were preparing meal after meal.

I said to Jojo: "You remember when we drove past Camp Crame, and you pointed out where you had been tortured. What happened?"

When they had come for Jojo in his house, the soldiers had been quite ruthless. From the way they stuck a gun in his aged grandmother's face, he had known that they wouldn't scruple to kill. They almost had killed the old woman. When they took Jojo and his fellow students to Camp Crame, they had beaten them up and tortured them for several days. They had a photo of Jojo in his martial arts outfit. "So you're a martial arts expert," they would say, smashing him in the chest with a rifle butt. They had tied electrodes to his hands and feet, but when they tried to get his pants off to do the same to his genitals, he had resisted, said, No, and held on to his pants. So they hadn't persisted, although they perfectly well could have done, and although they had done so to his two friends.

"What did you tell them?"

"I tried to tell them all the details they knew already, everything that was public. I stood for election in the students' association and got so many votes and the other candidates got so many votes. Things like that."

"Were you tempted to give them false information, just in order to have something to say?"

"It's very, very tempting, and you mustn't do it. If you tell them where to find somebody, and then they take you along and he's not there, they'll kill you."

"Did you give in, and tell them things they actually wanted to know?"

"No."

"How did you manage to resist?"

"One thing is, after a while, you become so angry. But the other thing you have to remember is that, if you do start confessing and giving information, when they've finished with you they'll kill you. Your only chance of survival is to tell them nothing at all."

As Jojo talked, and was filled with remembered anger at his torturers (who were known to have been involved in other salvagings), his voice turned thin and quiet. I'd known him now for four weeks, and I could see that there was a great survival value in never raising your voice in anger. When Jojo was in danger or a passion, only his eyes spoke, and the muscles around the eyes. The voice trailed off, and you had to strain to hear it. But if you were in danger with Jojo, and you knew what an expression meant, you would be in very good company. Torture had taught him a lot. He was an expert survivor, and he had perfected that art of seeing without seeming to see. It was Jojo who had noticed that arrest in Davao.

"Do you still meet the people who were tortured with you?"

"We used to meet for a while, but I've lost contact with them now. Some people, after they've been tortured, don't want to have anything to do with anybody they've known before. If they were communists, they avoid the communists. It's as if they can't bear anything that reminds them of the past."

"What were you like when you'd been released?"

"For a year I suffered from paranoia. If somebody knocked at the door, I wanted to jump out of the window."

"That's not what I call paranoia. What you mean is you were really scared. And it sounds as if you had every reason to be scared. If they'd done it once, they might do it again. Paranoia is when you think there are green men from Mars keeping tabs on you. *Your* fear was perfectly rational."

Jojo laughed. "And all the time I thought it was paranoia. Well, I was like that for a year. I kept on with my martial arts. One thing about being tortured is that afterward, when you meet this kind of person, you can tell immediately. I can recognize them by the way they walk, even the way they smell. You know, when they were torturing me, they were laughing and joking and fooling around. I got to know them very well indeed."

I looked down toward the breakers. "Jojo, if we were walking

211

along the beach now, and some people came along and you recognized them as your torturers, what would you do?"

"I wouldn't talk to them. I wouldn't do anything. That wouldn't be a solution."

"So what would be a solution?"

Jojo was speaking very softly again. "Well, to be brutal: They should be killed. They've killed people and tortured people. *They* should be killed. Unless of course . . ." He thought a moment. "Unless they'd really changed. But it would have to be a *real* change."

I could guess how he felt about a real change. Before we had left Manila, the television had been showing interminable discussions with time-servers who said they'd changed. Not torturers, of course. Small fry. Pop stars who had sung at KBL rallies and were now getting it off their chest. One of them described how, on his way to Marcos's *miting de avance,* the vehicle he was in had been stoned by the crowd. "And that was a real eye opener to me, I mean, man. . . ." As if he hadn't noticed anything wrong in the Philippines until somebody picked up a stone and threw it at him.

The glib talk of reconciliation would never bring about a solution, a real reconciliation. A change in the society would have to count as a real change if it was to satisfy people like Jojo or Comrade Nicky, whose whole psyches had been changed by what they had been through, or if it was going to dismantle the slums of the Tondo, stop starvation on Negros or release the peasant from the predators. Everything was yet to be done. Most of the prisoners were still to be released; there would have to be a new constitution; the communists would have to be either coopted or defeated, if the Aquino government was to succeed in its aims. And I was quite sure that nobody really knew what would happen, or what actually was happening. The communists had got it wrong. Bayan had got it wrong. The KBL had got it most spectacularly wrong. Laban had won but was now in a position where expectations were so hysterically aroused that disenchantment of some sort must follow. The struggle of the future was, quite simply, the battle for the definition of justice.

Jojo glanced at the figures on the beach. "D'you want a swim?" he said. It was evening and the sand was cool enough to walk on. People were keen to photograph the sunset. I picked up my Imelda towel, and we walked down to the water's edge. Pedro was being buried in the sand, and, for one morbid moment, I thought it odd that all over the world there should be a traditional game of giving yourself a shallow grave. Jojo was thinking something quite different. He took a large handful of sand and fashioned for Pedro a spectacular erection. Pedro lay there and giggled, as the erection shook and cracked and broke.

The Truce

1

Sotero Llamas was proud of the price on his head. Ten thousand dollars. This made him the most wanted man in the Bicol region. The rumor was that Sotero, or Teroy, or Nognog, was the NPA Commander of southern Luzon. It was as a spokesman for the NPA that he was due, one Saturday late in 1986, to go down from the hills into the town of Legaspi, to help set up the regional ceasefire committee.

On the whole Teroy thought that the military would respect the ceasefire, but he was worried about Colonel Abadilla, a notorious killer and inquisitor of the left, who had been sent down to Bicol after his involvement in the Manila hotel coup (the first of the military attempts to get rid of Cory). Abadilla just might use the occasion to bump him off.

So Teroy asked me if I would mind accompanying him in the first car of the motorcade. "If they see you there, " he said, "that would make our precautions more iron-clad."

The car belonged to the local radio reporter, who sat in the front seat giving a live commentary. In the back were two guerrillas, aged about fifteen or sixteen, called Marlon and Archie. When Teroy and I joined them first, we sat by the window. I thought: Good, he's sitting by the window.

Then we had a flat.

When the tire was changed and we were getting back into the car, Teroy asked if I would mind swapping places. "Not at all," I breezed, taking the exposed position.

So now, if Colonel Abadilla's men wanted to shoot Teroy, he was protected on one side by innocent-looking kids, and on the other by a foreigner. Teroy offered me a sandwich, but I refused. I could see that he was a charming man who was used to getting his own way and involving other people in slightly larger adventures, perhaps, than they had bargained for.

"The trouble is," said Teroy as the car moved off, "we have not yet received our safe-conduct passes."

All over the Philippines the NPA had been coming down from the hills. In the southern Tagalog region, they had even been allowed to bring their weapons into Lucena. But here, Teroy said, they were not to be armed.

So the two heavy bags he had placed in the car were innocent after all. I decided they probably contained exceedingly heavy sandwiches.

Sotero had not been into Legaspi since 1971, he said. He had been an activist at Aquinas University, where he studied law. But after he had disclosed some irregularity in the university's affairs he had been blacklisted. He had taken to the hills where he had helped to form the first generation of Bicol NPAs. Thirty-three people had been in that group. Many gave up early on. Others were captured, others killed. Of those who stayed with the NPA, only three are still, as he put it, "vertical."

When Teroy uses words like this, he laughs disconcertingly. He relishes the disconcerting. He keenly watches the effect his words have on the listener, and he is always happy to talk. This is partly because he knows very well how much he is at liberty to say. He's in command after all.

But there was something else, during this period and on this occasion particularly. Teroy the university activist, the clever and funny public speaker, who had gone underground a decade and a half ago, was coming out, dropping his disguise. Before that day, even within his own group, there were people who did not know who was the legendary Nognog. But from now on anybody could have his photograph and anybody could know that Nognog, and Ka Willy (for "wily"), and Teroy were the same person. Short, jovial, with a face like Socrates and a peaked cap like Castro, Teroy was going public.

When the NPA first began work in Bicol, they acquired arms by confiscating them from the private security men of the local landlords. Then "enlightened elements in the middle class" had helped them, after which they began to recruit among the peasants. In the late Marcos years it had been easy to identify the enemy (Marcos = Fascism) and to gain support from the peasantry. True, the beginnings had been hard, and there had been black years in 1974 and 1975. But all in all, according to Teroy, the basic issue was simple to understand and put across.

Since the February revolution things had changed, and in Bicol the situation was complicated. On the one hand, there was a popular government—reactionary, in the view of the NPA, but not fascist. There were still fascist elements in place among the military, in Teroy's analysis, with all kinds of pressures creating a new situation. This meant that there had to be intensive political work among the NPA and their supporters—but still, ceasefire or no, they had to be prepared for the resumption of armed struggle.

But the Bicol NPA needed arms. They needed explosives. They had just managed to buy an antitank weapon, but they needed more of these, and mortars—and they couldn't get such supplies without outside support.

They also needed doctors. Nothing demoralized them, Teroy said, so much as having a comrade wounded and being unable to get medical help for him. Finally, they also needed uniforms. They wanted fatigues, and they had asked their supporters to give them these as Christmas presents. After today's events, they had home-printed T-shirts, with a design of the Mayon Volcano.

That morning, representatives of the clergy and the cause-oriented groups had come up into the hills from Legaspi, to meet the NPA and escort them down into town. A service was held on a basketball court. The Assistant Bishop of Legaspi was full of memories of Teroy when young. Nuns handed out boiled sweets. Peace workers stuck flags into the NPA guns. The local radio interviewed Teroy as our lad from Tabako (a town noted for the manufacture of excellent scissors and unnerving knives). When Teroy spoke, it was to make people laugh—and I could see he must have been an excellent student leader.

When his colleague Celso Minguez tried to speak, he wept

instead. He had been seventeen years in the movement. He was another of the three remaining members of the founding group. And then there was Alberto David, Jr. from the second intake. It had been a moving scene in the barrio, with people greeting each other ecstatically. Some of them were friends who had left the underground, but now had come back to meet their old colleagues. I had seen several of the NPA-organized events since the truce had come into effect, but none of them had quite this emotional, provincial intimacy.

"Is it really fifteen years since you've seen Legaspi?" I asked Teroy, as we drove down. He claimed it was, but it was amazing how often, along the route, he would point out areas as being particular strongholds of the NPA, and how little seemed to surprise him in the landscape.

I asked him how it felt, coming down.

He said he was still worried.

Would he see his family?

Teroy said he hoped they wouldn't be there. His children and his wife, whom he rarely saw, would cry—and then he would cry too.

We passed a military camp, where he used to do his reserve officer's training. "I'm reserve officer," said Teroy with what seemed a touch of pride.

"You mean, you're *still* a reserve officer, officially?"

"Yes," he said, "but the question is—reserved for whom?"

People at the side of the road, hearing the loudspeaker van announcing the motorcade and its purpose, waved in a somewhat surreptitious way. I saw one man, for instance, who was definitely waving with the four fingers of his right hand, but with his thumb he was pretending to scratch his scalp. There was something intense and circumspect about the response along the way.

Fred and Bing, who were working with me at the time, had taken up a position by the first checkpoint into town. When the motorcade came close, a constabulary captain told them he was going to search every vehicle.

Fred asked him: "Who's the NPA bigshot here?"

"It's Nognog," he said, "Sotero Llamas."

Would he recognize Nognog?

"No," he said, "that's the problem—sometimes we are even talking with them and we don't know who they are."

The captain was a sympathetic man. His great hope for the ceasefire was that it might allow him to rejoin his family. He hadn't seen them for two years and he was afraid his children wouldn't recognize him anymore.

Now the captain tried to stop the loudspeaker van, waving it down. But people waved back at him and not a car in the line stopped. Then he seemed, simply, to give up the idea of searching every vehicle.

Inside the vehicle with Nognog, I thought the captain was waving us on. He peered at us for a moment. Instinctively I moved back my head a little to allow him to kill Nognog instead of me. Just half an inch, but enough to make me feel a little ashamed afterward.

Nognog/Teroy said to me again: "I hope my children aren't there, or I'll cry."

"There's nothing wrong with crying in public," I said. I was thinking: If *he* starts, I'll start.

We reached the Cathedral precinct, and waited for a while to disembark and for Teroy to make his face known to the public. The NPA surrounded us in their T-shirts. Then we got out and marched in close formation to lunch, Teroy holding my hands tightly. And there were Bing and Fred again, retreating in front of us, clicking away among the press.

At lunch, a small crowd watched us through the slatted windows of the *cursillo,* asking each other which was Teroy. Among the onlookers, he recognized his drama professor from university days. I met her later. She was floating on air. She said: "I taught them both, Sotero and Alberto David!"

I said: "They used to act?"

"Yes," she said.

"What did they play?" I asked.

She said: "It was in 1970! They both played leading roles!"

I bet they did, I thought. I was relieved my minor role was finished, and relieved too that, when my photograph appeared the next day in the national press, I was clearly identified as the Bishop of Legaspi.

2

Teroy actually owed me a favor, which he was keen to repay. Several days before, on the eve of the official ceasefire, Bing and I had come down to Bicol on the understanding that we would be able to interview the NPA, photograph them and even accompany them down from the hills, if all went according to plan. Because there had been doubt about the last bit, and because I needed a failsafe arrangement in order to have a story on offer to my newspaper (*The Independent*), I had chartered a plane. I had half a page of newspaper waiting to be filled, and I had visions of a truly elegant operation: Jojo was in Mindanao, Fred in Northern Luzon—between us all we should see something of interest.

Everything went according to plan: We were met at the airstrip and taken from place to place, made the inevitable river crossing and before too long were walking through a coconut plantation to meet the NPA. And we met the NPA, and they said, We're very sorry, but the man you were going to meet is not here and we have no authorization to talk to you. But this is absurd, we said. You've already brought us here—you must know the arrangement was official. They knew that all right, but because of a missing link in the chain of command they could do nothing about it. We had been promised access to a company-sized camp. We must have been a stone's throw from the place. But we were not to be allowed in.

Well, we said, could we at least interview some red fighters about their attitude to the ceasefire. Could they come out of the camp and talk to us? But that too was not to be. No provision had been made for such a thing. The red fighters were *there* all right, and sat in embarrassment at the edge of the conversation. But we couldn't talk to them, not even about the weather.

Hopelessly I began to explain through Bing the lengths to which we had come to secure an original story, with photographs, how we had the space waiting, the plane waiting, the enormous expense ($900) the hole in the budget, the necessity of cancelling the page . . . everything. But reasoning was useless. One act of authority was lacking.

Fury and despair overcame me. I left the conversation and began pacing around the trees beyond the scope of the lantern. Bing was being lectured on democratic centralism. I could tell he was becoming irritated: he was trying to say, Yes, I understand about democratic centralism, but it's not supposed to be a shield for stupid and petty behavior; while the voice that was lecturing him turned gelid—this is a revolutionary struggle, discipline is everything and so forth. I was glad that, however trivial the issue, we had stubbed our toes against democratic centralism, for much of the NPA propaganda recently had made the insurgents seem amiable to the point of insipidity. The foul-up in our plans had killed my story, but at least I was seeing how things worked. I was seeing one of those *displays of discipline* which form such a profound component of communist culture.

Such displays can be over great things or small. I met one woman, an early member of the NPA, who had been taking part on the trial of a comrade. The man had been voted guilty and the death sentence chosen. The woman had been in the minority who believed that the comrade should be given another chance. But once the decision had been taken, she had *volunteered* to execute the sentence. She had wanted, she said, the experience of executing a sentence with which she had disagreed.

It is a terrible thing to want an experience in this way. It is a desire that arises not out of practical necessities of membership of a guerrilla movement, but out of a pathological need for an obedience. Killing a comrade is anticipated as a supreme test of belonging, and there is a parallel here with another Filipino underground: that is the criminals. It is standard practice for the criminal gangs to demand of a new recruit that he commit a murder. The fact of having killed a man seems to be a kind of social glue.

3

News spread rather quickly through the underground about a foreigner who had chartered a plane to visit the NPA and been turned away at the last moment. Teroy said to me later: "We've very sorry about what happened that night"—and here the mischievous look broke through—"and they tell me you even cried because you couldn't get your story."

I laughed. I wasn't going to contradict him. Faced with a petty display of discipline by one of his *apparatchiks*, I had given a tenebrous display of rage and frustration. I could easily have cried. And afterward, when I was offered the chance of free access to one of his areas, to meet and talk to whomever I pleased, I took care to point out that it would not be free access, and nor would conversation be free. Democratic centralism would not permit that—and nor would the normal security precautions taken by any guerrilla movement. I might have access, but it would not be free access.

Teroy agreed. It is under his controlling influence that the Bicol NPA has become notoriously strict on discipline. He is the original democratic centralist. Every year there is one—but only one—month of discussion. It takes two months to organize the meeting, and fifteen days for the comrades to arrive. They can't descend on a barrio like delegates on a conference hotel. Roads are watched. Unusual movements would be noticed. And so arrivals must be staggered. Then they go through everything: organization, military, financial, and personal matters. Political decisions are made, and for the rest of the year they must be faithfully carried out. (This applies to the Bicol NPA. But the Communist Party of the Philippines has never held a congress since its foundation.)

It's a tried and tested system: recruitment, discipline, organization have all been worked out and can be explained, neatly, point by numbered point. When Teroy said he would explain the whole thing to me when we had our interview together I did not feel it necessary to tell him that the interview began the moment we first met, and had continued through those early weeks of the truce, as we drove around Bicol to public meetings, sleeping in schools and seminaries, being ministered to by nuns.

When the NPA went to mass I refused to join them. Teroy was amused and intrigued. Why not? "Because *I'm* an atheist," I said affecting a certain superiority. There followed a deal of eyebrow music between us: Teroy of course is a nonbeliever, but . . . diplomacy . . . and he enjoys humoring the nuns.

————

4

Here we are, then, guests of the Augustinian Sisters of Our Lady of Consolation, eating and sleeping in the science room of the Consolation Academy, among the bottled specimens and reports. A banner on the wall reads: "If I have seen further than other men, it is by standing on the shoulders of giants." Some of the young guerrillas are learning a song, set to a beautiful tune which sounds Spanish or even Neapolitan in origin. The tune became popular in Filipino prison: It was a song of the underworld. Now the tune has taken to the hills, with new words:

> *We are the poor people, with no strength except our industriousness,*
> *No wealth at all except our strength—sweat, blood and honesty.*
> *What happened to this creative force?*
> *Why did the others steal and leave nothing over?*
> *Since we joined the bloody uprising*
> *Our aim is liberty with the broad masses.*
> *Firmly, valiantly, shouting and struggling*
> *We'll carry the flag right on to total victory.*

I imagine that the tune began life as a love song, traveling around the Mediterranean in the seventeenth century. Then perhaps it was press-ganged and found its way out here.

Teroy is writing notes. The *apparatchik* is doing the accounts. At an adjacent table, the red fighters are practicing drawing the hammer and sickle—a task they are finding difficult. The wrong paint was used on their silk-screened NPA special truce T-shirts, and the Mayon Volcano is flaking off after the first wash.

Teroy starts telling me about sex, which can be a problem in the NPA. Rape is a capital crime, and I've heard it said that in the early days of the movement comrades were killed for illicit affairs. Teroy says that ordinary sexual abuses are carefully investigated and that demotion is the discipline. He has taken care not to fall into any sexual trap himself. And he has, of course, a system, which he explains to all his men.

The first thing is: never to be alone. Secondly, when you go to bed, try not to sleep near female comrades. Thirdly, keep active—it's when you're idle that you begin to think about these things. Write poetry. Read a book. Play Scrabble. Teroy and Celso Minguez are extraordinarily good at Scrabble, although Teroy has a way of laying down a faintly improbable word and quickly removing it at the first sign of objection. Once we acquired a Scrabble set which turned out to have only two vowels represented. But this seemed to cause no difficulty: the whole was played with O's and U's.

Another way of coping with the sexual problem, of course, is conjugal visits. In wartime these are classically dangerous moments, if one partner is in the underground and the other not. The truce was a sexual boon with the NPA. On Christmas Eve, in the Legaspi classroom where we have been billeted, Teroy points with pursed lips (Filipino-style) toward the *apparatchik,* who has been padding around all evening, inconspicuously getting things done. Now he's opening a briefcase and producing shirt and trousers, perfectly pressed. "You can always tell," says Teroy, "if someone is carefully getting his work done, like that. It means he's got a conjugal visit."

Now other wives, including Teroy's, arrive, and the senior comrades retire, leaving us to listen to the fireworks in the town. The guerrillas have no relish for fireworks. Their ears are trained to react swiftly to all kinds of explosives—except fireworks. It is a disturbing sound.

For the twentieth time that day, a young guerrilla picks up the guitar and sings "Boulevard." We read. We keep busy. We do all the things Teroy has recommended to keep our minds off sex. We are awakened after the midnight mass by the nuns who come with carols and a cake. Then a group of pretty girls from the town arrive with sweetmeats. We drink hot chocolate and feel a little sorry for ourselves, like seminarians.

5

One thing Teroy regrets is the lack of opportunities for reading. He carries a lot of books around with him (that was what was in the heavy bags we took down into Legaspi), and I noticed that he is currently dipping into John Reed's *Insurgent Mexico*. This was perhaps on some central committee reading list on insurrection, which has been very much a topic for debate.

In February, as the Snap Election turned into a revolution, the NPA were completely left out of events, and not surprisingly there was debate and discontent afterward. People were saying: We should have been in there; we should have staged an insurrection. So Teroy asked the central committee to prepare a study of insurrections—ones that have succeeded, ones that have failed. Within three months a paper on insurrections was distributed, together with books for Teroy. But he is a busy man. He has difficulty reading ten pages before falling asleep. There is something enviably out of touch about the Filipino guerrillas. Books are hard enough to come by in the cities anyway, let alone in the hills. And those political contacts with the outside world that the NPA maintains are not necessarily the most useful: Teroy was able to explain to me at some length what had happened to the Canadian Maoists. And what had happened to them? They had split. Over what had they split? Over the women's question, and over the language question. So much for the Canadian Maoists.

He also began to tell me that what had happened in Cambodia had not been nearly as bad as has been made out. And from what he started to say I soon worked out that he had received a visit from an old friend of mine, a Japanese photographer who was apparently never able to face up to the truth of what happened.

The Cambodia question is a hard one for the NPA, partly because of the effectiveness of *The Killing Fields,* which was widely distributed here. "Black propaganda!" the leftists tended to say, although I never heard one of them find serious fault with the film's presentation of events. Just before Marcos fell, an article in *Commentary* by Ross Munroe depicted the NPA as being the Khmer Rouge of the future, and referred to their increased ruthlessness and brutality.

The man cast by Munroe in the role of Pol Pot, Rodolfo Salas, had been arrested by the military during the truce negotiations. As for the negotiators themselves, Satur Ocampo and Tony Zumel, it would be hard to imagine them in the Cambodian context. Nevertheless the stories of brutality told in the article are not to be dismissed. The NPA admits that it has thorough phases of paranoia in which massacres have occurred.

These are referred to as infiltration periods, when "Deep Penetration Agents" (DPAs) were causing havoc in the movement: 1974 to 1975 and 1982 to 1983 are two periods mentioned by Teroy, the worst areas being Mindanao and southern Tagalog.

Anyone will tell you that, in the attempt to root out the DPAs, good comrades were killed: When the truth of the matter finally became clear, those responsible for the killing of innocent comrades were shot in front of their own men. The responsible cadres might themselves have been fine comrades—Teroy in some cases sympathized with them. But they had let their reason be ruled by their emotions. Justice had to be given to the dead.

Teroy's guidelines for the detection of DPA:

1. They often have relatives in the military.
2. They have "lumpen experiences"—criminal backgrounds.
3. They have unresolved personal problems.
4. They are extremely active within the movement.
5. But they regularly visit their families—which is when they have a chance to contact their friends in the military.

6. And finally the army follows closely the units in which
they work.

Just as you can see the thinking behind these indicators, so you can see the scope for paranoia. The presence of a DPA is suspected when some particularly bitter disaster his befallen a unit—they realize they were being fired on from behind, for instance, or that a carefully laid plan has been leaked.

But imagine an NPA unit which is being successfully shadowed by the military. How many of its members are likely to have no relatives in the army, to have no "lumpen experiences" or unresolved personal problems? Most of them will be "very active in the movement." But that's also the ethos. Keep active. (If only to keep your mind off sex.)

So the detection of DPAs could be a very bloody business indeed. There's another thing. While nobody doubts that the military has its agents, and that some of these get well entrenched in the NPA, you would have to know a great deal about what went wrong in, say, southern Tagalog before you could be sure that the problem had been created by DPAs. In most communist movements, power struggles or ideological purges have at some time or another been presented in similar terms. Unfortunately, despite all our vigilance, we were sabotaged by foreign agents, fascists, crypto-fascists, DPAs . . .

The DPA phenomenon seems to recur. I heard of a recent case in Surigao which sounded like the field of dragon's teeth. A whole company destroyed itself with imprisonment, torture, and executions. If such an event can be provoked by the presence of government agents in a unit, then the government has a truly awesome power at its disposal, and the guerrilla movement an awesome susceptibility. Mistakes were made, they will say, or excesses were committed, and those responsible have been seen "severely" punished.

But one must always ask why NPA should be prone to this kind of "mistake." To understand the success of the NPA, its fearful strengths as well as its fearful weaknesses, one might begin with the question of justice. Not justice in the abstract, but concrete justice at

the end of the remote, dusty road. You can stay in the Philippines—
you can be born and bred there—without ever getting a sense of life
in the distant barrio: the devastating helplessness and defenseless-
ness.

It might be that you are at the mercy of the weather or of
disease. It might be a mortgage or a loan on a crop. It might be cattle
rustlers or land grabbers. The cattle sleep beneath your hut—you live
with them for safety. Every night you tie the carabao's rope around
your neck, so that you will feel its every movement. But one morning you awake—the rope is cut and the animal is gone. That, they
say, "is like losing a limb."

A local landlord allows his fences to fall into disrepair. When
you complain that his animals are destroying your crop, his men
come and build new fences taking part of your land. At this point
you know that if you complain further you may be killed.

An illness in the family sends you straight into debt, a debt into
a mortgage, a mortgage into a foreclosure and a forced sale of land.
It can all happen slowly. More likely it will happen very fast. As with
a man I know who lost four children, in just over a week, during an
outbreak of measles. Then his wife had to go into the hospital . . .

At any moment the trapdoor may open under you. You are
responsible for your own physical protection: the long knife—the
bolo—you carry with you to the fields is more than a knife—it is a
sword. You have some reason to visit the next village. You strap on
your sword and you take a companion.

You can drive the length and breadth of Luzon, sticking to the
main road, and get no feeling for this. The roads attract houses and
small sums of money. They are ribbons of enterprise. You can
observe their economy very clearly from the air, beyond the ribbons,
the fields. Beyond the fields, the plantations. An hour's drive from
busy Laguna de Bay, a silent town with not a single private car. On
the plains of Mindanao, hidden Muslim villages still living in fear of
the last Christian massacre.

On a bleak, typhoon-swept shore, a community settling down
to the knowledge that for the next three months there will be strong
winds and no work.

There is the justice of the state—a complicated algebra of
money, gasoline, influence, luck, and time. There is the justice of the

gun—but who owns the gun? There is the justice of the sword in this world, and of God in the next—and the two are not exclusive, not at all. There is a Christ for the pickpockets, a Christ for the cutthroats, a Christ for the communists, and a Christ for their sworn enemies.

And the enmities go deep. Once, during the truce, I saw a police spy being caught during a peasant demonstration. The stewards surrounded the man while his ID was checked, and sure enough he was some kind of agent. The stewards kept the crowd at bay, but once or twice people slipped through the cordon, punched him once or twice and slipped away again. Finally, the stewards took the man to the police and handed him over, minus his ID. The police were at first uncertain what to do. But suddenly the man, who had hitherto looked only very frightened, remembered his pride. He wanted his ID back. He demanded it. He broke away from his captors and lunged into the crowd. He was going to get his ID even if they killed him.

At that point, police assumed responsibility. And if they had not taken him away, I could well believe that the man would have been killed. As it was, he was left with a burning sense of honor unredeemed. Maybe that night he would go out and kill someone.

Spy, informer, traitor—imagine the words on the lips of the distant village where you live. I know a group of friends among the poor fishermen of Quezon. They were an inseparable gang of mates—always joking together and amusing themselves with a highly developed comic routine. One day I arrive at the village and Baloloy's hut is empty. All that is left of his possessions is a light anchor made of stone and rattan, hanging in a tree.

"Baloloy is dead," laughs a woman, "No more *Kapitbahay*." I called him *Kapitbahay*, or neighbor, because his hut is next to the cottage I am renting. It turns out that, according to the village, Baloloy has made wholesale accusations against his friends, involving the illegal sale of milkfish fry. Now neither he nor his family can show their face in the village. As long as they stay where they have gone, three miles or so along the coast, they can remain nonpersons. All the old friends shake their heads and smile. Beyond the smile lies something absolute. "It's a shame," I say. Yes, they concede, it's a shame—no more *Kapitbahay*. Baloloy was so poor he had not yet even been able to have his three-year-old daughter baptized.

This preyed on his mind. He must have felt that he was being undermined by the other fishermen—he was working for the legal concessionaire; some of them weren't. But he must also have known that his protest was a kind of suicide, a suicide protest against the injustice in his life.

6

Teroy and I are sitting within sight of the Mayon Volcano. It is an object of national pride—a perfect cone. The smoke from the crater streams a short way down one side, then disperses horizontally into the atmosphere. It is as if people were standing on the edge emptying bags of feathers, which roll in lumps for a while until the air currents lift them off. Teroy has just explained how, in his system, you organize and consolidate a group of barrios.

"The next phase," he says, "we call cleaning."

Cleaning is when you kill the informers. "You get the masses with their *bolos* and you go to the informer's house and you say: 'Comrade, you have something to pay.'"

As he explains this, Teroy, in an instant, demonstrates his technique, and I am his model. He is coming at me, with one hand outstretched to grasp my shirt and the other holding aloft the imaginary *bolo*. Teroy smiles during the demonstration. I flinch. I can easily see him coming up the garden path with his *bolo* men.

I ask him how he can be sure who the informers are. There are three ways. First, most of them don't know how to keep a secret— they give themselves away. Secondly, the military doesn't know how to take care of its informers—they are seen with them. Lastly, the NPA have their own informers among the military.

And what happens to the families of the informers? Don't they become implacable enemies of the NPA?

Teroy points to a tall young man from his group. He is one of the best of his soldiers, has led several successful raids. This man's father was an informer, and from what Teroy said I concluded he had been executed at Teroy's instructions.

But such a strange case of transferred loyalty must be exceptional. On another occasion I was told that the best way with informers was to exile them from the village—precisely because of the reactions of the families.

But still, in general, revolutionary justice is marked by a series of strategic killings. When an area is being organized, the "semi-legal team" of two or more people move through the barrios making their first contacts and an ocular survey of secret trails and escape routes. They stay one night only in each barrio, moving backward and forward across the area setting up their initial organizations, the "Barrio Liaison Group," who begin the social investigation. They are looking for the poor or "lower middle" peasants. The middle-middle, the upper middle and the rich peasants are not good recruiting material. In a mixed group, the poor peasants will defer to them. What Teroy looks for is the peasant whose initiative and leadership qualities can be released from his lowly background. He will discover his own abilities—as it were, invent himself as he goes along. It is precisely the opposite approach to that of the Philippine Military Academy, which begins with the elite as its material.

Only when an area has been consolidated, with a complex set of groups, will the "cleaning" begin, and only when the cleaning has been achieved will the land reform be effective. For the land reform is like a surreptitious strike: All the peasants unite to report bad crops to their various landlords. Everyone has the same story, everyone will stick together. And thus the land rent is reduced.

You do not abolish the rent overnight, or take over the land. To do so is to ask the landlord to bring in the military or the private armies. Instead, you have to quietly let the landlord know that you are now an organized presence to be dealt with: "Time has changed, comrade. You can no longer have the deal you once enjoyed. But if you want to play straight with us, we'll play straight with you . . ."

The NPA often say that when they first move into an area it is the killing of cattle rustlers that wins them the decisive support. After that they are greeted like heroes. A man's family's way of life can change. Instead of living with the cattle they can put them in the pen overnight. The thieves are eliminated—the hoodlums go.

At the same time the NPA have acquired a monopoly of firearms, for among the first of their actions is the confiscation of guns from the farmers, and it is only after the consolidation has been completed that these may be handed back to their (trusted) owners.

But once an area has been consolidated it may soon receive the attention of the military. At this point the NPA makes a calculation about the level of activity they themselves will indulge in. If they go too far, they will "destroy their own mass base." There will be reprisals, mass evacuations, hamlettings.

And thus begins a period in which the advantages and disadvantages of being "consolidated" will be bitterly contested. If the regime works peacefully enough, it may look like a kind of justice. But if not, you will find that the answer to the question "What has the NPA done for you?" is a sharp "You mean, what have we done for them?"

————

7

Teroy is an extrovert—a revolutionary more in the Latin American than the Southeast Asian mode. He may use euphemisms like cleaning, but he, basically, tells you what he is up to and why. By now he is the overall NPA commmander for southern Luzon. The boast of his group is that it is they, the Bicol troops, who will in the end take Manila. And Teroy is a power-broker already, not just on the military fronts. During the truce he told me that traditional politicians of every shade of opinion approached him for this, that or the other deal. The constitution has been voted in (the NPA would have nothing to do with it) and that meant that there would be elections, first national, then local. Everyone was interested in the fact that people like Teroy had come out of hiding for a while, but the people most interested were the traditional politicians. Businessmen, landlords, and politicians have all been keen to deal with them—for a strict, perceived advantage. If you wanted evidence that the truce was working to the advantage of the NPA, Teroy would be evidence.

Jeff Tugawin, who comes from northern Luzon, is very different. Again, he was one of those leaders chosen to surface and make themselves known during the truce, but this was against the better judgment of men in his area, who had been fighting a hard battle in the Cagayan Valley and believed they were winning. Jeff and his group arrived late in metro Manila: they too had trouble with their safe-conduct passes, and trouble in believing in their validity once they had them. If Teroy had feared Colonel Abadilla, the man Jeff didn't trust was Colonel Rodolfo Aguinaldo—as it were, his opposite number in the Cagayan region.

By the time Jeff arrived in the capital, the talks which had taken so long to set up were proving something of a barren exercise. Each side felt that the other had nothing to say or offer. And in the meantime the military became increasingly outraged at the presence of the communists—on television, on the streets, even joining demonstrations, and with their own office in the National Press Club.

Jeff went on television and gave some interviews. In public he stuck to the agreed line. In private he was never expansive. I had known him for quite some time when he suddenly, to my surprise, asked if I would like to hear a song. He picked up a guitar and sang. "Suicide Is Simple" from *M.A.S.H.* He is a good guitarist and singer—you can easily imagine him as—when he was one—a Methodist youth leader. When he had finished his song, and I asked him for an NPA song, he looked at me as if I was mad. Jeff in the city— truce or no truce—was underground.

After January 22, when a group of protesters for land reform were massacred at Mendiola Bridge, everybody else went underground. The talks were finished. The office in the National Press Club was closed, and word was put out that all the communist delegates had gone to the hills.

Actually they didn't all go at once. They had a month left of safe conduct, for what that was worth. And a mass exodus from the capital would have made them particularly vulnerable.

Jeff had a long journey up north ahead of him. He was going first to a wedding of some comrades, and he invited me along to see a communist wedding. Nothing would arouse my curiosity less, in normal circumstances, but I did wonder if, one day, Jeff would actually talk.

He said of Teroy: "I like him—I wish I'd had more chance to meet him in Manila. He's amusing and full of ideas." Jeff's style was so different, so quiet and reserved, and I thought that in what he said about Teroy that he was implying a comparison with himself.

We eventually went up north, and Jeff hardly spoke along the way. But at the end, somehow, he seemed to explode. He said that now that the truce was over he could speak his mind, whereas before he had wanted to do so but had been constrained by party discipline. Jeff was dismayed at the sacrifices they had made for the truce—they had even released hostages they were holding—whereas his wife, prisoner of the military, had not been released. In Cagayan they had been winning against the military—why stop fighting now?

Indeed, as Jeff warmed to his theme, he said was it not a terrible thing that Salas, Rudolfo Salas, had been arrested in the course of the setting up of this truce. Salas had been right all along—said Jeff. "I even dare to say," he said, his eyes bright with outrage, "that the boycott in the Snap Election was right." When Cory stood against Marcos they had been right to have nothing to do with it. And after the victory of Cory, when Salas demoted and asked him to admit his mistakes, he had been defiant: "History will absolve us," he had said. And Jeff agreed. He is the convinced hardliner—have nothing to do with Cory or that junk about a truce.

There was only one thing that made people respect the NPA, he said, in all their struggle in Cagayan, and that was guns. "Politics is guns, guns, guns and it is nothing else." The idea that they could enter some kind of junior partnership in politics was rubbish. Until they had a leading position (fifty-five percent was how he put it) there was no point in talking to anybody.

"Guns, guns, guns and nothing else. Guns, guns, guns—and nothing else." I remember vividly how he spat the words out.

I asked him: "If it comes to the point where the communists take Manila, whose troops will do it? Will it be the guys from Bicol, or will it be the ones from Cagayan?"

Jeff laughed.

"You mean," he said, "will it be Teroy or me?"

"Yes."

"What do they say in Bicol?"

"They say they'll be the one to do it."

Jeff said: "If Teroy gets to Manila first," slight pause, "I'll be very happy for him."

KOREA

Kwangju and After

———

1

In 1980 I had, for personal reasons, to revisit Thailand. I hadn't wanted to. Indeed I had often vowed that I would never go back to the Far East. Also, I was absolutely determined never again to work as a foreign correspondent.

But there I was, staying at the Trocadero with several other journalists, and the conversation began to turn to South Korea. It seemed that the students had managed to throw the army out of a city called Kwangju, that they had armed themselves and taken the place over—an extraordinary event, an improbability, armed insurrection in one of the most authoritarian countries in the world.

Before long, the journalists' luggage began to appear in the hotel lobby, and anxious trips were made to travel agents. I watched all this with superior detachment. As far as I was concerned, they could keep South Korea, that terrifying place. It had one of the world's most efficient secret services. It crushed dissent at home and pursued it ruthlessly abroad. Its power struggles were bloody. Its soldiers had been the most detested foreign troops in Vietnam. It was a place to avoid.

But there was no question of my being sent there. I was a theater critic, on holiday. As I bade farewell to my departing colleagues, I congratulated myself on my escape.

Then, passing the reception desk, I noticed I had a cable. "Sorry to interrupt your holiday, James, but would you mind going to South Korea. . . ." Immediately I found myself thinking: South Korea! Of *course*, I'd *love* to go to South Korea. Just to *see* for myself what it's like. Having *heard* so much about it. Sounds *fascinating*.

I telephoned the *Sunday Times*. They wanted me, if possible, to get into Kwangju, which was by now sealed off by the army, but "Don't take any risks," they said; "we don't want blood and guts. . . ."

2

I didn't want "blood and guts" either. I arrived on a Sunday evening, which meant that I had five days or so before writing my piece. Somehow in that time I was going to have to acquaint myself with the broader issues in Korean politics. If I spent this time hanging around the roadblocks trying to get into Kwangju I might learn and see nothing. I knew nobody in Korea and hadn't any idea what I was going to do.

When the hotel bellboy extracted from me the information that I was a journalist, and when he immediately said, "You must go to Kwangju tomorrow," I became suspicious. I thought he was setting me up for some kind of trap. I paid him off and proceeded to run a bath. Just as I was stepping in, the phone rang. "Bellboy here!" A journalist from one of the agencies had just returned from Kwangju and was in the lobby. I must come down right away.

Quickly drying off the bathfoam suds, I pulled on my clothes and went down. The agency journalist was of Australian build, an intimidating figure in a Saigon safari suit. The tiny bellboy pointed him out and more or less ordered me to go and talk to him. The journalist was covered with the dust and sweat of the day. He didn't see why he should talk, nor could I see why he should. I did my best, before retreating in tongue-tied shame. And I had lost face with the bellboy. He couldn't see why I hadn't tried harder.

I retired to my room, took my clothes off, and stepped into the bath. At precisely that moment, the phone rang again. It was the bellboy. A French photographer had just flown in and was looking for someone with whom to share a car to Kwangju; we would have to take a car, because a public transport was blocked, and we would need packed lunches from the hotel, because there was no food in Kwangju: The bellboy had already found us a driver and was negotiating on our behalf; could I please come down at once.

By now, I thought: Either this bellboy is a genius, or I am about to fall into some horrible trap laid by the Korean CIA. But what can I do? I was already beginning to panic about my article. Even the *bellboy* seemed to be panicking about my article: I would have to leave at four in the morning, he told me; I would have to sleep early—he'd thought of everything.

The French photographer, slim, dark, hungry, and doomed, had just, he told me, flown over the North Pole to reach here, and the way he said it gave the impression that the polar route was something he had discovered, against all the odds, with a team of dogs. We made our arrangements and parted—I to my bath, which this time the bellboy allowed me to enjoy for five minutes before announcing the return of several more journalists from the south. By the end of the evening I had already met some people who had tried to get into Kwangju. Progress had been made. The bellboy watched me beadily as I pressed for the lift. "Did you order the packed lunches?" he asked. "I'm sorry, I didn't," I said, feeling drained and incompetent. "It's okay," he said, "*I* did."

3

In the dark, Etienne seemed to huddle for warmth against the rear seat of the car. "I wish I was back in Paris," he said, "in bed," and he paused before emphasizing "with a woman in my arms." He sounded as if he'd learned his French accent from a bad film whose lines kept coming back to him.

I'd seen Etienne before in Cambodia, and I wasn't entirely happy to be in his company. He gave the impression of a man forever traveling toward his death—a death that he was inviting you to mourn in advance. He was avid for nicotine and sympathy.

The highway was eerily empty, and the countryside at dawn was extremely beautiful. I felt as if we were traveling down the *autostrada del sole,* where a mysterious power had changed the vineyards into paddy fields. The agriculture was neat and intensive. Many of the fields were wrapped in polyethylene. The children went to school wearing cadet uniforms modeled after the Japanese style, which was in turn copied from Germany in the last century. Many of the houses had blue ceramic roofs. It was a cheerful sight.

Our driver seemed to be cast in the same mold as the hotel bellboy, for he was completely unfazed by the roadblocks. We left the highway and headed off into the hills, in order to approach Kwangju from the flank. And even on these narrow roads there were checkpoints, but each time—how, I couldn't tell—the driver managed to get us through by talking, talking, talking. By now, the countryside seemed much poorer—it felt as if we were going back centuries—and most of the villagers were in traditional dress.

We came down out of the hills to a town with broad streets. This was Kwangju. Or at least the driver said it was. Etienne was dismayed. There were soldiers everywhere. We thought that the army must have come back in, and that the insurrection was over.

Then came a moment of intense drama. We suddenly realized that the soldiers were not soldiers at all—these guys in uniforms and black, lobster-tail helmets were actually the students. Somehow or other we had crossed the lines.

The driver stopped. We left the car and walked a little way along a street. People hurried past us with averted faces. We stopped for a moment by a military truck, thinking that the slumped, helmeted figures in the cab were dead. But they were only sleeping. Then Etienne seemed to experience a rush of adrenaline. He shot off and I never saw him again.

I was very nervous. It takes a while, in any new country, to learn to read facial expressions and gestures. But here, barely able to guess who was who and what was what, I was completely disoriented and felt particularly unsafe. The driver could scarcely speak any English, though he was very keen to help. People gathered around the car and he asked them questions. An intense discussion followed, of which I was able to understand practically nothing, except the name of Chun Doo-hwan, continually repeated.

I walked toward the building that houses the regional admin-istration, which had been taken over by very frightened-looking armed students. In front lay a row of sixteen open coffins, containing as yet unidentified victims of the earlier massacre. In all, that day, I saw eighty coffins, but people were already saying what has been rumored since, that many, many more people had been killed. The military had, it seemed, run amok in the city. The students, in response, had raided the civil defense arsenals and with the help of the people forced the military to withdraw. And now, here they were, stuck with an insurrection. But the armed students were few in number—I reckoned there were about two hundred of them.

A woman made a signal to me to follow her, which I did, at a few paces. We went down a side street and, to my surprise, into the United States Information Service building. The janitor opened it up for us. The woman had been afraid to talk in the open. She said the place was full of spies. She was not from Kwangju herself—she had come down from Seoul at the start of the troubles, being a member, I supposed, of some dissident group. Now she was stuck here, and terrified they were all going to be killed.

She was desperate that the world outside should be told the truth of what was happening. Only if the foreign press reported the truth would there be any chance of saving the students. "You are our corridor to life," she said. Later in the day, I kept being asked by people: "Are you going to tell the truth about us?" Government propaganda had branded the insurrectionists as communists. They were not communists, they insisted. They wanted democracy. They wanted an end to the power of General Chun Doo-hwan and the KCIA.

Some people said they were not "with" the students. They were not in favor of the use of arms. But they were of one voice in saying that the students were their sons, and that if the army came in the students would be put to death. That was why they kept saying: "Tell the truth about us."

I didn't meet up with any of the foreign journalists there, but afterward everyone had had the same horrible impression of doomed children. A couple of school students took me around the hospitals in what turned out to be a vain search for casualties. There were reasons why both bodies and the wounded might be whisked way by families, for many people would want to hide the fact that a child of theirs had been involved. The disgrace would spread. Relatives would lose jobs. They would fall under suspicion. I remember my schoolboy companions saying that they too might soon be killed.

The day was as scaring as it was frustrating. It was so hard to find anyone who spoke more than a few words of English. Hard, too, to find people who wanted to talk in public. When the driver finally said it was time to go, a part of me was relieved that I did not have the money simply to pay him off, and stay. To the voice that said, "Don't go now, coward," another voice replied, "You must only take calculated risks." And: "Anyway, you're a theater critic." And: "These people have told you to go out and tell the truth about them."

Etienne was not to be found. I knew anyway that nothing would make him leave now. We got in the car and drove along the wide empty streets, the way we had come in. People were standing in doorways and on the low roofs of the houses. Suddenly I noticed we were driving straight toward a line of tanks and soldiers. Maybe we couldn't get out after all.

I tapped the driver on the arm. With astonishing calm, he took stock of the situation and performed a very slow U-turn. We tried a few side streets and soon enough were out of the city and back in the hills. We remembered the bellboy's packed lunches. Neither of us had eaten all day.

The driver stopped in a small village, where he astonished me again by walking straight into the police station and asking if we might eat our lunches there. It was the last thing I would have expected to do in a police state.

As we ate, the driver chatted away to the policemen, who were friendly types and clearly avid for news of Kwangju. I suddenly thought: So that was it—the driver was an agent all along, and I was simply being used as his cover. Now he is making his report.

But later, as we drove along the expressway through the dark, I noticed that he and the other drivers always flashed their lights at each other to warn about upcoming checkpoints. The people on the road seemed to be in prudent league against the forces of the state. Nor did it seem so likely that the village police of Cholla province were playing much part in the military operation to clear up Kwangju. I liked the driver. He had done a great job. I was less happy about the job I had done.

The next morning, on waking, I phoned Reuters to introduce myself. "Well, you've heard the news then, I suppose?" said a tired voice. "It's all over. They went in last night and fought it out."

4

When President Park Chung-hee was assassinated on October 26, 1979, his place was taken by Choi Kyu-hah, who, while in no sense the power that Park had been, became the focus of expectations. He was supposed to be going to rewrite the constitution. People saw the chance of having a democracy.

General Chun Doo-hwan, who had commanded the Armed Forces Security Command, was placed in charge of investigations into Park's assassination. On December 12 that year Chun mounted a coup with the aid of General Roh Tae-woo, removing some twenty generals and cutting short a series of hitherto promising military careers. There followed a rash of resignations from the military, as people realized they had no future any longer. A new group was at the helm.

Quite what the future held was uncertain. There were three leading politicians: Kim Jong-pil, of Park's group; Kim Young-sam, from the opposition; and the hero of the students, Kim Dae-jung, the man who had once been kidnapped from exile in Japan and brought back to house arrest in Korea. Kim Dae-jung had run against Park in 1971. His capture in 1973 might well have led to his death, thrown overboard in the Sea of Japan. But an American plane spotted the KCIA boat, and diplomatic pressure saved him.

By the spring of 1980, the so-called Seoul Spring, the pressure for democratization was very strong. The business community, uncertain which of the leading candidates to support, dug into its pockets and supported them all. Meanwhile the military clammed up, uncertain about its own structure, and maintaining its intense dislike of democracy.

The kind of democracy being talked about was not, at least in the eyes of the business community, anything radical, idealistic, or necessarily libertarian. The businessmen felt, though, that they were storing up trouble for themselves if they put off the establishment of free trade unions. They looked at trade unionism and democracy as things to be installed as part of the modernization of society. The military was anachronistic. That was the trouble with them. People felt they had outgrown dictatorship, censorship, and the other forms of repression. The military was diverting attention and effort away from the development of a modern society.

But at the same time as people talked, debated, demonstrated over these issues, General Chun was moving toward total power. In April he was made acting head of the KCIA. On May 17 he arrested all the key democratic leaders and extended martial law. The next day he sent in the paratroopers to Kwangju and the killings began. The insurrection that followed, and its crushing, marked the end of the Seoul Spring.

A couple of hours after I left Kwangju, the army delivered its ultimatum. The students who were defending their building called to the people to come out onto the streets. But the people stayed indoors. The journalists who had spent time with the students remembered one leader in particular as having been extraordinarily impressive. He had said he would die at his post. And the next morning they found him shot in the chest with the grenade he had been about to throw still in his hand.

Etienne's photographs told the last of the story—the beating into submission of the students, the mass arrests.

People talked, unrealistically, about Chun being made to take the blame. But Chun was unstoppable. A week after crushing Kwangju he relinquished his post in the KCIA: He no longer needed that power. He became instead head of the Standing Committee for National Security Measures—which exerted military control over the civilian government. By mid-August, Kim Dae-jung was on trial—he would be made to take the blame for Kwangju. By the end of the month Chun was "temporary president." The next year he was "elected" to that office.

At the time of Kwangju, people had only recently begun to worry about the character of Chun. He had a reputation for puritanism, conviction, and a dangerous sense of mission as his country's only savior. The students detested and feared him. The businessmen looked on him with distaste and apprehension. I remember a man asking me, in those days, wasn't it true that we in England had once had a character called Cromwell, and hadn't he, well, not been such a bad thing after all? This was said in a spirit of weariness that seemed to mean: maybe we *have* to suffer Chun, maybe it's just a stage we have to go through, as other countries have suffered before us.

5

The Official Chun

The blessed will not care what angle they are regarded from,
Having nothing to hide.

—*W. H. Auden*

But the rest of us, whether we are dictators or doormen, we *do* mind. And if we are dictators we take steps—or people take steps on our behalf—to see that we are viewed in the best possible light. The following stories are retold from *Chun Doo-hwan, Man of Destiny* by Cheon Kum Sung, translated by W. Y. Joh, North American Press, 1982.

245

Remarkable Circumstances Attending His Birth

Mrs. Chun had produced other sons, but they had died, and only the daughters survived. Because of this, Mr. Chun was thinking of leaving her. Then Mrs. Chun had a dream in which three men and one woman walked down a rainbow to her house. The first was clad in cobalt blue. The second had broad shoulders and a majestic face. There was a crown on his head.

The second dream figure was her second living son, and he was christened Doo-hwan. He had a dark spot on his right wrist, which was connected with another premonitory dream in which Mrs. Chun had tried to catch the moon in her skirt. This birthmark earned Chun the childhood nickname Spotty.

On the Character of Mrs. Chun

When Spotty was one year old, a monk came begging at his home. Mrs. Chun gave the monk a handful of barley. He lingered at the gate, as if wanting to say something. Later a neighbor came running to Mrs. Chun, exclaiming: "I overheard the monk saying to himself that you would see one of your sons grow up to be a great man, but your buck teeth might hinder that."

Mrs. Chun chased the monk and asked what he was on about. The monk said: "I wanted to tell you that your physiognomy indicates you are going to be the mother of a great man, but your protruding front teeth may get in the way. Being a novice monk yet, I had no nerve to say that before. Anyway, may Buddha bless you!"

Mrs. Chun determined to get rid of her teeth. She tied herself to one of the log pillars of the house and struck it hard, thinking: "I'll do anything for my children, no matter what!" She lost the teeth, but was ill for two and a half months.

On the Character of Spotty

————

Spotty was strong, honest, and brave. Other people, forced by hunger, used to rob the local potato field. If the owner caught them, he would strip them of their clothes.

One day the owner grabbed Spotty and accused him of stealing potatoes.

"No, I did not," said Spotty. "I never do anything I think is wrong. Look at my clean hands."

"You are Doo-hwan, the Spotty, aren't you?" said the owner.

"Yes, I am," said Spotty.

"You are different from the others, Spotty," said the owner of the field.

Spotty was not yet eight.

On the Character of Mr. Chun

————

Under the Japanese occupation, Spotty's father was administrator of their village. This brought him into conflict with the local Japanese police chief. One day, the chief insulted Spotty's father on a lonely road. The father picked the police chief up by the waist and threw him over a cliff. Then he threw his bicycle after him.

Mr. Chun thought: Good riddance. But "he also felt some compunction for he had committed a crime for the first time in his life."

It turned out, however, that the police chief survived the fall, with some broken bones. The family was obliged to flee to Manchuria.

At Primary School, Manchuria, 1940–41

————

Spotty did well. Soccer was his favorite sport.

Back in Taegu, Korea

Unable to afford school, he bought the second-grade textbooks and mastered them in under two months. He had a newspaper round of fifty homes nobody else was prepared to visit. Once he was almost bitten by a huge dog. "Scared to death, he fainted on the early morning street." He still does not like dogs.

Abraham Lincoln became his idol. He "made up his mind to become a man of strong will like the American president."

Just Before the Korean War

Taegu Public Technical High School was infiltrated by leftists, with destructive slogans such as: "Refuse classes and drive out the reactionary teachers!" Doo-hwan challenged the infiltrators, in spite of their threats and their seniority to him. To a club-wielding student he said defiantly: "Don't be silly! What do you think we know about politics? We are just students. We are supposed to study, not boycott classes. Concentrating on our study is our way of contributing to our country!" and so forth.

The leftist students flinched. His classmates shouted: "Doo-hwan is right! We are students. We must study!"

The machinery department, thanks to Doo-hwan's leadership, was the only part of the school to refuse to join the boycott.

The Korean Military Academy

In 1951 the Korean Military Academy began its first four-year courses. That year's intake was called the eleventh class (it is they who came to power after the assassination of Park Chung-hee). They were the first to be subjected to the full West Point treatment, which included four hundred examinations a year. If you went below sixty-seven percent in more than one subject, you were obliged to leave.

Doo-hwan was below average scholastically. His math dragged him down. On the other hand, reading philosophy he "acquired insight into the meaning of the universe, human beings, and life and death." His grades were not good, but he comforted himself with the thought that General Dwight D. Eisenhower, also no genius, had been an outstanding athlete at West Point. Doo-whan was good at soccer, basketball, and boxing. He was captain and goalkeeper of the academy soccer team.

Lieutenant Principle

Of the 228 admitted to the eleventh class, only 156 graduated from the academy. Some were flunked, others expelled for lying, stealing, or cheating. You were also expelled for failing to report lying, stealing, or cheating.

Commissioned as a second lieutenant in 1955, Doo-hwan earned a new nickname—Lieutenant Principle. He always went by the book. He eschewed moral slacknesses such as bribery. Two officer candidates brought him a gift of cigarettes. It was a sweetener. Spotty ordered them to stretch out in the push-up position, and paddled them five times each with a pole.

Well, thought the officer candidates, he is not called Lieutenant Principle for nothing.

When one of his academy classmates was discovered to have borrowed some money from an officer candidate, Spotty persuaded a meeting of the classmates that this man too should be paddled. The officers took turns, with a bat, in the "spirit of the military academy."

Spotty was also known as Lieutenant Jet-Plane. He had a habit of arriving out of nowhere.

In the fullness of time, although poor, he won the hand of the daughter of the head of the academy.

On the Character of the New Mrs. Chun

She gave up medical school to marry him, took up hair-styling instead, and graduated from the course "at the top of her class." Then, to be at home more for his sake, she changed to piece-work knitting. A friend found her at home one day with a book of military strategy and an English-Korean dictionary. The friend asked if the new Mrs. Chun were studying English or military science.

"No," said the new Mrs. Chun, "I was just looking up in the dictionary those words my husband had underlined."

Doo-hwan and Democracy

It was in one of his training courses in America that Spotty decided his countrymen were mistreating democracy because they had not understood it: They confused democracy with freedom without responsibility.

Something had to be done about this problem.

Doo-hwan meets General Park

In a fiercely proud encounter, on the second day of Park's coup, Spotty (then a captain, with well-built body, piercing eyes, and firm jaw) argued his way into the office of Park Chung-Hee and blatantly challenged him as to whether he was just a corrupt military officer like the rest. Convinced by Park that the revolution was just and necessary, Spotty made his contribution to the coup—he persuaded the Military Academy to join Park. This action "helped the Americans and other foreigners to understand the situation in the country better."

Park later said: "That Captain Chun Doo-hwan is *some* man. He did what I had not even thought of!"

Doo-hwan in Vietnam

He made a point of always being prepared for death. He used to say to his men: "Do you want your enemy to see your dead body, should you die, in dirty underwear?"

Doo-hwan in Seoul, 1979

By now he is a general. We see him in his modest home, sitting "face to face" with his wife and four children. It is December 12— the twelfth of the twelfth. The air is "tense as if something [is] going to happen that night."

He asks his family: "Would you let yourself be swept away in a big stream which you do not think is flowing the right way, or would you try to make the stream flow in the direction you think is right, even if you have to risk your own life doing that?"

And his children reply with one voice: "The latter, father." But his wife stares out of the window.

"All right, children," says Doo-hwan firmly; "should the worst happen to me tonight and should disgrace, contempt, and hardship befall you, never panic or despair."

"Leaving these words behind," our biographer concludes, "the General went out into the darkness of the bitterly cold night. The rest is history."

6

. . . a phrase that seems to imply that everyone knows what happened on December 12, and why twenty generals were either arrested or killed. But these matters were never publicly discussed until late 1987, when they were used in the election campaign to discredit Roh Tae-woo, who, as a putschist, helped Chun to power.

It is the same with Kwangju. I know a former soldier who was involved in the massacre, but he has sworn never to say what happened during those ten days. The parents of the dead have often been vocal in their demands for a full inquiry. But they were soon split into two camps, one group accepting compensation and agreeing to move their children's graves from the cemetery, the other group refusing, and claiming that there was yet a third group who had never come out and admitted the loss of their children. To substantiate a figure of two thousand killed, you would have to know exactly what happened on May 21, when the martial law police started firing at citizens in front of the provincial capital (before that, they had been using bayonets, and it is said that on the outskirts of the city they were using guns). You would have to know whether it was true that citizens who died on the outskirts were ferried away by helicopter. You would have to be able to count the graves in the mountains, and so forth.

For my own part, when I finally returned to Kwangju several years later, I was appalled at my inability to recollect the places I had seen: A main square and a fountain that were firmly fixed in my mind turned out to have been imported from some other city somewhere in the world, as if they had been refurbished in a dream. All I could definitely retrace was the route down a side street to the USIS building, where I had followed the frightened woman. The confusion of the day had triumphed over the other impressions.

———

7

Economically speaking, Chun's Fifth Republic was a triumph. And a part of that triumph expressed itself in the architecture of the dictatorship: the grandiose zoo outside of Seoul, with its staggering parking lot; the Great Hall of the Nation, with its adjacent museum devoted to the history of the Korean struggle against the Japanese, and its hideous chamber of Japanese horrors; and then, above all, the remodeling of the capital for the Olympic Games, with so many sports facilities that the world could not wait to participate.

The propaganda value of all this was consistent not only with Chun's vision of himself as the sporting man of destiny, the goalkeeper general, the referee. There was also a totemic significance to the Games. It is deeply felt and believed that it was the Tokyo Olympics that marked the moment when Japan took its place among the great nations of the postwar world, and it is a deeply held belief, in the obscurest regions of Korean thought, that a great future lies in store for the divided country. After the Olympics, Korea can take its rightful place in the world.

As the Olympic plans progressed, many people expected that Chun would choose the moment of his victory to retire in the post-Games euphoria. He had made emphatically public his desire to be the first president of South Korea to enjoy a peaceful transition from power. Now here he was saying he would step down *before* the Games. And everyone was certain he would want to fix the succession.

Thus it was that an immensely complex set of rival plans began to shape the future of the nation: Chun and his one-time Sports Minister Roh Tae-woo, planning to install the stadiums, the roads, the underground, the succession of power; and the opposition, planning to install the democracy—*their* contribution to the modernization of the country. Thus it was that the South Korean government, which had never been shy of defying the Americans, suddenly became anxious about the International Olympic Committee. Korea in general, North and South, had been immune to world opinion. Now came the great diplomatic offensive.

Another thing had happened, which had changed a great number of minds: A popular uprising had overthrown President Marcos in 1986. A bloodless revolution! Filipinos, who are notably sensitive to the way they are treated around the world, soon began to report that in South Korea they were considered celebrities. I saw this myself when I returned to Seoul in November 1986 in the company of a Filipino photographer. People were avid to talk to Bing. I basked in his reflected glory.

In those days, Seoul was still very visibly kept under tight control. Plainclothes thugs stood with folded arms at the entrance to every underpass and in front of the large downtown buildings. The opposition held protests which it broadcast by loudspeaker from an upper story of an office block. There were protests on the campuses, but the downtown streets were absolutely off limits.

Kim Dae-jung, whom I interviewed under house arrest, was very alert to the Filipino comparison. Like Ninoy Aquino, he had been condemned to death, allowed into exile in the States, and had then decided, after Ninoy's assassination, to "do a Ninoy" and return to his country. That had been in February 1985. Now he was full of talk about people power.

The opposition was adamant that the touchstone for the democracy would be direct presidential elections. The government was adamant that these would not happen. Kim Dae-jung had just announced that if the government gave in to the opposition's demands, he would not run for the presidency. The government was not impressed by this: Kim's political rights had been suspended. There was no question, in their view, of his running for anything.

I remember one day sitting in the garden of the Toksugung Palace, near the City Hall. There were rumors of disturbances outside, and police had been placed near the palace gates to prevent any students coming in and demonstrating. One plainclothesman was keen to talk.

In a short while he knew where I came from, what hotel I was staying in, and what my job was. That seemed par for the course. When I told him that I now lived in the Philippines, his interest became intense. He asked me what I thought of his country. I told him what had long been the truth—that I liked his country and his people very much. When he asked what I thought of the political situation, I made some kind of diplomatic reply. I had only, after all, been here twice before in my life—once for a quick visit as a tourist, and once in 1980.

The date hung in the air between us.

"Yes," I said, "it was at the time of Kwangju."

"You were *there?*"

I changed the subject. He had been a sociology student. Now he was doing his national service. His job today was to keep an eye out in the direction of the American ambassador's residence. I asked him what he would do after finishing his national service. He said he would resume his studies.

I asked him why the students were so angry now. He said in a measured way, "Because *they* think they are the only hope for democracy."

And from now on in the conversation there seemed to be an understanding between us that if I refrained from asking him *his* views, he would tell me what some people thought. For instance, he said that *some* people were very shocked at Kim Dae-jung's announcement that he would not run in a direct presidential election. *Some* people hoped that he would change his mind.

Of course there was always the possibility that I was being egged on to say something subversive. But what I felt, during our conversation, was that I was meeting a man with a very common predicament. He had to sit out his national service. In the end, he would return to the university and be able to speak for his former beliefs. Today, however, his job was to stop the students from demonstrating. He couldn't do anything about that fact.

As you would expect, wherever there is national service, the armed forces contain a broad representation of popular opinion. The views of the officer class are only part of the story.

In exchange for what he had told me, I told him what little I knew about Kwangju. And he made absolutely no comment.

8

One Day in June 1987

"They don't use guns or truncheons particularly," said somebody's ambassador, "but they do use an awful lot of tear gas. And it's terrible. It sticks to your clothes and your skin. And they fire it practically at point-blank range." The ambassador sneezed. "There," he said, "it's begun already." And he looked vaguely out of the sealed window.

I couldn't smell anything. I could hear in the distance the

broadcast voices of the opposition, calling out like muezzins over downtown Seoul, but this was hours before the demonstration was due to begin. My companion sniffed again. "Oh," he said, "in this place, whenever somebody sneezes they think it's tear gas."

And he began to elaborate, very elegantly, on a line of argument that was not uncommon among foreigners in Seoul: In the West, the Two Kims (Kim Young-sam and Kim Dae-jung), being opposition leaders, were identified with the cause of democracy. But it would be quite wrong to believe that if either of them took power there would be democracy in South Korea. You had only to look at the way they dealt with their own followers to see that they were autocratic and uncompromising. A political party in South Korea is not a group of people with a common platform—it is a loose coalition around certain personalities aiming at power.

And indeed you had only to look at the way Kim Dae-jung's followers behaved to feel that such an argument was attractive. There was a kind of awe with which he was treated, within the confines of his house arrest. He was a king in his living room.

And yet if the argument between the ruling party and the opposition was simply about power, it seemed incomprehensible. Why would Kim Dae-jung have risked his life for so long, as he indubitably had? And why would the supporters of the Kims risk theirs? Why were so many people prepared—people who enjoyed no kind of indirect protection from international opinion, or from the United States—to risk everything: not just the possibility of torture and death, the certainty that if arrested they would be banished to the margins of the society.

I tried to put this to the ambassador but we did not get very far. A remarkable thing began to happen to him, as we talked. He appeared to have been tear-gassed. At first he was too polite to show it, but soon he was coughing and his eyes were watering. I thanked him very much and left.

Back in my hotel room, I looked down at the adjacent building site, a deep pit cut in the rock. Every afternoon they would set little explosive charges all over its surface, and I used to be fascinated to watch the progress of the work.

On my desk lay a photograph of much the same city view, taken in 1951. If you had known Seoul before the Korean War, and now you returned, you might find your bearings perhaps from the skyline of granite mountains, still visible from so much of the city. Then there were the large Japanese buildings in the Wilhelmine style—the Capitol and the railway station—and then the soon-to-be demolished City Hall. But as my photograph showed, you wouldn't recognize much more because the rest was burned during the retreat of the United Nations forces.

After the war, a generation of buildings grew up on modest plots of land that must correspond to the old street design. There is a complex system of back alleys, where you can still find (but they are disappearing) areas of traditional architecture—small private houses built around courtyards, inns, restaurants, bathhouses, artisans' shops.

With prosperity came the latest generation of high-rise schemes, which radically obliterated the street plan—schemes like the great hole into which I was gazing, where a large corporation would build a prestige block. The old entertainment district which I remembered from my first visit seemed to have disappeared beneath these prestige ventures or to have moved either upmarket or elsewhere.

No doubt somewhere in this great exploded hole they would accommodate the "room-restaurants" and high class saunas for the daily comfort of the businessmen, along with the proliferating luxury shops. But the tendency of the city, as it modernized, was to simplify and to drive the street life literally underground into the extraordinary network of granite-lined underpasses. You can walk through much of Seoul without emerging into the daylight more than once or twice.

Should the city be bombed or shelled, this complex underground might be very useful—or a deathtrap. Its role in the defense of Seoul is demonstrated during the regular monthly defense routines, when the sirens clear the streets in a trice. (London during the Blitz seems to have been the inspirational example: Once, in the remote countryside of Korea, I met a man who talked at some length about the discipline the British had shown then—it was almost the only thing he knew about my country.) But during the weeks of rioting there were parts of the underground that became intolerable because of tear gas.

At the nub of one of these underground arcade systems rises the Lotte Hotel, which was built by a chewing-gum magnate of a romantic disposition. (He named the chewing gum, and the hotel, after the heroine of Goethe's *Werther*.) This enormous complex has doubled in size since I first saw it. I would never dream of staying at the Lotte, but on a cold day it makes an excellent place to take a walk—visit the department store, the arcades, the bakery, the dentist, the health farm, whatever you fancy.

Hotels like the Lotte are built to impress the Japanese (Seoul really doesn't bother to impress the Americans anymore—money seeks to impress money). The showpiece is the atrium lobby/lounge, with its large picture window behind which a waterfall cascades over a natural arrangement of rocks and trees. Late at night, when the band has finished playing and the bar closes down, they throw a switch—and turn off the waterfall.

On this day, a demonstration was due to start outside the Lotte Hotel at five in the evening and to make its way to the Anglican cathedral, just on the other side of City Hall. But the cathedral had already been cordoned off the previous day, and the plaza in front of the City Hall was forbidden as usual to demonstrators. There were rows of riot police, with their black leather lobster-tail helmets—the Kagemusha brigade, as we used to call them.

In the morning, the Kagemushas were joined by the snatch squads, the plainclothesmen in crash helmets and matching parkas. Tens of thousands of men were going to stop the demonstrators from reaching the Anglican cathedral—a simple enough task, since the cathedral is in a little back street. But no chances were being taken. The government had declared the demonstration "impure." Anything was impure that gave comfort to the enemy. Anything at all could be said to give such comfort.

Shortly before five, I put on my paper smog-mask and began to stroll toward City Hall, looking for demonstrators. The police were all around, and the tear gas was already strong. I was not properly kitted out. The journalists and photographers, who were by now used to the rules of rioting, had taken to wearing hard hats, gas masks, and plastic armbands identifying them as press. My paper mask was inadequate for the tear gas.

And it felt odd to be in a large city, looking for a riot, when all you could see was a thin sprinkling of civilians and a thick sprinkling of actually rioting police. I looked down the broad streets and wondered: Who are those troops in medieval armor actually attacking? Nobody's attacking them—with their personal mini-fire-extinguishers tied to their belts, and their side-vented gas masks giving them the look of cubist wolves.

It was only later that I began to understand that the police were not necessarily wrong to consider every bystander a rioter, for the Korean crowd on these occasions had in fact developed the habit of loitering innocently, then suddenly attacking opportunistically. And it was true, too, in those days, that the most respectably dressed businessman might suddenly turn into a demonstrator. The buzz was that this time the middle class was on the side of the students, and it was rumored that the students themselves had taken to dressing up like businessmen in order to reinforce this impression.

Still, the most committed of the demonstrators were instantly recognizable. The skin of their faces was burned and bleached from the gas. They wore Clingfilm over their eyes, or they smeared toothpaste over their cheeks. When they ran away from an attack, they ran backward so they would not be hit by the lobbed shells. Every civilian knew that you must never rub your eyes when they stung. Everyone carried handkerchiefs.

When the tear gas really hits you for the first time and you burst into tears, the first thing you feel is sorry for yourself. You think: My god, I'm crying—a tragedy must have befallen me. Then, if you can bear to think at all, this weeping strikes you as funny—this sudden illusion of grief. And then, *then* you really do feel sorry for yourself.

Outside the Lotte Hotel, I began to recognize members of the opposition. The demonstration was about to begin in earnest. But such was the strength of the gas, as the demonstrators came past me with their faces in their hands, I gave up. I couldn't see anymore.

I went into the hotel. I needed to talk to people. I had an article to write that night. But the trouble is, in those circumstances, you can't bear to go up to somebody who has been gassed because you know that the stuff (which is in fact a fine powder) will be all over their clothes. And you don't want to approach someone who has not been gassed, because you will be doing them a disservice.

Now I saw that it would be hard to leave the hotel, because the crowds were rushing the revolving doors. I could see that even if I got into the revolving compartment, I might get stuck there, revolving, with a host of other people drenched in gas. A hideous fate.

I turned to the atrium lounge, with its high ceiling and its welcome open space. A few foreign businessmen and tourists were sitting drinking there, served by beautiful ladies in teapot skirts. Sitting as far away from them as I could, I stank and wept by myself. The understanding ladies brought handkerchiefs, peanuts, and beer. An absurd range of fancy drinks was available. The demonstration became smellably closer, the foreigners departed, and the ladies burst into tears.

And now a riot broke out in the lobby. You could hear it, but it was literally true that if you walked from the high lounge into the lobby you couldn't see a thing. You were blinded. You could hear scuffles. You could hear people singing patriotic songs and the Korean version of "We Shall Overcome." It was hard to imagine how anyone could physically sing in such conditions.

The wall of tear gas advanced. I found myself backed up against that gigantic plate-glass picture window, looking out at the waterfall, the miniature pines, the Japanese maples, the pretty rocks, and the koi carp in the pool. I wished I could get out there, but we were all trapped.

There was a great noise of fighting in the lobby, and suddenly a nimble figure with clingfilm over his eyes vaulted a rococo glass-and-metal barrier and rushed across the lounge in my direction, looking over his shoulder as if in fear of pursuit. Reaching my chair, he crouched behind it, trembling and breathing heavily. I made him understand that the best thing for him to do (since no one had yet pursued him) was to sit down and join me for a drink.

Taking the clingfilm off his eyes, the student (he was in business management) suddenly became formal and immensely respectful. He accepted an orange juice and calmed down.

When the time came to talk, I asked him the question that had been at the back of my mind all day: Did he and people like him believe that with the two Kims they would get democracy.

What he said was just this: He didn't believe that victory of the two Kims would guarantee anything—it was simply that, under them, the country had a better *chance* for democracy. Nothing more.

Such were the people who were facing the tear gas and the police snatch squads that June.

9

It was a remarkable time, and I developed a most unusual routine. In the mornings, I relaxed in my room, reading Wordsworth. The students normally began rioting after lunch. By now I had my kit—gas mask, hard hat, armband—which I would set off with, in the direction of the universities. Evenings were for writing stories, and comparing notes with friends.

Seoul was everywhere contaminated. People moved into the upper stories of hotels, only to find that the air conditioning sucked up the tear gas and made their rooms uninhabitable. One prayed for rain, or the hoses of the municipal authorities. People stopped in the streets to listen to the loudspeakers of the opposition. Around the city there were illuminated signs counting down the number of days to the Olympic Games, which were now, with all the disturbances, in jeopardy. There is a Korean superstition about the number 4, which is the character for death. (Hotels and office blocks either do not have a fourth floor or, in the elevators, they spell the number out.) There was an idea that, when it was 444 days to the Olympic Games, a major catastrophe would occur.

The government and the ruling party made menacing noises about the opposition. The situation had been deteriorating since April 13, when President Chun had put a stop to the constitutional debate. On June 10, Roh Tae-woo had been proclaimed the presidential candidate of the ruling party which meant in effect that he was president-elect. From that day on, the country was in an uproar, which the widespread arrests did nothing to contain.

On June 24, Kim Young-sam was finally able to meet with President Chun to present the demands of the opposition. Their conversation was formal, meaningless, and absurd.

K.Y-S: "I believe all political leaders are seriously concerned about the current situation. And yet I understand, Mr. President, you are the one who is most painstakingly working on it. I hope we will be able to exchange frank views. Some [people] doubt that the seriousness of the situation has been accurately reported to you."

Chun: "I have been receiving detailed reports from various sources. In fact, I have been smoking heavily because of the pressure of reading so many reports."

Kim Young-sam came away having made all the obvious suggestions, with cringing politeness, and without anything by way of results. But within the ruling party itself, the pressure for reform was beginning to be felt. The riots had forced a new realism.

It was Roh Tae-woo who, in the end, made the public gesture of capitulation, and he did it with such style, and so absolutely, it took the breath away. Somebody somehow decided that the only way to outflank the opposition was to take all their central ideas and turn them into orthodoxy. From now on, Roh Tae-woo said, there should be direct presidential elections. There should be amnesty for political prisoners. Kim Dae-jung should have his rights restored. Habeas corpus should be extended. There should be a free press. He—Roh Tae-woo—was making these demands, and if the president did not agree, then Roh would resign from his presidential candicacy and from his chairmanship of the ruling party.

So Roh went and stood before Chun, like God the Son before God the Father in *Paradise Lost,* ready to make the sacrifice of becoming a man, ready to be crucified at the ballot. And of course there was an element of the charade in this: Roh threatening Chun, Chun taking a couple of days to agree to Roh's demands. But there was also something real in the capitulation. From now on, the ruling party became the proponents of the demands of the Seoul Spring— albeit in their own subtle version—while the opposition was lost for a platform.

You saw the effect immediately on the industrial front. Suddenly there was a wave of strikes. Official unions were disbanded and new ones took their place. And the government supported their wage demands. Suddenly large numbers of prisoners were released. Suddenly people were allowed to demonstrate.

Throughout the period of the disturbances, a student called Lee

Han-yol had lain in a coma after having been hit on the head by a tear-gas grenade. Really it was astonishing that there had not been many more such casualties. But life is not cheap in Korea, and much attention had been focused on the fate of this young man and on his death.

On the day of Lee's funeral, political rights were restored to Kim Dae-jung and two thousand others. The placatory gestures of the government continued, and, to the surprise of many, the funeral procession was allowed to pass through the city center unopposed. There was an enormous crowd—even those who claimed expertly that it was not as enormous as all that had to reach back to the days of Eisenhower for a comparison.

For once, now, you could see the strength of the opposition, rather than, as before, a confusing blur of running figures with streaming eyes. The traffic stopped. The City Plaza and the roads leading off were filled. Every building was obliged by the students to lower its flags to half mast. On City Hall, the Olympic flag itself was removed.

But one veto remained. There would be no march in the direction of the Blue House, Chun's residence. And it was only later in the day, when this veto was challenged, that the riot police moved in and the pitched battles began.

Watching the scenes that day, awed by the solemnity and determination of the crowd, I doubt if most people would have realized that the movement had reached its peak, that the insurrection was over. Unless perhaps someone very cynical, in the ruling Democratic Justice party perhaps, knew in advance that the key to the future lay in the reenfranchisement of Kim Dae-jung. Already since his release from house arrest Kim had given interviews to four hundred members of the foreign press. Already he had been visited by the U.S. ambassador. Though he had said before that, given the concession already made, he would not run for the presidency, he was now back in the legitimate arena. He would be able to revisit Kwangju, and his own province of Cholla. He would hear the call of the people. He would have to run.

And if he ran, it followed absolutely that Kim Young-sam would run. He too would hear the voice of the people. The rivalry of the two Kims was an ineluctable fact of political life. They dogged each other's steps. They copied each other's moves. They fought inseparably.

For weeks and months they assured the people that they would sort this matter out—that there would be only one opposition candidate. And to the very last, Kim Dae-jung said that if it seemed that his candidacy was going to lose the opposition the election, he would step down. People went to the lengths of committing suicide to beg the two Kims to see sense. But they had rival courts and rival certainties.

In the meantime the retired four-star general, Roh Tae-woo, was hiring his image-builders and planning his campaign. He was to sell himself as the Man with Big Ears, the good listener, the Ordinary Man. He would usher in, his advertisers said, a Great Era for the Ordinary Man.

10

On the Road with Mr. Roh

Early one morning in December, I joined the press bus at the Democratic Justice party headquarters to accompany Mr. Roh to Kunsan, Kim Dae-jung's birthplace, and Chonju—barnstorming Cholla province, enemy territory. It seemed an obvious thing to do, although not many people came down from the foreign media. A rumor had gone around that someone was about to burn himself to death. That, if it happened, would be the picture of the day.

All three major candidates had suffered their own humiliations at the hands of the electorate, and it was part of the deal that they should suffer them unflinchingly. Neither Roh nor Kim Young-sam had lasted long in Kwangju—in fact the latter had lost face by being unable to speak there. Kim Dae-jung had been pelted in Taegu, Roh Tae-woo's home ground, but had defiantly told the audience that they could throw what they liked at him—he was going to give his speech. For Roh, it was important that he should dare to show his face up and down the country, and the Korean press corps were used to the consequences. They boarded the bus with hard hats and protective clothing.

We drove south down the highway toward Kwangju, and when we turned off we began to encounter strategically placed knots of loyal demonstrators at the roadside. The photographers began strapping on their helmets. We were warned that the moment Roh finished making his speech, we must all be on the press truck or we would be left behind. The warning seemed faintly bossy until you saw what was in store.

Along the approach road to Kunsan were lines of parked buses. A crowd had been imported to protect Roh and his entourage from the real, hostile crowd they would meet. We got off our buses. Roh and his bodyguards took their places in the candidate's open truck, which was preceded to the rally site by a press truck. The streets were full and hostile. People crowded on rooftops to see one of the men they held responsible for the Kwangju massacre.

It was extraordinary to be at a rally where ninety percent of the audience were attending because they hated the speaker's guts. Around the platform, the thugs from the snatch squads chanted pro-Roh slogans. But as soon as Roh began speaking (telling the people of Cholla about a massive investment program that would involve their part of the west coast in the future development of trade with China), the crowd turned its back on the speaker and began looking toward the periphery, where supporters of Kim Dae-jung were demonstrating.

At the end of the speech, we rushed to the press truck and the crowd edged closer. There were scuffles and tear gas ahead of us. Mr. Roh took his place on his open truck, surrounded by bodyguards with transparent shields. As we set off, he was wearing his usual smarmy smile. Then the rocks began to pour down. Mr. Roh's shoulders hunched slightly. His face seemed to say: You don't hate me *that* much, do you? Oh, I see—you *do* hate me that much. Finally he disappeared beneath the plastic shields, and the two trucks wobbled at high speed along the road.

Several of the press on our truck received minor injuries, and two were hospitalized. For the Korean press was very much despised—and the TV more so. Watching Mr. Roh go through this performance, I thought: This is the first time in my life I have been literally stoned; I wouldn't have missed it for the world, but I don't want it to happen ever, ever again. The most astonishing sight, as we reached the buses, was that of the plainclothes thugs, rushing for their transport, dashing to get out of town. I was used to seeing these men evenly matched against the students—dangerous, too. They were the most hated of the police and were popularly believed to have been recruited from the prisons. Here, however, not a man was going to wait a moment longer. We were all shooed out of town.

Further along the road we regrouped for lunch. A street had been sealed off. Outside Mr. Roh's restaurant, within the cordon of police, a loyal demonstration was taking place. Quite who was deriving satisfaction from it would be hard to say. It was like a chamber demonstration—*Tafelmusik*. An aid to the digestion.

That afternoon, as we approached Chonju, we could see that most of the men were making their way toward the rally site. The Korean press corps were expecting bigger trouble here, in a city of some half a million people, with many students. We waited for the Roh cavalcade to begin, until suddenly it became apparent that it was not going to begin at all. Mr. Roh was stuck in his hotel.

The rally site, by the railway station, had been ill chosen. Small hills surrounded it, with a quarry and many other sources of rocks such as half-finished construction sites. There were the riot police, fantastically outnumbered by the crowd, trying to hold off the demonstrators, who were tearing down the Roh banners and burning them. There was tear gas everywhere.

What ensued was like a medieval battle. When the crowd on the surrounding slopes saw that the police were on the retreat, they would come storming down, running across the loose stones and thinking nothing of jumping an eight-foot drop off sheer rocks. Attack and counterattack followed. Behind the police, the hired supporters performed their rehearsed routines until it became clear that Roh could never show his face in this city.

And when that became clear a group of students went and sought him out in his hotel in the center of town, where they kept up the hostile pressure through the evening. It was an impressive display of sheer dogged detestation. Mr. Roh said it was a pity for democracy. A member of the government said publicly that Chonju should be punished for the insult it had delivered. But he had spoken out of turn in the Era of the Ordinary Man, and he lost his job in consequence.

When it came to playing the democrat, Mr. Roh was more adept than his colleagues.

———

11

Election spending by the ruling party was so high it showed up in the money-supply figures. The Mint was said to be working overtime, turning away foreign orders. The rib-of-beef restaurants were booked up with political banquets. Bus rental companies across the country were booked up. It was, they said, a great time to be in the small sewage-farm business—every politician was combing the countryside promising small sewage farms. Around Seoul, it was the influential figures at the precinct level who organized the attendance at Mr. Roh's rallies: You could see the various groups having their names checked off lists at the rally site. Most of the large companies told their employees to attend, but did not necessarily enforce the order. Nevertheless, by a mixture of money and gifts, and then threats, the momentum for the ruling party was sutained. It was not a free election—it was a very expensive election. There was no expenditure ceiling for Mr. Roh. I remember the drunk men, stunned by his generosity, at the end of his last big rally, and I remember walking back toward Seoul, over the Map'O Bridge, at sunset, and watching the great drift of political literature into the Han River.

Each of the two Kims seemed confident. Either they would win, or the public outcry at a rigged defeat would be so intense that, even if Roh "won," he would lose. He would lose on the streets. He would be driven out by the righteous fury of the people. At his final rally Kim Dae-jung was particularly threatening on this point.

Nobody knew what would happen. The Americans, in their briefings to the press, made circumspection a fine art. They were going to have to "work with" the victor—that is, if the victor's victory proved workable. The pollsters continually found a high proportion of "undecideds"—and the question was, were these the voters who secretly intended to go for the dangerous Kim Dae-jung (whom the military considered a communist), or were they planning to make the "unpopular," the "realistic" choice of Roh Tae-woo? How many could have been bought and how many forced? In every calculation, the armed forces vote, made in advance, in the barracks, belonged to Roh—whatever the real opinion of the rank and file might be. But how far could his influence stretch beyond that?

When the results began coming in, the outcome was soon obvious. Whether by fair means or foul, the ruling party had achieved a plurality large enough to be decisive, but small enough to stand forever as a reproach to the opposition. From the early projections and through the night, suspiciously consistent but still—there it was—consistent, the figures said: If only the two Kims had got together, the opposition would have won. That there had been foul play, there was no doubt—but most people doubted there had been a sufficient amount of foul play to thwart the opposition. Whichever Kim you supported, the obvious fault lay with the other Kim, or with both.

It was Christmas. Along the streets of the downtown shopping area came the students, with gift-wrapped boxes containing Molotov cocktails. And there were other students, who could see that the support for the rioters had been dissipated, campaigning among the shoppers, explaining how they thought the elections had been rigged, and what had happened in one notorious incident in Seoul, where the vote-riggers had been caught red-handed. In this place, Kuro, the protesting students had been brutally arrested, and the name of Kuro became a rallying call. It was a miniature Kwangju.

My interpreter was dejected. He was a student, but at his university there were no student leaders he could consult because they were all, he said, under lock and key. In the ruling party, people began making menacing noises about anybody who failed to accept the results. When Kim Dae-jung appeared before the press he looked shocked and deflated. Before long both Kims would have to wear sackcloth and ashes, to apologize to the people they had betrayed. For the people themselves were not buying the story of election fraud: They were pointing to the crucial, brute fact of the divided opposition.

After a few days the foreign press went home to their families, and the international observers left town. Those who had been expecting an explosion were disappointed. Apart from anything else, it was too cold for an explosion. And then there was all the shopping to be done.

Tired of Seoul, we went off to Mount Sorak and spent some days walking in the national park. My interpreter was in love, and his girlfriend was thinking of becoming a nun. She had seen us off on the train, then gone to a covent for retreat.

I was reading Coleridge. My interpreter was writing poems in the next room. We walked in silence through the astonishing pink granite ravines. Once we discussed the definition of happiness, which, said my interpreter, was to be free from the shackles of desire. We were surrounded by frozen, gurgling cataracts. The mountaineers hurried past us, properly equipped, but we were outclassed on the icy, difficult tracks.

"What happened in the Philippines?" asked my interpreter. I told him how Marcos had been declared winner, and how Cory had had herself proclaimed, in defiance of the results. Every day we watched the newspapers. My interpreter had heard that Kim Dae-jung would also have himself proclaimed.

Countries watch each other in this way—with aspiration, with alarm. What happened in the Philippines? What happened in Vietnam, in Cambodia, in Poland . . . ? Anxious questions, disappointment, disbelief.

We sat Christmas out, in the deserted resort, then went back to Seoul before the New Year influx.

FOR THE BEST IN PAPERBACKS, LOOK FOR THE 🐧

In every corner of the world, on every subject under the sun, Penguin represents quality and variety – the very best in publishing today.

For complete information about books available from Penguin – including Pelicans, Puffins, Peregrines and Penguin Classics – and how to order them, write to us at the appropriate address below. Please note that for copyright reasons the selection of books varies from country to country.

In the United Kingdom: Please write to *Dept E.P., Penguin Books Ltd, Harmondsworth, Middlesex, UB7 0DA*

If you have any difficulty in obtaining a title, please send your order with the correct money, plus ten per cent for postage and packaging, to *PO Box No 11, West Drayton, Middlesex*

In the United States: Please write to *Dept BA, Penguin, 299 Murray Hill Parkway, East Rutherford, New Jersey 07073*

In Canada: Please write to *Penguin Books Canada Ltd, 2801 John Street, Markham, Ontario L3R 1B4*

In Australia: Please write to the *Marketing Department, Penguin Books Australia Ltd, P.O. Box 257, Ringwood, Victoria 3134*

In New Zealand: Please write to the *Marketing Department, Penguin Books (NZ) Ltd, Private Bag, Takapuna, Auckland 9*

In India: Please write to *Penguin Overseas Ltd, 706 Eros Apartments, 56 Nehru Place, New Delhi, 110019*

In Holland: Please write to *Penguin Books Nederland B.V., Postbus 195, NL–1380AD Weesp, Netherlands*

In Germany: Please write to *Penguin Books Ltd, Friedrichstrasse 10–12, D–6000 Frankfurt Main 1, Federal Republic of Germany*

In Spain: Please write to *Longman Penguin España, Calle San Nicolas 15, E–28013 Madrid, Spain*

In France: Please write to *Penguin Books Ltd, 39 Rue de Montmorency, F-75003, Paris, France*

In Japan: Please write to *Longman Penguin Japan Co Ltd, Yamaguchi Building, 2–12–9 Kanda Jimbocho, Chiyoda-Ku, Tokyo 101, Japan*

A CHOICE OF PENGUINS

Fantastic Invasion Patrick Marnham

Explored and exploited, Africa has carried a different meaning for each wave of foreign invaders – from ivory traders to aid workers. Now, in the crisis that has followed Independence, which way should Africa turn? 'A courageous and brilliant effort' – Paul Theroux ·

Jean Rhys: Letters 1931–66
Edited by Francis Wyndham and Diana Melly

'Eloquent and invaluable . . . her life emerges, and with it a portrait of an unexpectedly indomitable figure' – Marina Warner in the *Sunday Times*

Among the Russians Colin Thubron

One man's solitary journey by car across Russia provides an enthralling and revealing account of the habits and idiosyncrasies of a fascinating people. 'He sees things with the freshness of an innocent and the erudition of a scholar' – *Daily Telegraph*

The Amateur Naturalist Gerald Durrell with Lee Durrell

'Delight . . . on every page . . . packed with authoritative writing, learning without pomposity . . . it represents a real bargain' – *The Times Educational Supplement*. 'What treats are in store for the average British household' – *Books and Bookmen*

The Democratic Economy Geoff Hodgson

Today, the political arena is divided as seldom before. In this exciting and original study, Geoff Hodgson carefully examines the claims of the rival doctrines and exposes some crucial flaws.

They Went to Portugal Rose Macaulay

An exotic and entertaining account of travellers to Portugal from the pirate-crusaders, through poets, aesthetes and ambassadors, to the new wave of romantic travellers. A wonderful mixture of literature, history and adventure, by one of our most stylish and seductive writers.